Strange Sounds

Music,
Technology,
& Culture

TIMOTHY D. TAYLOR

ROUTLEDGE

NEW YORK   LONDON

Published in 2001 by
Routledge
270 Madison Ave,
New York NY 10016

Published in Great Britain by
Routledge
2 Park Square, Milton Park,
Abingdon, Oxon, OX14 4RN

Routledge is an imprint of the Taylor & Francis Group.

Transferred to Digital Printing 2010

The publisher and author gratefully acknowledge permission to reprint the following:
An earlier version of chapter 7 appeared as "Music at Home, Politics Afar" in *Decomposition: Post-Disciplinary Performance,* edited by Sue-Ellen Case, Philip Brett, and Susan Leigh Foster, © 2000 by Indiana University Press.
Example 4.1, an exceprt from "Moon Moods," music by Harry Revel, © 1946, reprinted by permission of Michael H. Goldsen, Inc., and William C. Schulman.
Figure 4.5 used courtesy of Capitol Records, Inc.
Figure 7.2 and figure 7.3 reprinted by permission of Geert-Jan Hobijn.
Figure 8.1 and figure 8.2 reprinted by permission of Synthetic Sādhus.
Figure 8.3, figure 8.4, and figure 8.5 reprinted by permission of Tsunami Enterprises, Inc.

Cataloguing-in-Publication Data is available from the Library of Congress.
ISBN 0-415-93683-7 (hbk.) — ISBN 0-415-93684-5 (pbk.)

Publisher's Note
The publisher has gone to great lengths to ensure the quality of this reprint
but points out that some imperfections in the original may be apparent.

FOR SHERRY,
MY NUMBER ONLY

I'm crazy about technology. I'm hooked on it.
—Roni Size, "Better Music through Technology"

CONTENTS

EXAMPLES, FIGURES, AND TABLES

LIST OF MUSIC EXAMPLES

LIST OF FIGURES

LIST OF TABLES

ACKNOWLEDGMENTS

Writing acknowledgments, for me, is the most pleasurable part of writing a book. This is in part because it is the last section to get written, but mainly because thanking one's friends, colleagues, and students is a wonderful and humbling experience.

The idea for this book took shape in a seminar I taught at Columbia University in the spring of 1997, "Technology and Its Effects on Music since the 1980s," and I would like to thank those students who participated: Allison Armstrong, Maja Cerar, Timothy Mangin, Jason Oakes, Heather Willoughby, and Paul Yoon.

I would also like to acknowledge those institutions who provided support of various kinds: Columbia University, for its Humanities Council Grant; the American Council of Learned Societies; and the National Humanities Center, which supported me with a grant from the National Endowment for the Humanities. I would also like to thank the NHC staff, particularly those in the library: Jean Houston and Eliza Robertson; and Karen Carroll, who copyedited most of the chapters.

Other people, organizations, and agencies that provided help along the way also deserve thanks: my old friend Lori Garver at the National Aeronautics and Space Administration, and her colleague Diana Hoyt, for help with sources about NASA in the early days. And Vanguard Records, which provided me with some press kit materials and recordings.

I would also like to thank the New York City psy trance folks, especially Hugh, and also Ascher, Holly, Joe, Rudston, and Tom.

People at Routledge have been their usual helpful and supportive selves: first and foremost, my editor and friend, Bill Germano; Matt Byrnie, assistant editor; Lisa Vecchione, the production editor; Brian Bendlin, the copy editor; and the indexer, Lydia Lennihan.

Various friends and colleagues read bits of the manuscript or participated in discussions with me about some of the ideas presented here, and I would like to thank each of them: Philip Brett, Sue-Ellen Case, Luther

Elliott, Steven Feld, Aaron Fox, Brad Garton, Nancy Guy, Charles Keil, George Lipsitz, Carol Muller, Paul Rabinow, Dan Sherman, David Suisman, Christopher Waterman, Glenn Watkins, and Hans Weisethaunet.

Several old friends have provided much intellectual sustenance, both as I wrote this and long before: John T. Canaday, René T. A. Lysloff, and Deborah Wong. These three college and graduate school friends helped put me on the right intellectual track more than anyone else during that part of my life, and they still help me to find my way.

A few indefatigable people read the entire manuscript and offered invaluable comments: Joe Auner, Steve Feld, and Louise Meintjes. Also in this category goes Susana Loza, who knows more about techno music than anybody I know. I could not be more grateful to these friends for their careful readings, which helped make this a better book. I am humbled and awed by the collective knowledge and generosity of these good people.

My sister Kristin Taylor, of Amadeus Music in Portland, Maine, helped track down obscure albums, for which I am always grateful.

I would also like to thank my parents, Jane and Lee, who breathed a sigh of relief after helping to pay off my student loans during the completion of this book.

Last, the support of my immediate family has always meant more than anything. They are: Paddy the Cat, my stepdaughter Gwen, and, most of all, Sherry B. Ortner, as always my model in scholarship and life.

THEORY

WILL

THE REVOLUTION

BE DIGITIZED?

The advent of digital technology in the early 1980s marks the beginning of what may be the most fundamental change in the history of Western music since the invention of music notation in the ninth century. This is a rather bold statement, so let me explain. The earlier innovation was brought about because Charlemagne wanted to standardize the music of all the churches of Christendom. Yet, as is usually the case with any technology, the resulting uses were different from the original intent. Standardization was eventually achieved by and large, but perhaps more noteworthy is the fact that notation changed the ways music was made, stored and distributed, and heard.

The invention of movable type for music printing in the beginning of the sixteenth century made the mass publication and dissemination of music move easier, faster—and thus, farther—than before, but had less of an effect on a trio of features that have proved to be so important historically: production, storage/distribution, and consumption. It wasn't until the invention of the player piano and, more importantly, the gramophone in the late nineteenth century that production, storage, and portability were once again greatly altered (especially the latter two). This time, however, music as *sound* could be moved about, bought, sold, and, with the invention of radio, broadcast.

Digitization accomplishes many of the same things as the gramophone: music storage and retrieval is greatly facilitated, though this time it is not simply music as sound, but music as bits—combinations of zeros and ones. These digits are more portable, more easily disseminated, than ever before, thanks in large part to the Internet. But it is not just storage and retrieval that have changed; production has as well. Anyone who recalls television programs from the 1970s or earlier might also remember that the soundtracks usually featured orchestral music, attributed to a composer in the program's credits. In those days and earlier, television, film, advertising, and, indeed, all music was written by a person, perhaps orchestrated by another; parts were copied and distributed to orchestral musicians, often employed by the major television and film studios, and the music was recorded for each program and edited to fit the specific program. Now, however, this music can be realized by a single person with a home studio consisting of a computer and a few electronic musical instruments, and much of it is. No performers are required; indeed, there is no "performance" in a conventional sense.

While in some ways digital technology seems to be merely increasing the efficiency of music storage and distribution, it is important to remember that all previous modes of the distribution of music were *physical*: the notated or recorded object had to be moved from place to place; broadcasting changed this somewhat, but broadcasting fidelity has never been high, and ways of capturing broadcasts forfeit even more fidelity. With digital technology, however, sounds can be recorded and then perfectly and endlessly copied with no loss of quality. And digitally recorded music can be transmitted electronically over the Internet, a fact increasingly worrisome to the music industry. On- or offline, digitally recorded music can be copied exactly, unlike all previous modes of reproduction; making a perfect copy of digitally recorded music is pretty much the same thing as copying a floppy disk, and these copies can be easily compressed and sent over the Internet.

With each historical technological breakthrough, each technological shift, there are changes in social organization. The invention of movable type in the early sixteenth century meant that music could escape its former boundaries of the centers of power and move farther than it had before; a musical "public" was born. Composers climbed the ladder of social respectability; and, by the late eighteenth century, copyright protected their works. The early nineteenth century saw the rise of the composer as artist, as genius; "the artist was born, at the same time his work went on sale," writes Jacques Attali.[1] And both of these events were facilitated in part by music printing and publishing.

With music publishing, people could take music home and make it for themselves (which practitioners of orally transmitted musics had always done, of course). But with the gramophone, people by and large stopped making music on their pianos and other instruments at home and started buying it instead, ready-made, turned into consumers rather than producers by the modern Western inventions of talent, genius, and masterpiece.

I am not unaware that this chronology of events—notation, printing/publishing, and gramophone/radio—has been noted before as pivotal points in the history of Western European music, as in Attali's widely cited *Noise*. While Attali never explicitly theorized technology, it is interesting that his four stages of music—sacrificing, representing, repeating, and last, the not-yet-realized composition—correspond neatly to the most important stages in the development of music technologies. The (premodern, oral) era of sacrifice was halted by the rise of music notation, in which music could be "represented"; the dominance of this era gives way to, first, printing with movable musical type, but more significantly, gramophone and radio. Failing to theorize the technological aspect of these stages means that Attali slips into a deterministic model of technology in his book, as if each of these new sociotechnical systems simply produced new musics rather than being caught up in complex webs of music, technology, society, and history, all of which presuppose each other.

Still, Attali's optimism about "composition" is infectious. With digital technology, there is some hope that people—at least those who can afford computers—will begin to make music for themselves again using their computers and cheap, easily available software; it isn't even necessary to buy much hardware anymore. There are also sites on the World Wide Web that allow people to remix (that is, manipulate previously recorded music) recordings—sites such as MusicHall 2000, which lets anyone make music quickly which they can then save and share with others on the web.[2] I will talk about the claims of the democratizing potential of technology in later chapters, so here I will just observe that such arguments are frequently so hyperbolic as to take one's breath away. It is not uncommon for authors seemingly with both feet on the ground to take potshots at "the media," who (to take one example) "are constantly feeding us exciting and imaginative stories about how information technology will change our lives. Most of them are pure fantasies. . . ."[3] This same author, Michael Dertouzos, goes on, however, to write passages such as, "The final dynamic the Information Market-place will bring to the creative world is the *democratization* of art. It may not be the most exciting development, but it will be the most important. Suddenly, all the worlds' art will be available to all the world's people. Already, the world's museums are putting their most popular works on CD-ROM and on the World Wide Web."[4] And so forth; as if there were not already high-quality reproductions of art-works in books, reproductions that preserve to a greater degree than do digitized images the physicality of the artworks. Such claims always operate under the assumption that everybody has a computer, which for the foreseeable future is far less the case than is the current availability of books in libraries (to which access is free). There is also the question of computerized access, since, as is almost never stated (or, I suspect, recognized), most of the people on the planet do not have access to a telephone, much less a computer with an Internet connection.

Such statements are always made without realizing that claims for the democratizing potential of almost any technology have been around for a long time. Langdon Winner writes that the airplane was heralded as a democratizing force in the 1920s, for example.[5] There are ways it was, I suppose, but the claim that a particular technology is democratizing should always be accompanied by questions: In what ways? For whom?

In the following pages you will read about all kinds of technology used to make music: tape recorders, turntables, synthesizers, computers, drum machines, electronic basses, computer software, and more. Already a question arises: what distinguishes one item of technology (musical or otherwise) from another? Is a computer used in making music a qualitatively different form of technology than an analog tape recorder?

There are no easy answers to such questions. One of the ways technology works in Western culture is to call attention to itself when new, for at that moment it has no social life. It is true, of course, that it was produced as the result of a complex series of interconnected social processes, but at its moment of development—and, more importantly for my purposes here—distribution and use, it has no social history. After a period of use, most technological artifacts are normalized into everyday life and no longer seen as "technological" at all, while whatever is new becomes viewed as "technological." Turn on MTV's popular *Unplugged* program, for example, to see how plugged in it really is.[6] So, if today someone says that she is interested in technology, this is generally taken to mean computers or other kinds of current digital technology. But if she says she is interested in, say, kerosene lamps, then most listeners would assume that she is interested in antiques, not technology, even though, of course, kerosene lamps were once considered cutting-edge technology.[7]

Any musician at any time uses a jumble of different technologies. A symphony orchestra, for example, is comprised of many different instruments that were developed at different moments in history and in different places, and thus have quite different histories, quite different social groups and trajectories that contributed to their development. Even individual instruments are not single objects of technology; the development of the Boehm-system clarinet, for example, was completed in the mid-1840s, but today's clarinetists are constantly experimenting with different reeds, ligatures, and mouthpieces, all of which have their own histories. And not all of today's clarinetists—even classical clarinetists—use Boehm-system clarinets; the term *clarinet*—even *soprano clarinet in B-flat* (the most common clarinet today)—does not refer to a single, final, technological artifact.

Goa/psychedelic trance (the subject of chapter 8), a music made with computers and other kinds of electronic technology, raises more issues. The preferred mode of storage and reproduction—"performance"—of the music is the old-fashioned vinyl LP and not something more recent such as a compact disc, a minidisc, or an MP3 (a kind of music file easily played back on a computer or portable MP3 player).

Whatever music technology is, it is not one thing alone. It is not separate from the social groups that use it; it is not separate from the individuals who use it; it is not separate from the social groups and individuals who invented it, tested it, marketed it, distributed it, sold it, repaired it, listened to it, bought it, or revived it. In short, music technology—any technology—is not simply an artifact or a collection of artifacts; it is, rather, always bound up in a social system, a "seamless web," as is often described.

And any new technology is never wholly new, even though it is usually accompanied by a discourse trumpeting its novelty and innovativeness. This practice bespeaks one of the deepest ideologies surrounding technology, for it has a long history as riding the crest of the wave of one of the most exalted of Western European ideologies, that of progress and scientific advancement. Technology is often identified with tools, and as many authors have written (or endorsed), it is the use of tools that separates us from all other animals.[8] This distinction is so important in Western European culture that by the middle of the eighteenth century one of the most important and sometimes *the* most important way that Europeans judged other cultures was by their scientific and technological advancement.[9] It is no accident, then, that most studies of technology concentrate on innovation and invention, or the moment of introduction into the larger society, in order to gauge the "impact" of a particular tool or machine.

Technology, then, forms an important part of the modern West's idea about itself, an observation as useful as ever in this era of information technology. The relatively recent rise of digital technologies, which most of this book is about, cannot be separated from the current phenomenon usually called globalization. I have examined the globalization of popular music in my previous book, *Global Pop, World Music, World Markets*, and in some sense *Strange Sounds* is a kind of distant companion.[10]

The various "world music" connections in this book—discussions of Western musicians sampling other musics, the flow of musical styles in and out of Goa, India, for example—help illustrate and dramatize the inseparability of globalization and information technologies. Manuel Castells writes of the complex intertwining of the information age and globalization that today's economy can be called informational "because the productivity and competitiveness of units or agents in this economy . . . fundamentally depend upon their capacity to generate, process, and apply efficiently knowledge-based information." It is global, he says, "because the core activities of production, consumption, and circulation, as well as their components . . . are organized on a global scale. . . . It is informational *and* global because, under the new historical conditions, productivity is generated through and competition is played out in a global network of interaction."[11]

On Strangeness, Methods, and Transcriptions

Strange Sounds: Music, Technology, and Culture examines a rather eclectic group of musics. Some are stranger than others. But I confess to being fascinated by many of these sounds on the fringes. I would argue that the strange, the relatively unheard, often affords greater insights into the largest issues I want to examine here—agency, ideologies of technology, pro and con—than does other music. It is not that the mainstream offers no avenue to understanding people and their music in a particular place and time. But the odd—the marginal—can often tell us more, for the margins often have much to say about the centers that those in the centers might not be aware of.[12]

In attempting to grasp these strange sounds, this book also employs a diverse assortment of theories and methodologies: part historical, part ethnographic, also utilizing the World Wide Web for the glimpses it offers into how real people hear music when it isn't possible to learn this through more conventional ethnographic methods.[13] I am continuing, in other words, the kind of "virtual ethnography" I advocated in *Global Pop*, gleaning whatever ethnographic data I can from various electronic sources. I also continue to read and listen ethnographically and historically; that is, texts of whatever variety aren't merely texts, but statements that need to be understood both as texts and as culturally and historically specific utterances.[14] A favorite passage from Michel Foucault puts this approach succinctly: "How is it that one particular statement appeared rather than another?"[15] In other words, what are the historical, cultural (and other) reasons that resulted in a particular statement, defined broadly as any text? Thus, historical and ethnographic methods are used.

What I mean by "history," however, is Terry Eagleton's History (uppercased).[16] That is, history as it shapes peoples' real lives and the things that they make, such as music and technology. This may not sound like a necessary argument, but there are a growing number of theoretically informed writings, including some about music, that ignore history altogether, or reduce it to an effect, an anecdote—what Eagleton has called history (lowercased). But History is always more than this, and if we are going to find out why a certain piece of music is the way it is—one of the small handful of guiding questions of this book—then we must attend to History.

I also want to make it clear that when insisting that we study history (uppercase assumed hereafter), I am not talking about history as something (co)incidental to music, a zeitgeist. A recitation of historical facts that precede a discussion of a particular work without any connection between one and the other is as unenlightening about why the piece is the way it is as an absence of a historical discussion altogether. Studying the work in history/culture isn't easy, but that's what cultural theory is for: connecting a text (broadly understood) to larger and deeper social and historical realities.

I also need to comment on the paucity of music examples in the following pages. My earlier book contained many notated musical examples (there were more, but I could not get permission to use all of them from their copyright holders), some of which were quite long. I thought it was important at the time to argue against scholars who are neither musicians nor musicologists who purport to write about music without writing about the music, for much of the meaning of music resides in the sounds and styles, meaning that can't be apprehended through analyses of song lyrics alone.[17] Unfortunately, that argument still needs to be made. But with these electronic musics, which are less concerned with pitch than any music I have ever studied, transcriptions would be difficult, even impossible, most of the time. The sounds and effects—and affects—that interest most of the following musicians are sounds achieved not so much by moving notes around but by moving knobs and sliders. And there is no notational scheme for these sounds.

I have thus in a few instances provided tables that attempt to track important sonic events in a work; and there are a couple of transcriptions where possible. But most of the more technical discussions of music in what follows are simply technical discussions, in prose—discussions that I have endeavored to make user-friendly to nonmusicians and nonmusicologists.

Last, in the writing of this book it has become increasingly important to me to try to address workers in the growing field of science and technology studies (STS). For whatever reason, no book—indeed, almost no published writing of any kind[18]—about music and technology by any scholar of music has seen fit to engage in any substantial way with the voluminous and fast-growing literature in STS. And yet, we in academia are supposedly inhabiting an era of growing interdisciplinarity. I have learned much from the writings of many of these STS scholars, whose work has helped make this a better book, and I hope that, should they read it, they find something of use.

Strange Sounds opens with a section, entitled "Theory," that examines the technological developments that are shaping this digital transformation and situates them in historical context and theoretical literatures. These innovations change the ways that media are produced, stored, transmitted, and consumed. It is now possible to make music using nothing other than a personal computer, and it is as possible to disseminate that, or any, music over the Internet. Chapter 2, "Music, Technology, Agency, and Practice," begins by considering the existing literature on technology, particularly with respect to agency. This chapter also offers a practice theory of technology in which technology is seen neither as a controlling factor in musicking, nor as merely a symptom of cultural shifts—the two opposing positions usually taken—but as a social practice that in part changes our modes of musicking while at the same is susceptible to changes we might make to it.

Following "Theory," the book is divided into two additional parts, "Time," and "Space." This division helps underline some of the major goals of this book. Part 2 introduces a historical dimension to contemporary discussions of technology, which all too frequently view our technological culture as unprecedented. Histories of technological progress, however, are often frequently histories of past visions of the future, as is the case in various ways with the chapters of part 2. Second, digital technology has in part driven the trend toward an increasingly global economy. Music is no less caught up in these changes, and so part 3, concerned with space rather than time, listens to various musics with respect to their role in this globalized world, but at the same time, endeavors to show that this globalization, like this technological moment, has a history.

The first of the chapters in part 2, "Postwar Music and the Technoscientific Imaginary" (chapter 3) examines *musique concrète*, the earliest form of electronic music made with magnetic tape, and is primarily concerned with late 1940s and early 1950s debates about the one true path of postwar music, which centered on the composer's control over the work, both in acoustic compositions and electronic ones (*musique concrète* and *elektronische Musik*). *Elektronische Musik* musicians were also concerned with situating themselves and their music in a historical trajectory that linked them to the great works and composers of the past, and much of their discursive efforts at valorizing their mode of composition were directed toward connecting their music with the most prestigious music from before World War II by Arnold Schoenberg (1875–1951) and other members of the Second Viennese School (a group of composers associated with Schoenberg, mainly his pupils). One figure, however, remained largely aloof from this fray and was comparatively unconcerned with these debates. Perhaps as a result, the *musique concrète* composer Pierre Henry (b. 1927) has had the most success with popular musicians through his career, and is currently being rediscovered by a new generation of DJs, some of whom credit him with being the founder of techno music itself as they construct their own historical trajectory that connects them and their musics to earlier practices and sounds.

Chapter 4, "Men, Machines, and Music in the Space-Age 1950s," considers, like chapter 3, the beginning of the postwar era. But unlike the previous chapter, the setting is the United States, and the music is popular, what is now called "space-age pop"—that is, popular music that thematized the exotic, whether terrestrial or in space, intended to be played on hi-fis, all the rage from the late 1940s into the 1960s. Space-age pop was caught up in a new postwar technological drivenness in which gadgets such as hi-fis were parts of an ideological complex that propounded the benefits of science and technology, while at the same time attempting to deemphasize the dangers of some technologies, such as nuclear weaponry and power. These albums usually featured optimistic and futuristic titles and cover art, but the music itself was often far darker in affect, as if registering the anxiety and ambivalence over technology in this era.

Chapter 5, "Technostalgia," examines the recent revival of space-age pop from the 1950s and early 1960s, resurrected both by intrepid collectors of old vinyl recordings and by bands who emulate the styles of their 1950s progenitors and cultivate the use of old analog (that is, predigital) electronic instruments, which allow them greater control than newer machines that have more automated functions.

Part 3 begins with a discussion of one of the many ramifications of the increased availability and dissemination of digitized sounds. Music now travels faster and farther than ever before. This issue is raised particularly clearly in an episode with the Germany-based band Enigma and their sampling of a Taiwanese folk song in their hit "Return to Innocence," from the 1993 album *Cross of Changes.* Unusually, the people who first recorded this folk song, an elderly couple living in a remote area of Taiwan, heard Enigma's song on the radio and sued; the case was recently settled out of court. At the same time, however, these same Taiwanese musicians were making their own recording of traditional music that was mixed by a European producer utilizing drum machines and other digital music equipment. I will devote chapter 6, "A Riddle Wrapped in a Mystery," to this saga, paying particular attention to issues of ownership made more complex by the growing global traffic in sounds, hastened by digital technology, and the new dynamic of appropriation, accusation, and, sometimes, restitution that is beginning to constitute this traffic.

Digital technology also makes home music making possible as never before. One can create complex, polyphonic music at home with a computer and other digital equipment without having had years of piano lessons, for every sound an "electronica" musician might require can be synthesized or digitally sampled (that is, perfectly copied) from previously recorded sources.[19] Chapter 7, "Music at Home, Politics Afar" thus engages with questions concerning the nature of the "public" in contemporary life, and focuses on those musicians who produce their music largely apart from more social and public realms. ("The public" for my purposes here refers not so much to the "public sphere" of Jürgen Habermas as to the use of urban spaces, and so draws on Mike Davis's and Edward W. Soja's studies of the changing geography of cities). The musicians of this chapter also espouse distant political causes (one is pro-Palestine, the other pro-Tibet), and their music samples sounds from these places as part of their political messages.

If digital technology may be contributing to a retreat from the public, these new technologies and musics are bringing people together in new communities, communities that profess neither anxiety nor ambivalence about technology. One such community centers around a music known as Goa trance or psychedelic trance, referred to by insiders as "psy trance." The young people in this scene cultivate a music and what Grant McCracken has called a "little culture" (cultures that are relatively whole in and of themselves) that facilitates their momentary loss of self in the collective effervescence of the group, [20] all accompanied by electronic dance music provided by a DJ. Chapter 8, "Turn On, Tune In, Trance Out" is based on fieldwork in the Goa/psychedelic trance little culture as it manifested itself in New York City in 1999. It reviews youth subcultural theory in order to point out its shortcomings when examining little cultures such as this one in which there is no sign of any oppositional politics, boundary policing, "resistance," or indeed any of the practices one has come to expect from a youth subculture. More useful here are classic theories of religion and ritual, mainly by Émile Durkheim and Victor Turner, which helpfully illuminate the quasi-religious activities of this group.

Chapter 9, "Anxiety, Consumption, and Agency," returns to the practice theory of the beginning and the question of agency. Instead of viewing technology generally and music technology in particular as something separate from society, separate from individual social actors, this concluding chapter takes issue with those who are revising Marshall McLuhan's deterministic arguments about the media to understand digital technologies. Rather, we make machines for our own ends. I am hoping instead that, like the Goa/psy trance dancers, we are instead becoming postindividuals—that is, more aware of ourselves as social beings.

MUSIC,

TECHNOLOGY,

AGENCY,

AND PRACTICE

In direct contrast to German philosophy which descends from heaven to earth, here it is a matter of ascending from earth to heaven.

—*Karl Marx*, The German Ideology

This chapter examines the ways that digital technology shapes the three areas that have historically been so affected by technology: music production, storage/distribution, and consumption.[1] However, in keeping with my interest in the agency of everyday people and their use of everyday technologies, I will focus on distribution and consumption more than production and the practices of the music industry, which others have usefully done.[2] Following this survey, I will discuss the problem of agency in existing theories of technology and society, and offer an adaptation of an existing social science body of theory for use in the study of technology.

It may seem odd that I am insisting that a theory of technology in society take into account everyday technology and everyday users of it, but it is important to recall that, at the moment of its invention, any technological artifact does not yet have a social history or use, even though it was produced in a social setting. That is, the social production of technology is quite different from its subsequent social uses.

Raymond Williams writes that "virtually all technical study and experiment are undertaken within already existing social relations and cultural forms, typically for purposes that are already in general foreseen. Moreover, a technical invention as such has comparatively little social significance. It is only when it is selected for investment towards production, and when it is consciously developed for particular social uses—that is, when it moves from being a technical invention to what can properly be called an available *technology*—that the general significance begins."[3] It is this "general significance" of the social life of technological artifacts that interests me.

Music Production, Storage, Distribution, and Consumption

Technological changes are occurring so rapidly, and lawsuits mounted so quickly, that it would be pointless to attempt to examine every new piece of hardware and software, which would only render this book woefully out of date practically overnight. Instead, I will confine the following discussion to what I think are general trends that new technologies has helped bring about.

MP3s: The .Wav of the Future?

Digital technology is helping to challenge—even, in some instances, break down—the difference between production and consumption. Nowhere is this convergence—or confusion—of production and consumption more evident than in the rise of the MP3. Most people in the so-called developed countries are familiar with compact discs and the claims of greater fidelity and convenience. But the technology that has really changed storage and portability for consumers is the Internet. Early in the days of the World Wide Web, there were technologies available for transporting and transmitting audio, but most of these formats either sounded as though the sounds were coming over a phone line (which, of course, they were if the user had a modem); or the file sizes were so huge that they would take a long time to download over a dial-up connection, and would then be difficult to store. The advent of more affordable CD burners has changed this somewhat, but large file sizes are still a problem for dialup users. Who wants to wait for hours to download one song that is then too large to store conveniently?

The MP3 format has changed all this. MP3 (short for MPEG-1 Audio Layer 3), boasts quality approaching that of the CD but with far smaller file sizes than CD audio (though they're still large). One three- to four-minute song from a compact disc might occupy, say, 40 megabytes on a CD, but this song can be "ripped" from the CD using free and easily available software and converted to an MP3 using the same software (or other free and easily available software). The resulting MP3 file is far smaller (perhaps less than one-tenth the size of the original), which means it can be easily uploaded to the Internet and sent to any receiving computer. This is still a large file, which would deter some people with slow modems from downloading it, but more and more people have Ethernet connections (such as college students in their dorm rooms, who, with their relatively high amounts of cultural and educational capital, seem to be the biggest group of users), and these files can thus be downloaded quickly.[4]

Once downloaded, MP3s can be stored as any file is stored: on the hard disk, on a Zip disk, on a CD if the user has a CD "burner." Users with a sound card that permits a connection to a stereo can record MP3s with whatever audio equipment they have. Until recently, however, the problem was portability, but in 1998, San Jose-based Diamond Multimedia Systems released the Diamond Rio MP3 player, which easily attaches to the computer for downloading MP3s from the hard disc. In a small, portable size, it can store about sixty minutes of music, and since there are no moving parts, unlike a Walkman or Discman, it never slows or skips. Since the Diamond Rio was introduced, many similar players have hit the market. Most of these were released by small companies, but in the fall of 1999 RCA entered the fray, a possible indication that the MP3 is here to stay. Prices of the players are coming down as well; the Diamond Rio was introduced at $179, but it later sold for $89 (after a $50 rebate).[5]

This mode of storage and distribution marks the beginning of a radical change. M. William Krasilovsky and Sidney Shemel's indispensable guide to the music business offers several flowcharts that show the changes in distribution in the recording industry from the 1930s to 1990. What we see is a trend toward increasing complication, with growing numbers of middlemen and more specialized services. The earliest flowchart, the 1930s through the early 1940s, has only two intermediaries between manufacturer and consumer; the second, for the late 1940s to 1955 (marking the entry of the jukebox), has five; the third chart, 1955 to 1957, has six intermediaries, including the then-new record clubs; the last chart, 1957 through 1990, has eleven.[6] Online downloads will not change this chart much, at least at first, except to make it possible, for the first time ever, for consumers to purchase recordings directly from the manufacturer without joining a record club.

MP3s aren't used solely to disseminate prerecorded compact discs; DJs, producers, and musicians send their music around the web this way as well. Unknown musicians can put their music on their own websites, or send it to such sites as MP3.com, which has thousands of different selections, organized by seventeen different genres (and many subgenres).[7] DJs are increasingly bringing a couple of laptops to gigs with hard discs full of MP3s, instead of toting their more familiar box of vinyl LPs. There are a growing number of software applications, such as Digital 1200SL by Visiosonic (the 1200 refers to the preferred turntables of DJs, the legendary Technics 1200), that allow them to cue up their MP3s just as though they are cueing up vinyl recordings.[8]

Some companies such as Music Point are also developing kiosks that allow customers to select the tracks they want and then wait while they are burned onto a CD that the listener can then take home.[9] This may not sound that similar to MP3s, but what is noteworthy, is that, with both of these technologies, listeners can pick whatever track they want from any recording. If they don't like some songs from a particular album, they don't have to get them.

Music Consumption

> [Radio, gramophone, and film have made available a] boundless surfeit of music. Here, perhaps the frightful expression "consumption of music" really does apply after all. For perhaps this continuous tinkle, regardless of whether anyone wants to hear it or not, whether anyone can take it in, whether anyone can use it, will lead to a state where all music has been consumed, worn out.
>
> —*Arnold Schoenberg,* Style and Idea[10]

Since I am concerned with the issue of agency and technology, I want to turn now to examining changing patterns of music consumption—the main way that most people today interact with music. If history is any guide, Simon Frith tells us, those technologies that catch on are ones that lead to the decentralization of music making and listening, and more flexible ways of listening, and so MP3s or their successors are here to stay.[11] This increasingly personalized nature of music consumption, made possible with digital modes of distribution, whether Internet or kiosk, is therefore worth thinking about. MP3 technology means that listeners will be able to avoid buying a prepackaged bunch of songs on CDs or cassettes and instead put together whatever combination they want.

Today's technology makes possible a greater degree of eclecticism in consumption than ever before because of purchases (or downloads) from the web of single tracks of recorded music.[12] While in the past a consumer with eclectic tastes might have cultivated an interest in several genres (it is easy to imagine someone whose record collection boasts selections of jazz, blues, rock, and world music), it is now easy to acquire, cheaply or for no cost at all, just about any kind of music one might want from the Internet.

So how do we speak of this new flexibility? David Harvey's notion of "flexible accumulation" is meant to describe the post-Fordist or disorganized capitalist mode of production today: just-in-time production, production of small batches for carefully targeted groups, with accompanying niche marketing.[13] But Harvey (as well as those who emphasize post-Fordism as the current mode of production) tend to be production oriented, which begs the question: what about changing patterns of consumption?

Scott Lash and John Urry also critique Harvey's and others' tendencies to be too concerned with production and not enough with consumption. Neither Lash and Urry nor I would go as far as some—most famously, Jean Baudrillard—have, arguing that patterns of consumption have become so flexible or confused that consumers are overwhelmed by the plethora of available signs.[14] Lash and Urry's "reflexive accumulation" is their attempt to theorize new modes of consumption that have not jettisoned the agency of the individual consumer. A subcategory of this general term is of direct interest here: "reflexive consumption," a kind of consumption made possible by the decline of social forces that once influenced, even determined to a significant extent a particular consumer's choice—family, corporate groups, and social class.[15]

Lash and Urry, however, overlook the fact that not everybody can afford whatever they want. Credit card debt, organizations such as Spenders Anonymous, innumerable self-help books on how to quit spending, and other forms and symptoms of irresponsible consumer behavior are proliferating, to be sure, but it is still the case that not everyone can afford everything (though those who can't may have to cope with heightened desires for that which they cannot afford). Another critique revolves around a more historicized reading; America has been a mass consumption society for most of the post–World War II era, and identity formation has been caught up in consumption for decades, even for the entire modern era, as some have argued.[16]

This degree of eclecticism, this notion of reflexive accumulation facilitated by the digital distribution of music, is related to the increasingly technologized social life. Today's music fan may not hang out physically with a group of fans with similar tastes, but instead can find fellow music lovers on the Internet by visiting websites devoted to particular musicians (some of those made by fans are incredibly detailed and complete); newsgroups devoted to particular bands, styles, regions, or eras; or by joining similarly specialized mailing lists, which put e-mail messages in users' inboxes. I have seen many messages on the mailing lists to which I subscribe saying that the particular writer is alone in her tastes, how few of her friends are interested in whatever music to which the mailing list is devoted. It may be that the era of the Phish fan, and the Canadian Madonna fan magazine that refers to all other musicians as NMAs ("Non-Madonna Artists"), will disappear.[17] But today's isolated fans can find like-minded friends on the Internet.

Until recently, music was pretty much used as manufactured— companies made recordings, consumers played them back. Playback situations varied hugely, of course. Yet, whereas in the past only someone with a studio could alter recorded music (the main, and important, exception being hip hop musicians scratching their LPs), with digitally recorded music and with inexpensive software or even free Internet websites, it is now possible for music fans to remake and remix somebody else's music. With an MP3, one can play the music, or one can play with it, using any one of a number of available software packages; the listener can be a DJ, a remixer, a soundscape artist, and engineer. And much of the software that makes this possible is free or cheap (by which I mean under $100). Some of this software seems to be popular; I tried many times to download Visiosonic's PCDJ Phat, a free MP3 DJ application, with no success.[18] After a week or so, I tried again and found that Visiosonic had added two servers to handle what I take to be a far greater than anticipated demand. Their motto for this product: "Don't just play, MIX with PCDJ!" There are other such applications, such as Virtual Turntables ($42), which emulate a DJ's pair of turntables.[19]

One can remix using Mixman Studio ($34.95) or Mixman Studio Pro ($89.95), software applications that allow you to make your own remixes of prerecorded (available from Mixman) music and save them as MP3s.[20] Software that permits remixing of MP3s was slower to arrive on the scene but is quickly being developed and is already appearing.

Additionally, online companies are now springing up that allow users to make their own music on the web. Take one example, MusicHall 2000. Visiting their website results in the following message:

> Welcome to the first global online music community.
> Music is the mother tongue of all people.
> mH$_2$0.com marks the beginning of a music evolution that will enable anyone to create, exchange, share and distribute music regardless of experience or ability. mH$_2$0.com is the first true online music community to take full advantage of the World Wide Web's interactive potential by offering a new way to create and share the gift of music.

Such language pushes all the buttons of those inclined to "cyberlibertarianism" (Langdon Winner's term to describe conservatives who have embraced the computer[21]). Discourses of community, liberation, and democratization are combined with older notions of the "international language of music" and the imperializing assumptions of Western companies with respect to the rest of the world's music.

MusicHall 2000 asks the user to select samples from anywhere in the world by clicking on a map of a revolving globe. These samples can then be dumped into a sequencer (a kind of software that allows one to manipulate sounds, as a word processor allows users to manipulate words), Sonic Foundry's Acid DJ 2.0; samples can be edited using Sonic Foundry's Sound Forge XP 4.5. Once the music is done, one can upload it to MusicHall 2000 for others to listen to, download, sample, and remix. The same can be done to anybody's music. To accomplish all this one registers and pays a monthly fee of $3.99, or $19.99 for a year. Registration brings a "free" CD-ROM with the necessary software, as well as some sound samples, messaging capability, and other goodies. MusicHall 2000 is competing with the aforementioned Mixman, a CD-ROM that comes with a few tunes that listeners can remix. Additionally, record companies and retailers such as Virgin include a "Remix" button on their websites. Users can not only hear music before buying it but can also remix it, though they can't save their remix.[22]

Classic Theories of Consumption

It has not been widely noticed that arguments concerning consumption form the core of some of the most influential theories of mass and popular culture going back to the Frankfurt school and continuing to the present in various theories of postmodern culture. The main two positions historically have been essentially "top-down" and "bottom-up": that is, that the so-called culture industries promulgate their products on a public that accepts them unquestioningly or, that people make their meanings out of mass-produced and mass-mediated cultural forms. Thanks to the work of the so-called Birmingham School, in the realm of cultural studies there has been a rejection of the top-down notion of *mass culture*, a model mainly associated with Max Horkheimer and Theodor Adorno of the Frankfurt School, in favor of a somewhat more bottom-up notion of *popular culture*, as if the first is entirely malevolent and the latter only salutary.[23] If forced to make a choice I would happily ally myself with the Birmingham School rather than Horkheimer and Adorno, but even their position is not wholly unusable. Horkheimer and Adorno's characterization of the "culture industry" doesn't mean that people can't make their own meanings out of the things they buy, even when they know that they might have been manipulated into buying them.

There are arguments to be made on both sides: sometimes industries' desires prevail, sometimes people's do. As an example of the former, take the well-known example of Microsoft Windows versus the Apple Macintosh operating system. Macintosh's was (and remains, at least when I write this on my Windows machine that crashes with maddening frequency) the superior system—famously more user-friendly—but Apple's decision not to make the operating system source code available prevented "clones" of their machines, which meant that Windows, and thus, the IBM-compatible computer, now rules. In this and many cases, business and/or marketing decisions trumped consumer preferences—the top-down approach prevailed.

An example of the latter is the history of 8-track tape, a form of playback technology that didn't survive, beaten by the cassette despite the latter's inferior sound quality—putting sound on half the amount of tape as in 8-track, and playing the tape back at half the 8-track's speed. Cassettes, despite the inferior sound, prevailed because blanks were cheaper, tapes and machines smaller and thus more portable, and they could hold more music (up to ninety minutes).[24] It was the flexibility afforded by the cassette that made it more desirable, and flexibility, as we have seen, is generally what has made the difference historically, as we are seeing once again with the inferior sound of the wildly popular MP3. Today, the 8-track tape is often mentioned as one of the more common examples of wrongheaded technology, even though it was the first tape format to achieve a national market.[25]

The Frankfurt and Birmingham Schools represent two poles. While the Birmingham School seemed to prevail for a while, the rise of what we now call globalization and new kinds of technologies such as satellite television, computers, and fax machines meant that cultural forms traveled farther and faster than ever before, a condition that in some quarters prompted a resurrection of arguments resembling those of the Frankfurt School. Jean Baudrillard, perhaps the most influential theorist of consumption in the last couple of decades, is in some sense a neo-Frankfurter. For my purposes here, what is most noteworthy about Baudrillard on the subject of consumption is that he, like so many authors, takes a position on what is to me the crucial theoretical issue of structure and agency. Baudrillard, like his earlier German forefathers, assumes a structure that dominates individuals. Rather than the culture industry, however, the dominating structure is the code, the system of signs that has replaced actual products (referents, or "finalities" in Baudrillard's language, which are thought of as having functions), which were once what people consumed. This system of signs structures reality itself, even produces it. Objects are no longer defined by their functions, by their relationships to people, but now are defined by their relationships to each other in the absence of the social that is assumed to have been effaced—and along with it, individual agency.

But studies of consumption have not been ethnographic.[26] Researchers who conduct ethnographies are not finding changes as dramatic (or negative) as Baudrillard and others predicted. James G. Carrier and Josiah McC. Heyman, for example, argue that contemporary patterns of consumption in the United States are far more connected to household interests and needs, whereas the familiar "cultural studies" notion of consumers as individuals "who contemplate, desire and acquire commodities" describes a fairly small subset of consumers and consumption patterns.[27] They preface this empirical argument with a trenchant critique of the recent academic interest in consumption—a turn, they say, that suffers from its synchronic approach, its use of psychocultural explanations (that is, explanations that are concerned with what goes on in people's minds as reflections of collective values), arguing that the literature on consumption represents consumption and consumers unidimensionally.

Carrier and Heyman are not arguing that previous theorists of consumption are wrong, simply that, without an ethnography or at least attention to specific social groups in specific times and locations, a practice as broad and ubiquitous as consumption cannot be theorized totally as either Horkheimer and Adorno on the one side, or Stuart Hall and the other "New Times" proponents on the other.[28]

Daniel Miller, another anthropologist of consumption, has written extensively about consumption and shopping and similarly finds that, contrary to a Baudrillardian top-down argument (and, perhaps more surprisingly, also contrary to what Stuart Hall and others have said), people shop as "an expression of kinship and other relationships."[29] This helps explain the massive popularity of Napster, a program that allows users to congregate in various chat rooms devoted to specific styles and genres of music and trade MP3s; they have access to your MP3s and you have access to theirs, effectively turning everyone's computer temporarily into a server. This means that MP3 distribution can be accomplished without any need for the music industry whatsoever except in the initial production of the distributed music. There is no need for a centralized distribution system, either physical or virtual (such as MP3.com). Napster permits fans to come together to converse and share their music, unlike other websites such as Gnutella that similarly offer free exchange of files but without a centralized website or meeting place.

These arguments about consumption make sense even from a commonsense perspective (though it is interesting how theorists of consumption never discuss their own, presumably commonsense, experiences of consumption). For me, at least, some shops are simply more fun to go into than others; some categories of items—such as books or CDs—are more fun to shop for than, say, shoes. Grocery stores with lovely displays of organic produce are far more inviting to me than shops featuring food from factory farms.

Despite the work of Carrier and Heyman and other ethnographers, the two poles, represented by the Frankfurt School (essentially top-down) and Birmingham School (more bottom-up), remain dominant. You are probably thinking I am about to propose some sort of middle ground between these two positions, but I am not. Facing facts, sometimes some consumers in some places and times are duped; sometimes some industries in some places and times fail to fool their customers. Practices of marketing and consumption, from being either top-down or bottom-up, are instead more like Stuart Hall's memorable characterization of the dynamic between dominant and subordinate cultures, "the double movement of containment and resistance" that never ends.[30]

Technology and Agency

This double movement can only happen because individuals have agency, albeit in varying degrees. And at this point I want to step back and attempt to put the foregoing into some kind of larger theoretical framework, always keeping in mind the issue of agency. There are a wide variety of writings in science and technology studies useful here that I will attempt to reconcile with social theories of practice.

The problem of top-down and bottom-up characterizations is not confined to models of consumer culture, but is much more widespread and is in fact one of the most intractable of all problems of social theory. It should thus be no surprise that technology is caught up in a similar set of debates and assumptions, with the idea of technological determinism as a kind of top-down model and voluntarism its polar opposite.

But first it is necessary to examine how this dichotomy has come to be possible in the realm of technology. The slipperiness of the term *technology* can lead to its reification, lifting it out of the social, cultural, and historical webs in which it is produced and used.[31] One would have to have been living outside our current moment not to have heard phrases such as "technology changes the way we see," as an ad for my local television news has it, as though it were technology and not our-selves making and using various technologies in a complex series of interlocking webs.[32] Anthropologist Bryan Pfaffenberger makes a simi-lar point, though for him, technology is usually fetishized in the classic Marxian sense, its social ties hidden.[33] Both points are useful; technol-ogy is both fetishized and reified, its social and historical existence understated or hidden entirely. But another anthropologist, Robert McC. Adams, reminds us that it is changes in the social world that have been more important in the direction of technological trends than the nature of the particular technology itself.[34] The same point may be applied to changes in technology itself: technological changes tend to occur for social and historical reasons rather than technical ones.[35]

The reification and fetishization of technology has resulted in assumptions about technology that can be characterized as usually falling on one of two poles. The first is the familiar voluntarism argu-ment: technology is a tool that people use, nothing more, and is thus essentially neutral; it is only good or bad depending on its use. The sec-ond is the position known as technological determinism, in which technology is assumed to transform its users directly. One could add yet a third position, what Langdon Winner has named "technological somnambulism," a term that refers to the uncritical attitude toward technology that assumes that, whatever it is, technology is made by engineers and used by everyone else; it is simply a tool and as such doesn't merit serious reflection or consideration.[36]

Technological Determinism

The most pernicious of these three positions is the notion of what has become known as technological determinism, in which technology is assumed to transform its users directly.[37] Phrases such as "technology is changing our lives," which attribute agency to technology, uncover one of the most potent and durable assumptions about technology—namely, that it changes us, perhaps more than we change it. Even though historians, sociologists, and other students of technology have labored assiduously to complicate this simplistic notion of technologi-cal determinism, it is nonetheless the case that this remains a salient viewpoint outside of the academy.[38]

But even in the academy, the idea of technological determinism has found new life in some studies of technology and media, where it usually appears as some kind of McLuhanesque idea that the nature of media alters our perceptions: "the medium is the message."

We are, perhaps not surprisingly, in the midst of renewed interested in the writings of Marshall McLuhan, whose work never strayed far from a fairly strict determinist idea of the effects of media. The Canadian scholar's works are being cited again and again in the face of new digital technology; a collection of his writings has recently been published, as well as a book by Paul Levinson called *Digital McLuhan*, in which the author posits that McLuhan's contemporaries thought he was talking about television when he was in fact presciently talking about the Internet.[39]

Despite Levinson's attempts to soften some of McLuhan's more extreme language, McLuhan's technological deterministic attitudes are unmistakable. For example, take the well-known statement that "the medium . . . shapes and controls the scale and form of human association and action."[40] "Shapes and controls"—there is little room for maneuvering or agency here. McLuhan's clearly deterministic language is not mitigated by later statements, only amplified: "The effects of technology do not occur at the level of opinions or concepts, but alter sense ratios or patterns of perception steadily and without any resistance."[41] All of this is not to say that McLuhan was entirely wrong, simply that he overstated the case.[42]

Since music is part of this "media" it is important to take McLuhan's and his revivalists' ideas apart a little bit. Friedrich A. Kittler's *Gramophone, Film, Typewriter* provides a recent example. Kittler is a Foucauldian-Lacanian, or Lacanian-Foucauldian, and in this conjunction ends up in or near McLuhanville. At one point, Kittler offers an argument about the decreasing necessity for human memory with the improvement in modes of storage: " 'The more complicated the technology, the simpler,' that is, the more forgetful, 'we can live.' Records turn and turn until phonographic inscriptions inscribe themselves into brain physiology. We all know hits and rock songs by heart precisely because there is no reason to memorize them anymore." Kittler goes on to quote Siegfried Kracauer about a typist he knows, " 'for whom it is characteristic that she cannot hear a piece of music in a dance hall or a suburban café without chirping along with its text. But it is not as if she knows all the hits; rather, the hits know her, they catch up with her, killing her softly.' "[43] Now, there is some truth to this. We have all had the experience of being reminded of a song or lyric, which seems almost to trigger our singing or humming it. But Kittler is unconcerned with whether or not Kracauer's secretary likes singing the hits, whether she derives some pleasure from doing so. To argue that the songs sing her is a defensible position, but it is not defensible to omit the possibility that she makes her own complex and personal meanings of them. I suspect, also, that if this secretary could hum along with Johannes Brahms she would have invited Kracauer's—and perhaps Kittler's—approbation instead of disdain.

Music Marketing

Arturo Escobar reminds us that the role of capital must be considered in the face of new technologies.[44] As a way of examining these changes while keeping an eye on the issue of determinism and agency, particularly the ways that technological/media determinism intersect with theories of consumption discussed above, I want to turn now to another brief discussion of the music industry. The flexibility afforded listeners by digital distribution, licit and illicit, isn't theirs alone. They may be agents in the ways that they listen, but the music industry has increased its own flexibility as well. Many music listeners are quite sophisticated about obtaining and even manipulating music found on the Internet, and the music industry, for its part, is learning to be just as sophisticated in the way that it brings this music to the fans' attention. When RCA Records—a division of BMG, one of the "majors" (that is, a handful of the biggest record companies in the world)—wanted to promote its new star Christina Aguilera, it hired an Internet marketing company to promote Aguilera's 1999 eponymous debut album. Electric Artists of New York City formulated a plan. Stage one consisted of surfing the web to ascertain the current buzz on Aguilera. There was some discussion already, for Aguilera had released a single that was getting some radio airplay. Most fans didn't know, however, that one of her songs, "Reflection," had appeared in a hit Disney film, *Mulan* (1998). Leaving what they had called stage one, information gathering, for stage two, information disseminating, Electric Artists passed that information around in messages such as: "Does anyone remember Christina Aguilera—she sang the song from 'Mulan,' 'Reflection'? I heard she has a new song out called 'Genie in a Bottle.' "[45]

Electric Artists sent out pleas to encourage fans to ask their local radio stations to request the song in mid-July 1999. "Genie" went to the top of the singles charts, but the full album wasn't due out for another six weeks. Electric Artists continued their campaign, sending out information on Aguilera's television appearances and other information.

The album was scheduled for release on August 24, 1999, and earlier that month Electric Artists stepped up its efforts. They posted song snippets on a fan website. RCA also hired a direct-marketing firm to compose an electronic postcard containing song excerpts and biographical information, which was mailed on August 23 to 50,000 web addresses of prospective buyers, identified from their previous album purchases. When the album was eventually released, it debuted at number 1 and reached double platinum (two million albums shipped) in record time; it remained in the top 5 for weeks after its release; by the end of November 1999 it had sold four million copies.[46] Early in 2000, Aguilera won the Grammy award for Best New Artist.

Officials from Electric Artists claimed in a *Wall Street Journal* article that their cybersurfer hirelings identified themselves as employees of Electric Artists, though this doesn't appear to be true; one of their marketers (whose job title is "Grassroots/Community Marketing") wrote in messages from earthlink.net (not electricartists.com), where, according to the firm's website, he has an e-mail address.[47] As of this writing, there has been only one online post about this marketing strategy in any Usenet group—at alt.fan.hanson.

"Leverage" seems to be Electric Artists' favorite verb, judging from their website, for it appears in the first and last sentences of their introduction of themselves on their homepage: "Leveraging the Internet and new technologies, Electric Artists is remarkably re-defining the way music is marketed and consumed." And, "If your business involves music, or if your company is looking to leverage music to help strengthen your brand, you've come to the right place."[48]

Doubtless some future fans of Aguilera became fans when they picked up on the phony buzz created by Electric Artists. But, like Kracauer's secretary, this does not mean that they haven't found their own reasons to enjoy Aguilera's music.

Raymond Williams wrote over twenty-five years ago that the two positions of technological determinism on the one hand and voluntarism on the other "are so deeply established . . . that it is very difficult to think beyond them," a statement even more applicable today.[49] Still, it is clear that to some extent the various media and technologies we use to disseminate and store information change our perceptions;

something like determinism does happen sometimes. I am just unwilling to go as far as the technological determinists in saying that our perceptions are *directly* or *wholly* changed or determined by them. The theoretical and methodological problem, however, concerns ways of navigating between the historically well-established poles of technological determinism (or the controlling nature of any structure) and individual voluntarism. Williams used the phrase "symptomatic technology" to refer to the opposite position of technological determinism, but it is clear that his term labels what I am calling here voluntarism. Technology, he writes, is seen as "either a self-acting force which creates new ways of life, or it is a self-acting force which provides materials for new ways of life."[50] Williams rightly rejects these positions, however, for both, he says, isolate technology from society. Thus, we must also take issue with definitions of technology forwarded by Jon Frederickson and also employed by Paul Théberge in their studies of music and technology, for they adopt a notion of what they call "social technology" (technologies with specific uses and social formations) and "machine technology."[51]

In attempting to modify or obviate the voluntarism/determinism dichotomy, however, I think some have gone too far. For example, Michael Menser and Stanley Aronowitz write, "Technology does not *determine* social organization nor does it *cause* the rise of global capitalism. . . . We claim that, although technology and science may be everywhere, there is no determinism anywhere, if by determinism we signify a one-to-one correspondence between the causal agent and its effects; rather technology *permeates*, or inheres in, all these regions, practices, and ideologies."[52] But there are ways, as we shall see, that technological determinism happens. It is simply not an accurate description of the way that technology works in culture.

Instead of the foregoing uses or reuses of the concept of technological determinism, I prefer to follow those historians, sociologists, philosophers, and other students of technology and media in science and technology studies who view technology as neither voluntaristic nor deterministic but as caught up in a complex, fluid, variable dynamic of each. This relatively recent perspective was first forwarded, albeit obliquely, by Martin Heidegger in "The Question Concerning Technology." Heidegger's argument continues the somewhat pessimistic view of Lewis Mumford and José Ortega y Gasset—that technology, while neutral in and of itself, runs the risk of decreasing our humanity or creating a rift between our creative sides and our scientific sides (as Mumford wrote in *Art and Technics*).[53] For Heidegger, technology is not technical, not a tool or machine, but rather, a process, a dynamic of "revealing."[54]

Agency in Theories of Technology in Society

In debates over determinism and voluntarism, it is clearly agency that makes the difference: people are either agents in the face of technology, or they are unagentic. But this is clearly not the case with the users of MP3s, the remixers of MP3s, and the DJs. A technological determinist argument would hold that the advent of the MP3 (which I am using here as an example, not as the only kind of new digital technology) in real ways *determines* how listeners use it, that MP3 technology is actively changing music itself. It seems, however, that hardly a day goes by without a new use of MP3s cropping up or a new software application being devised. MP3s are being used in ways that were inconceivable with the advent of this particular technology. So a theory that provides for some degree of agency is clearly necessary.

In several writings, Wiebe E. Bijker has identified three current modes of analysis that begin from a sociotechnical systems, or what he calls "sociotechnical ensembles," approach. (These approaches have been widely characterized and summarized and there is no need to rehearse them here except to introduce them to readers who might not know them).[55] The operating assumption is congenial: technology is never simply an artifact, but always caught up in social, historical, and institutional webs, an idea whose recent success Bijker credits to Donald A. MacKenzie and Judy Wajcman's *The Social Shaping of Technology*, first published in 1985 and since updated.[56]

But this assumption does not prescribe a particular method of study. There are three main approaches that Bijker labels: the "systems approach," in which large technological systems are the main focal point of analysis; the "actor-network" approach, which attempts to analyze any sociotechnical ensemble with the same analytical framework for both human and nonhuman actors, in a sense granting some degree of agency to objects; and, finally, Bijker's own approach, formulated with Trevor Pinch, called the "social construction of technology," or SCOT, which starts first by examining what Pinch and Bijker call "relevant social groups"—that is, those groups responsible for developing a technology.[57] This last approach has also been called the "social construction" perspective.[58]

While all of these approaches are useful, I think they have similar limitations. In attempting to get around, or minimize, the problem of technological determinism, which is a more complex and intractable problem than voluntarism, most of these theories sidestep the question of agency. Also, while it would be wrong to assume that there is no determinism or voluntarism, most agree that we need a way of building determinism into any theory so that it can be considered in the moments that it does happen, instead of resorting to a vague and slippery position somewhere in a putative continuum of "hard" or "strong" technological determinism at the one pole and "soft" or "weak" at the other.

Of the major approaches currently available, actor-network theory takes this into account, though in a problematic way. Actor-network theory, associated mainly with Madeleine Akrich, Michel Callon, Bruno Latour, and John Law, argues that human subjects and technological artifacts should be studied with the same methods; that is, no analytical distinction should be made between subjects and objects, which in effect ascribes agency, or potential agency, to artifacts. This is accomplished by acts of "translation," in which various engineers' ideas about design are thrown up against one another, and the resulting design is "inscribed" into artifacts, which then act on human users who are in effect objects of that artifact.

In the words of Bruno Latour, "actor-network theory (hence AT) has very little to do with the study of social networks. These studies no matter how interesting concerns [*sic*] themselves with the *social* relations of *individual human* actors—their frequency, distribution, homogeneity, proximity. It was devised as a reaction to the often too global concepts like those of institutions, organizations, states and nations, adding to them more realistic and smaller set of associations. Although AT shares this distrust for such vague all encompassing sociological terms it aims at describing also the very nature of societies. But to do so it does not limit itself to human individual actors but extend [*sic*] the word actor—or actant—to *non-human, non individual* entities."[59]

Agency thus becomes a kind of discrete, transferable entity, which in actor-network theory means that human agents are always already somewhat diminished; actor-network theorists therefore tend to prefer the term *actant* to the more common social science term *actor* in describing the human agent, a shift that demonstrates the ways that, in this theory, the agent, even when he is an agent, is less than an agent. The issue here is, first, that to ascribe agency to nonhumans is highly problematic; only humans can be agents in any meaningful social science sense. In attempting to permit some degree of technological determinism, or, at least, material effect, into their theory, these and other actor-network proponents seem to assume that determinism and agency are all-or-nothing propositions, but the real world of people and things is characterized by a dynamism and a variability that their theory fails to capture adequately.

What Latour and most theorists in science and technology studies (STS) accomplish by focusing on actors/actants and ascribing some degree of agency to objects is that they tend to evade that entity entailed by agency: structure. Structures act on agents, not objects. I will discuss this theoretical problem in depth shortly but here simply want to note the way that, in attempting to account for the actions of social actors with respect to technology, it is the *objects* that are appealed to, not *structure* in the classic social science usage of the term.[60]

In recent studies of information technology, a few researchers have forwarded an adaptation of Anthony Giddens's theory of structuration. Some of the familiar problems occur here, however, for as the name implies, structuration theory is more about structuration than agency, and the way that it has been used by most researchers has continued this bias toward structure. In the absence of an ethnographic perspective, most such studies—which appear mostly in the realm of the study of information technology—reduce agents to cogs in a structural wheel.[61] Rob Hagendijk, however, has argued that structuration theory provides some important answers that elude what he calls constructivist theories (which include actor-network, the main theory he argues against).[62] The reluctance of constructivists such as Latour and others to accept that there is a structure that exists independently of what a given set of actor/agents can make of it means that constructivists cannot satisfactorily explain why certain scientific ideas are accepted rather than others, for example.[63]

It could be said that I am focusing too much on agents and not enough on the technology. But my goal here is not to forward some kind of putative "balanced" approach to the study of technology in society; one could argue that that is what actor-network theory is, or at least is attempting, to be. Rather, I am simply more interested in people and music than gadgets. The people I am interested in, however, are not necessarily the innovators, the inventors, the engineers, or the agents of change—the usual focus of STS. I am interested in everyday people and how they use everyday objects of technology, new or old, to make, disseminate, and listen to music. And it is precisely they who are omitted from the established STS theories, actor-network theory in particular. Bruno Latour and the others who advocate the actor-network approach do write about everyday technology, such as door closers and European hotel keys, and it could be argued that it doesn't matter who uses these objects, or to what end; these objects are designed to have one function, and it is for that function that most users employ them.[64] But what about more complex technology? What about a typewriter, a camera, an automobile? Things quickly become much more complicated.

Toward a Practice Theory of Technology

In a field already littered with theories—some still in use, others moribund, and still others, no doubt, nascent—I am nonetheless proposing another way of looking at technology in society that takes the most useful aspects of actor-network theory and Anthony Giddens's (and others') ideas about structure and agency. There is an existing body of theory that one could turn to (though to my knowledge it has scarcely been used to examine technology), and that is practice theory. Sherry B. Ortner writes that "studies of the ways in which some set of 'texts' . . . 'constructs' categories, identities, or subject positions, are incomplete and misleading unless they ask to what degree those texts successfully impose themselves on real people (and *which people*) in real time."[65] Texts—and technologies.

For Ortner, practice theory constitutes the one body of theory that can grapple adequately with the problem of structures and individual agency, though Ortner is careful to note that practice theory is less a theory than a founding argument—"that human action is made by 'structure,' and at the same time always makes and potentially unmakes it."[66] Practice theory provides a way of avoiding the traps of theorizing the subject and agency in the face of technology without falling back into the polarized positions of voluntarism on the one hand and some kind of structural determinism on the other, which seem to be the only two available points from which to argue. Agency, for my purposes here, refers to an individual actor's or collective capacity to move within a structure, even alter it to some extent. "The challenge," Ortner writes, "is to picture indissoluble formations of structurally embedded agency and intention-filled structures, to recognize the ways in which the subject is part of larger social and cultural webs, and in which social and cultural 'systems' are predicated upon human desires and projects."[67]

Ortner proposes the idea of "serious games" as a way of indicating the part conscious, part intentional, part scripted nature of social relations and human activities: "The idea of the game is on the one hand drawn from a variety of past social theories . . . as a way of getting past the free agency question, and theorizing a picture of people-in-(power)-relationships-in-projects as the relatively irreducible unit of 'practice.'"[68]

Still, calling technology a "structure" in the classic social theoretical sense may seem to be problematic. Whatever technology is, it is clearly always changing, whereas the term *structure* seems to imply something that is comparatively static. I thus want to spend some time outlining the ways that technology can be considered a structure in the classic sense in which Ortner and other social theorists use the concept, and why calling it a structure helps us make sense of it as a social and historical phenomenon. (I should also note here that anthropologist Bryan Pfaffenberger argues that his idea of the sociotechnical system is harmonious with Giddens's conception of structure as discussed in *Central Problems of Social Theory*, though he doesn't pursue this.[69])

William H. Sewell offers a particularly cogent argument concerning the nature of structure. Pointing out that "structure" in Giddens's theory (or anyone's, for that matter) is notoriously ill-defined, Sewell undertakes to clarify what the term might mean, carefully critiquing Giddens's usage of the concept. This usage is quite similar to Ortner's in that structure is seen not as a monolithic entity, but always dual; that is, structure both makes and is made by people. Structure, thus, does not preclude agency, but rather, structure and agency presuppose each other.

Still, it is a long way from structure to technology. Or is it? Sewell tackles Giddens's murky definition of structure and carefully sorts through meanings and implications in it. Structures are rules, according to Giddens, which means that they are not patterned social practices themselves, but the principles that pattern social practices, patterns that are difficult, if not impossible, to perceive; they are "virtual," they exist as "memory traces" rather than as concrete entities.[70]

Giddens argues that structures are also resources. Sewell explicates this to argue that resources can be both human and nonhuman, which includes "objects, animate or inanimate, naturally occurring or manufactured, that can be used to enhance or maintain power."[71] It is possible to excise resources from the conception of structure, and argue that structures are only rules or schemas, and then posit that resources are an effect of structures.

This means we are assuming that technology, as a resource, is also an effect of rules or schemas. Is this tenable? Sewell does not consider technology in his article, instead confining his discussion to resources in an everyday use of the term; he discusses (for just one example) the resources generated by a factory and the ends to which these resources can be put, but does not consider the factory and its technologies as resources themselves. Whether or not technology is included in this formulation, Sewell would probably find the idea that technology is the product of schemas to be problematic, for it implies a causal relationship between schemas and resources. Schemas, in this usage tantamount to structure itself, produce resources, which means we have failed to get around the problem of causality in structure and agency.

So structure should be thought of as "schemas, which are virtual, and of resources, which are actual," which means that each is an effect of the other.[72] And, Sewell continues, "Sets of schemas and resources may properly be said to constitute *structures* only when they mutually imply and sustain each other over time."[73]

Since the term *structure* can connote stasis, Sewell is careful to argue that structures are not fixed, but are mutable by agents. Agency entails knowledge of schemas; schemas are less the "memory traces" as Giddens would have it, or invisible and unspoken, as in Pfaffenberger.[74] Agents, however—and thus, agency—are not all the same. "Structures, and the human agencies they endow, are laden with differences in power."[75]

Technology, I rather think, is a special kind of structure. It is both a schema or set of schemas, and a resource or set of resources. It is no accident that some have interpreted "technology" to refer both to tools and machines, as well as techniques and kinds of knowledge. Bryan Pfaffenberger uses the term *technique* to refer to "the system of material resources, tools, operational sequences and skills, verbal and nonverbal knowledge, and *specific* modes of work coordination that come into play in the fabrication of material artifacts."[76] It is possible to incorporate arguments by Heidegger and others who concentrate on schemas—that is, the intangibles—as well as those who prefer to think of technology as tools, as material objects. Technology is a peculiar kind of structure that is made up of both schemas and resources, in which the schemas are those rules that are largely unspoken by technology's users, thereby allowing for some degree of determinism, while technology as a resource refers to what we do with it—that is, what is voluntaristic.

While adopting a notion of technology as a peculiar kind of structure, and structure as something that entails agency, is a way of moving beyond the poles of technological determinism and voluntarism, it is nonetheless the case that some sociotechnical systems provide for greater and varying degrees of agency compared to others. That is, I am not rejecting the notions of technological determinism or voluntarism out of hand, but am instead saying that both positions are overtotalized and falsely binarized, and that opposing them masks the ways that some sociotechnical systems are more deterministic than others (though never wholly deterministic), that some provide for more voluntarism than others (though never total voluntarism), and that social actors do not have the same experiences with any sociotechnical system. Experiences vary in the familiar ways—based on social class, age, geographical location, gender, sexual orientation, religion, race, ethnicity, cultural capital, and so on. In short, while I am insisting that technology is a kind of structure, and that everyone is an agent, the positionality of any individual agent matters. As we shall see in chapter 7, sometimes actors *voluntarily* behave in ways that seem to be determined by the technology with which they have contact.

What a practice theory notion of structure—and, more generally, practice theory itself—forces us to keep in mind, then, is not only the founding argument, "that human action is made by 'structure,' and at the same time always makes and potentially unmakes it," but also the central question: what are these social actors doing in this time and place, and why?[77] By putting practice theory in the foreground of one's considerations, individual subjects and subjects-as-agents are always important, though never central, just as the structures that act on them are always important but never central.

Any music technology, then, both acts on its users and is continually acted on by them; MP3s—or any software or hardware—have designed into them specific uses, which are followed by listeners, but at the same time, listeners through their practices undermine, add to, and modify those uses in a never-ending process.

TIME

POSTWAR MUSIC AND THE TECHNOSCIENTIFIC IMAGINARY

[The] computer has given us the opportunity to tap into history in a way we could never do before, and that gives us the opportunity to create our own perspective of what we've been brought up with all our lives.

—*Derrick May,*
Detroit techno music pioneer,
as quoted on the Internet

While it may seem that technology has only recently become a central factor in social and cultural life, the current hype isn't new. In the post–World War II era, all kinds of technologies—televisions, hi-fis, kitchen gadgets, and much more—quickly infiltrated all aspects of everyday life in ways it hadn't before. Eric Hobsbawm describes a "technological earthquake"; he writes that the rapid economic growth in the postwar era "seemed powered by technological innovation."[1] Hobsbawm lists the inventions, many of which were developed or whose development was hastened because of the war: the transistor, digital computers, jet engines, radar. Perhaps more significantly, technology "utterly transformed everyday life in the rich world and even, to a lesser extent, in the poor world."[2] The problems of what Hobsbawm called "the era of catastrophe" (the two world wars) "seemed to dissolve and disappear"[3]: free market capitalism, coupled with technological growth, were thought to be able to solve all social and economic ills.[4]

Following World War II, a technoscientific worldview assumed a hegemony that it had never enjoyed before. It was this technoscientific imaginary that won the war, after all, with the Manhattan Project emerging as one of the most stupendous feats of science and engineering ever.[5] Whether or not the bomb was seen as a beneficial or a troubling invention, the increasingly salient role that science and technology played in the lives of everyday people following the war is unmistakable.

One wartime development that ultimately affected music was the invention of magnetic tape. Following World War II, magnetic tape technology had progressed to the point that tape was used not just as a means of recording but also as a new experimental musical medium. Foremost among the early experimenters with tape was Pierre Schaeffer (1910–1995), a writer, electronic engineer, and composer who published an article in 1950 in which he introduced the term *musique concrète* to describe the kind of musical "found object" works he was learning to fashion, first with turntables and later with tape recorders.[6] In this chapter, I will concentrate on Schaeffer and another *musique concrète* composer, Pierre Henry (b. 1927), because of their importance as composers in their own time and also because they have exerted influence on popular musicians outside the realm of "art" music today; there are hundreds of Internet postings, for example, on these and other early electronic musicians by fans and makers of contemporary popular electronic music.

With the possibility of making music with tape, composers and others began to be concerned with the place of this music in the great trajectory of Western European art music composition: how did this new music fit in with the masterpieces of the past? Another issue concerned signification: what does music communicate, if it does at all? This chapter seeks to situate these concerns in a postwar moment of composition. The two main schools of electronic music that emerged—*musique concrète* in France and *elektronische Musik* in Germany—offered different solutions. One figure, however, remained largely outside these debates and pursued a more personal musical path. Pierre Henry, originally affiliated with Schaeffer, did not share the fears of technology and was more concerned with music as communication than were most of his peers. Because of these positions, I think, Henry is currently being hailed by some in the new generation of DJs and techno musicians as the father (or grandfather) of techno music.

Postwar Culture and the Technoscientific Imaginary

Wartime and postwar technological changes affected every aspect of everyday life in the industrialized world, not just at the level of jet engines or computers. In France, the U.S. development of the atomic bomb precipitated a renewed drive to fund science and technology, and played a pivotal role in the rise of modern, technocratic France. Scientists did not hold back their rhetoric. Frédéric Joliot-Curie, who married Marie and Pierre Curie's daughter Irène and who became one of the most prominent and powerful scientific and public figures in France following the war, said in 1945, "I will state quite simply that if this country does not make the necessary effort to give science the importance it merits and to give those who serve it the prestige necessary for their influence to be felt, it will sooner or later become a colony."[7] This utterance betrays an underlying assumption that equates modernity, and thus prestige, with science, an ideology constructed explicitly against the French (and other) colonies' supposed premodern condition. In France, the process of modernization became linked with the role of science and technology, and proponents of this new technocracy successfully argued that pursuing this path would return France to its former glory. Joliot-Curie, speaking early in 1945, argued for "the importance of science and technology for the war effort and for the renaissance of the Nation."[8]

But it was the bomb that first captured France's attention more than anything else. Anyone who voiced moral reservations about the United States dropping the bomb on Hiroshima and Nagasaki was countered by Joliot-Curie's and other scientists' familiar voluntarism arguments about science and technology, that they are themselves innocent, it is only the politicians who are to blame. This position proved to be effective. Historian David Pace has written vividly of the French nation's infatuation with things atomic following the war, so that the word *atomique* "itself broke loose from its origin in physics and took on the abstract meaning of 'great' or 'striking.'"[9] And in 1946, the bikini swimsuit was named by its French fashion designer for the island where the first postwar atomic tests were conducted.

Pace writes that "the link between nuclear physics and France's prestige and position in the world quite naturally strengthened the sense of the importance of science. Virtually no one writing in France in the aftermath of Hiroshima contradicted Louis de Broglie's claim that 'henceforth, more than ever before, the grandeur and power of nations will depend on the ardor with which they seek to pursue and hasten the progress of science.' "[10] This resurgence of importance in science was rather utopian, however; all the discussions of what atomic power could accomplish were carried out in postwar conditions where there were many hardships, including power shortages; a cartoon published in December 1945 entitled "Chronicle of the Atomic Era" showed "a man lecturing on 'the formidable source of energy placed at the disposition of man' in a dark room lit by a single candle."[11]

Using the bomb and atomic energy as a foot in the door, Joliot-Curie and others managed to make science and technology important parts of the political landscape in postwar France. Even before the conclusion of the war, Joliot-Curie was named head of the new Centre National de la Recherche Scientifique, which oversaw most scientific research in the country. When Charles de Gaulle returned to power in 1959, it was clear that he wanted what Walter A. McDougall has called "permanent technological revolution," which in any event was already well underway.[12] It must be stressed, however, that the roots of French interest in science, and the connections between the arts and the sciences that have existed in French culture, go back to the utopian socialists Saint-Simons and Charles Fourier in the 1830s. Saint-Simon's utopia, Georgina Born writes, was to include a government that was to be an "elite at once intellectual, industrial, and managerial," a utopia that "centered on a dialogue between artists, scientists, and engineers, with artists having a leading role in the imaginative exploration of reality."[13] The detonation of the first atomic bombs provided the last motivation for the rise of the French technocratic society long envisioned by de Gaulle and others.

Postwar Music and the Technoscientific Imaginary

Given the ideological power of science and technology, the arts were inevitably affected; Eric Hobsbawm, in beginning his overview of the arts in postwar era, states simply, "As might have been expected in an era of extraordinary techno-scientific revolution, [the exogenous forces acting on the arts] were predominantly technological."[14] Leo Marx writes that "the cultural modernism of the West in the early twentieth century was permeated by [a] technocratic spirit," a "kind of technocratic utopianism."[15]

France and Musique Concrète

Music in France was as implicated in this technocratic spirit as any other art. French composers were pursuing different ideas about new musical directions. Pierre Schaeffer noted the two possible paths art could take in an era of high technology: either technology could come to the rescue of art (his position), or the ideas of science and technology could be adopted for use in making art.[16] Schaeffer clearly viewed technology as a way of rejuvenating music in the immediate postwar era while at the same time critiquing his rival composers, whom I will discuss shortly.

Rather than presenting an overview of Schaeffer and *musique concrète* (as Carlos Palombini has admirably done), I want instead to discuss the issue of meaning—both signification and communication, major concerns in the early days of this music—and, to a lesser extent, historical prestige.[17] A little introduction to Schaeffer and *musique concrète* is, nonetheless, necessary. The first point is to note that *musique concrète* was not, at least for Schaeffer, simply a genre, but a compositional aesthetic arrived upon in 1948 after several years of studio research: "We have called our music 'concrete' because it is constituted from pre-existing elements taken from whatever sound material, be it noise or conventional music, and then composed by working directly with the material."[18] The term *concrete* was probably borrowed from Max Bill's idea of "concrete art," which was reasonably well known at the time, referring to a style that was clear and antinaturalist; later, however, as we shall see, Schaeffer's idea of the concrete shifts to become virtually synonymous with Claude Lévi-Strauss's.[19] Thus, for example, Schaeffer said he intended that the term *musique concrète* "point out an opposition with the way a musical work usually goes. Instead of notating musical ideas on paper with the symbols of solfège and entrusting their realization to well-known instruments, the question was to collect concrete sounds, wherever they came from, and to abstract the musical values they were potentially containing," a process I will examine in greater detail.[20] Many years later, Schaeffer also made a comparison to painting: *musique concrète* was like figurative—not abstract—painting because it, like figurative painting, draws on objects from the visible world, in a way resembling collage.[21]

Lévi-Strauss argues precisely against this comparison in *The Raw and the Cooked*. For him, *musique concrète* is akin to abstract painting in that "its first concern is to disrupt the system of actual or potential meanings," since *musique concrète* composers endeavor to alter the source sounds so that they are not easily recognizable. As a result, "*musique concrète* may be intoxicated with the illusion that it is saying something; in fact, it is floundering in non-significance."[22]

This desire to make the source sounds unrecognizable was necessary, Schaeffer believed, in order to allow the formal properties of the particular work to emerge, for if listeners concentrated on recognizable sounds they would be distracted by these rather than the composer's skill. This problem of what we might call residual signification is central. Recognizable sounds might evoke residual meanings that listeners might associate with the sounds' origins, which would mean that the composer is neither creating, nor in total control of, a self-contained aesthetic object. Schaeffer wrote in 1952 that "even if noise material ensured for me a certain margin of originality in relation to music, I was . . . led to the same problem: the extraction of sound material from whatever dramatic or musical context, before wanting to give a form to it. If I succeeded there would be a *musique concrète*. If not there would be only trickery and procedures of radio production."[23] In an interview not long before his death, Schaeffer put the problem more directly: "You have two sources for sounds: noises, which always tell you something—a door cracking, a dog barking, the thunder, the storm; and then you have instruments. An instrument tells you, la-la-la-la (sings a scale)."[24]

In another publication, Schaeffer describes the engine sound in his first *musique concrète* work, *Étude aux chemins de fer* (*Railway Study*, 1948), as sounding like "casting in a foundry."[25] After this description, Schaeffer goes on, as though to justify the use of this metaphorical language: "I say 'foundry' to render it comprehensible myself, and always because a little 'meaning' remains attached to the fragment. I concluded from this that *musique concrète* will be opposed again to traditional music on a significant point. In classical music, C is C, whatever its register. For *musique concrète*, a sound, in general a sound 'complex,' is inseparable from its situation in the sound spectrum."[26]

But Schaeffer came to realize that listeners would inevitability associate *musique concrète* sounds with their origins, and so moved toward composition that included instruments and began devising ways of manipulating the sounds by playing recordings at different speeds and removing the initial attack (the beginning of the sound) of the recorded sounds, which renders them much less recognizable.[27] This would allow him to circumvent the possibility of listeners hearing residual significations and reexert control over the "quality" of the sound itself.

In fashioning this new music, Schaeffer appeared to feel no need to appeal to the great musical works of the past for either sustenance or prestige; indeed, prominent French artists and intellectuals—Olivier Messiaen, Henry Michaux, and Claude Lévi-Strauss—urged him to make a break with the past with *musique concrète*.[28] Also, Schaeffer was not a trained composer, and so music history was not of as much interest to him as it was to composers in Germany; thus the burden of tradition was lighter on his shoulders: in Foucauldian terms, he was less disciplined by a compositional tradition.

Germany and Elektronische Musik

Schaeffer soon found himself at odds with Austro-German composers, however. The disagreements are instructive, and in order to understand them it is necessary to spend some time outlining the state of composition in postwar Austria and Germany. There, finding music of the past to draw on for inspiration was still important for most composers. Postwar German composers wanted to emphasize what the Nazis had demonized. Thus, their Austro-music wasn't going to try to start afresh but build on the shoulders of the heroes of the past. Of course, there were many heroes available to be drafted: Igor Stravinsky (who was still alive but living in California, not Europe), Béla Bartók (who died in 1945), Maurice Ravel (who died 1937), and others. But the exiled Jewish composer Arnold Schoenberg (1875–1951) best fit the bill, and it was to him that the younger postwar musicians first turned.

Much of the installation of Schoenberg and the Second Viennese School as the predominant school of composition immediately following the war was due to the publication in 1948 of Theodor Adorno's *Philosophy of Modern Music*, in which Schoenberg emerged as the composer of courage and integrity who followed the inevitable historical path of increasing complexity and logic, while Igor Stravinsky was little more than a gifted prestidigitator who wallowed in older forms and sonorities while pretending that he was doing something new.[29] Despite Stravinsky's popularity with audiences, his influence on composers following the war quickly attenuated.

In an attempt to legitimate their music, and to show that it was not insular or strange, organizers of concerts following the war often juxtaposed new music with music from the Second Viennese School. Pierre Boulez (b. 1925), the most vocal proponent of the Second Viennese School, says that these programs were designed "Firstly, to show that contemporary music does not represent a historical 'break,' as has been too easily admitted, but that there is quite clear evidence of historical continuity. Second, to make up the balance sheet of the artistic generation immediately preceding our own."[30] Since the Second Viennese School composers believed themselves to be following an Austro-German tradition (a stance echoed by Adorno), postwar composers' alignment with them was even more potent.

Yet the link to Schoenberg was ruthlessly jettisoned after his death in 1951 in favor of one of his students, Anton Webern (1883–1945). Boulez was the hatchet man: in a 1952 essay entitled "Schoenberg Is Dead," he officially declared him passé at best, writing that Schoenberg's attempt to integrate traditional formal, textural, and rhythmic ideas with the method of composing with twelve tones (in which the composer, rather than drawing on a major or minor scale, constructs a "row" or "series" of all twelve pitches, which are then manipulated in various ways) "went off in the wrong direction so persistently that it would be hard to find an equally mistaken perspective in the entire history of music."[31] This judgment, however, had been foreshadowed for some time. In a 1949 essay, for example, Boulez was already rewriting music history so that Webern could replace Schoenberg, claiming "it is undeniable that Webern's soaring flight required that springboard; but, in truth, Webern's Five Movements for String Quartet, opus 9, dating from 1909, already showed him taking a position more virulent than that of his master's works of the same year, a position that in a sense would lead to their annihilation. Will that prove to have been Schoenberg's only justification? It almost seems so."[32]

Such advertisements for Webern were required, since he was the least celebrated member of the Second Viennese School triumvarite, which also included Schoenberg and Alban Berg (1885–1935).[33] Shot and killed by an American soldier in 1945 who hadn't known that armistice had been declared, Webern was in a sense a martyr of the war. Choosing him as their hero would allow his followers to connect their work with Webern's and not have to tangle with composers still living, such as Schoenberg himself, whose very existence connected them to a recent past that postwar composers were anxious to forget. Dropping Schoenberg in favor of Webern was relatively straightforward, for before the war Adorno and other writers frequently wrote of Berg as the more recognizably Romantic of the three composers—thus Schoenberg's link to the past, with Webern the bridge to the future. The cover of the *New Grove Second Viennese School* bears a collage of photographs that places Schoenberg in the center with Berg on the left and Webern on the right, as though music itself is moving from Berg to Schoenberg to Webern.[34]

Further, Webern's music was the most rigorous in its use of Schoenberg's method of composing with twelve tones, and the explosion of interest in compositional procedure and method following the war made Webern's supremely orderly way of composing compelling and attractive.[35] These followers of Webern attempted to extend twelve-tone techniques into the realm of electronic music and were concerned with composing music that was as rigorously organized as possible. As Boulez wrote, "Let us go back to the music itself. . . . The chief elected predecessor: Webern; the essential object of the investigations into him: organization of the sound-material."[36] This is a fortuitous juxtaposition for my argument here, for it shows what the two salient, and connected, issues were for Boulez and other composers of the era: finding a predecessor, which for them was the same thing as finding a method.

Yet resurrecting Webern out of the past meant constructing him as having been ahead of his time—it is with *this* music of the past that the music of the future can be made *against* the past. "It is with Webern, then, that there irrupt into the acquired sensibility the first elements of a kind of musical thought irreducible to the fundamental schemata of earlier sound-worlds," wrote Boulez.[37]

Elektronische Musik *versus* Musique Concrète

Much of this pro-Webern rhetoric was about serial composition (an extension of Schoenberg's method of composing with twelve tones to many more musical parameters—duration, register, attack, dynamics) of acoustic works. But German composers had their own electronic music, too. *Elektronische Musik* was produced by composers working under the auspices of the Westdeutscher Rundfunk. Their music was synthesized, and because they could make their own sounds rather than collecting them in the real world as the *musique concrète* composers did, *elektronische Musik* composers believed that their electronic music could be presented as the only possibility for the rigorous realization of serial music.[38]

Given the necessity that these composers felt for reestablishing the superiority of Austro-German music following World War II, pretenders had to be vanquished. Boulez wrote,"Happily, the composers who have attacked the problems of electronic music have a different scope [than the *musique concrète* musicians]. And if that domain does become important one day, it will be thanks to the efforts of the Cologne and Milan studios, not to the derisory, outdated magic of the amateurs, as miserable as they are needy, who operate under the tattered flag of concrete music."[39] The virulence of Boulez's language demonstrates what the stakes were: determining the only true path of greatest prestige of musical composition immediately following World War II. Boulez's image of the "tattered flag" is powerful, for it conveys not only the sense of battle, but the hoary nature of *musique concrète* itself from Boulez's perspective, as well as nationalistic overtones. Boulez may be French by birth, but in this skirmish he cast his lot with the Austro-Germans.

Contemporary Critiques of Musique Concrète

Because the composer was not able to conceal totally the residual significations listeners might find in the source sounds used in *musique concrète*, and despite Schaeffer's copious published efforts at supporting *musique concrète* theoretically in terms of new ways of listening (which most commentators think has been a more lasting contribution than his compositions), the genre was nonetheless criticized, perhaps most famously, and fatally, by Pierre Boulez.[40] In a brief article, Boulez writes, "Now one can be certain that its role is of no importance, that the works it evoked are not considerable."[41] Boulez critiques *musique concrète* on precisely the same grounds that Schaeffer feared it was vulnerable: that the musical material was too closely associated with its original sound sources to permit it the necessary abstraction to be under the complete control of the composer. Boulez: "The question of the material, though primordial in such an adventure, was not taken care of there [in *musique concrète*], where it was supplied by a sort of poetic display that prolonged the surrealistic practice of collage—painting or words. The musical material, if it is to lend itself to composition, must be sufficiently malleable, susceptible to transformations, capable of giving birth to a dialectic and supporting it."[42] Deprived of this dialectic, which Boulez refers to as "that primordial activity," composers of *musique concrète* were "consigned to nonbeing," that is, they were not in complete control of their works and as such were no longer eligible to be considered creators.[43] Again and again Boulez returns to this theme. *Musique concrète* works exhibit a "lack of directing thought" resulting in a "flea market of sounds"; they are "bare to the bone of all intention of composition."[44] Elsewhere, Boulez says that he found *musique concrète* composers "amateurs, as worthless as they are impoverished."[45]

The main locus of the criticism by Boulez and the other commentators on *musique concrète* revolved around the issue of signification that may reside in recognizable, "concrete" sounds, which thus called into question the determinacy (that is, the extent to which the composer determined every aspect of the musical work) of this music; Boulez and other composers were attempting to apply Webernian serial principles to all musical parameters in both acoustic and electronic music, controlling it utterly. ("Many of Webern's structures seem like premature electronic fragments," wrote one supporter in 1954).[46] Composers advocating "determinacy" thus viewed the relative looseness of *musique concrète* as highly problematic, with the composer as much a discoverer as creator and, in Boulez's eyes, not a creator at all.[47]

This was clearly the dominant position, both before and after World War II. Apart from Boulez and composers in Germany, general reactions to *musique concrète* were not always positive either. Histories of twentieth-century music produced in or not long after the onset of the postwar era greeted *musique concrète* with skepticism, if not outright derision. Well-known critic André Hodeir lambasted *musique concrète* in 1961: "The founder of this 'movement,' Pierre Schaeffer, is a dilettante with a bent for the wildest ventures, and had at first looked upon sound-objects as the makings of strange, poetic sound-effects and nothing more. Later, he rather ingenuously conceived the idea of arranging them in various patterns, much like visible objects."[48]

Russian-born American composer Vladimir Ussachevsky wrote an article on the tape music scene in which he quoted an unidentified source who said that the raw materials used in *musique concrète* and other kinds of tape music were " 'uncontrollable sounds, which belong to the acoustical but not to the musical domain.' "[49] And in a review of a *musique concrète* concert in England, Reginald Smith Brindle refused to call the composers "composers," but rather referred to them as "technicians."[50]

The how-to guides that began to proliferate after the rise of composition with tape similarly reveal contemporary attitudes toward *musique concrète*. For example, Terence Dwyer's *Composing with Tape Recorders*, published in 1971, begins with three short introductory chapters, but the fourth chapter, entitled "What Are We Aiming At?" tackles the issues of meaning and communication. This chapter, interestingly, takes the form of a dialogue between "A" (the author) and "B" (the beginner), a form of explication that recalls ancient philosophical writings, thus grounding the argument in a style of discursive presentation that lends it more credence than it might otherwise have if the author were merely writing paragraphs of explanation as he had been in all other chapters. "What Are We Aiming At?" thus comes across as "philosophy" (or aesthetics), not just technical or "how-to." In the following excerpt, note how a discussion of formal properties becomes a discussion about communication and meaning. "B" asks what would seem to be a reasonable question:

> You don't think people should know how we made our sounds?
> A: Not usually. We don't even want them to *wonder* what made them. The essence of true music is that we are interested in the sound itself, not the cause.[51]

"A" speaks again and again on the importance of how the piece is put together; organization makes the piece. "A" argues that electronic composers deliberately gave up all methods of organizing sound used in conventional music.

> B: In what way have they dropped the old rules?
> A: Briefly: no themes, no melody, no rhythm, no harmony, thin textures, great emphasis on single sounds and their tone-colours. Also the use of several channels to make sounds move around in space.
> B: That last bit sounds exciting. But surely the other things mean that it's not really music? You said music must be organised—how is electronic music organised?
> A: Well, there are three answers really. One is that each composer

invents his own organisation for each composition, and this may be considered successful because we can perceive it somehow, probably unconsciously. Another is that the composer may have organised his music in so private a way so that his audience *can't* perceive it. Thirdly, I can't help feeling that sometimes there's no real organisation at all, that frankly, it's bad music.

B: This all sounds very risky. Why can't I stick to the safer rules of earlier music? People would understand my sounds better then, wouldn't they?

A: This is something we all have to decide individually. It's a matter of communicating with other people. If you talk a language they are familiar with you'll communicate quickly. But in artistic matters ease of communication tends to link itself with lightness of worth. Significant depth often involves a new language. But it's a very involved subject.[52]

It is so involved, apparently, that it is not pursued further—either here or in the rest of the book.

Elektronische Musik composers' idea that electronic music should sound abstract was not new, though it had to be (re)argued after the war. Their arguments took hold quickly, mainly because the aesthetic of abstraction and the desire for the absence of signification were already the norms in the most prestigious modes of composition. Also, however, serialism became the hegemonic method of composition in Europe immediately following the war; even if one were not a serial composer, in order to be taken seriously one had to compose music that seemed to have something in common with it.[53] Composers of serial music—many of whom also wrote *elektronische Musik*—enjoyed the prestige of this mode of composition and used it against Schaeffer, in often vitriolic terms, as we saw with the language of Boulez. Schaeffer had questioned serialism's emphasis on rigor, which he elsewhere described as a "corset of abstraction," and argued for *musique concrète* as a kind of middle way between Schoenberg and Stravinsky—the two leading figures before World War II—perceived as occupying divergent, even opposite, musical aesthetics.[54]

Human agency in the face of technology proves to be an important issue here. The *Elektronische Musik* musicians attempted to preserve control over the work by devising the most complicated and abstract modes of formal organization ever. In the realm of purely electronic composition, they advocated synthesizing sounds so that listeners could not bring previous associations to them, which they saw as a major weakness in *musique concrète.*

Schaeffer, for his part, was freer in composition, but just as doctrinaire in modes of listening. Schaeffer writes in his magnum opus, *Traité des objets musicaux*, published in 1966, that "Each of us hears with different ears: sometimes too refined, sometimes too coarse, but in any event always 'informed' by all kinds of prejudices and preconditioned by education." So, "sound still remains to be deciphered, whence the idea of a sol-fa of the sound object to train the ear to listen in a new way; this requires that the conventional listening habits imparted by education first be unlearned."[55] Schaeffer advocated a kind of listening—*écoute réduite*, or "reduced listening"—that asked the listener to focus on timbral qualities of sound only, while attempting to ignore the origin of the sounds; the listener was expected to isolate and focus on an *objet sonore*, a "sound object."

One last note on the historical underpinnings of this battle over the issue of signification. There is clearly a residue of older debates about musical meaning resonating in the rhetorical war between the *musique concrète* composers and the *elektronische Musik* composers. Their disagreement essentially recapitulated—or continued—a nineteenth-century battle between Richard Wagner and his proponents and composers whom they thought were not grounding their music in the real truths of poetry and drama. Wagner's side was the side of "program music," that is, instrumental music with an explicit story or meaning; the other side rallied around the idea of "absolute music," instrumental music thought to be without any such story or extramusical meaning. The main figure on this side was Johannes Brahms, championed by the most influential critic of the day, the Viennese Eduard Hanslick, who had written in *On the Beautiful in Music* that the only meaning in music is in its form: "Forms moved in sounding are the sole and single content and object of music."[56] Although he and Richard Wagner were often at odds, and though Wagner's stature still remains high, Hanslick's opinion is the one that has been dominant since, though it undergoes periodic attack, or what is seen as an attack, which is how composers in German viewed *musique concrète.*[57]

After these battles died down somewhat, with Schaeffer and *musique concrète* vanquished, Schaeffer discussed this early period with striking scientific imagery: "At that time some of us were working at constructing robots, others at dissecting corpses. Living music was elsewhere, and only revealed itself to those who knew how to escape from these simplistic models."[58] Schaeffer's description is apt, and suggests an irony not immediately noticed by these protagonists in the 1940s and 1950s—in attempting to gain unfettered control over technology, they relinquished some of that control in their obsession with it.

Primitive Undertones

Clearly the Austro-German composers (including Boulez) and the French composers were embroiled in an aesthetic-discursive war. The roots of this war run deep, deeper than one might expect, for the poles of the arguments were constructed along well-worn binary oppositions. I can best demonstrate this by discussing the main historical and ideological complex that separated them: primitivism, and conceptions of otherness more generally. We had a hint of this earlier with Joliot-Curie's statement about France becoming a colony unless it embraced technology.

Before the postwar era in France, peoples, musical instruments, artworks, and other artifacts from other cultures poured in, as is well known, influencing artistic production from Pablo Picasso to Maurice Ravel in movements such as primitivism earlier in the twentieth century.[59] After the war, as Carlos Palombini writes, Pierre Schaeffer was quick to employ sounds from unfamiliar instruments in his theories. By 1953, Schaeffer was attempting to aggregate *musique concrète, elektronische Musik*, tape music, and exotic music under the single label of "experimental music."[60] Schaeffer's list of positions that had to be minimized (for some reason he put this in the negative) includes a paragraph on "exotic" instruments: "The recourse to prepared or exotic instruments, which now join the traditional [classical] means of obtaining sounds considered musical, has no relevance. Apart from the fact that these sounds, of a doubtful purity, disturb the practices of our ear, we are quite determined not to compose and not to hear any music other than that manufactured with the Western *lutherie* [lute making] which crystallized a century ago, let us say since Bach."[61]

Even before this embrace of nonwestern instruments and sounds, however, Schaeffer had been open to the influences of the musics of other cultures. The first *musique concrète* work ever, *Cinq etudes de bruits* of 1948, included a movement entitled "Étude aux tourniquets"

("Whirligig Study") that employed both "exotic and non-exotic thin-metal instruments,"[62] that is, "African xylophone, four bells, three zan-zas [another name for the instrument from southern Africa usually called an *mbira*], and two whirligigs," sounds assembled during Schaeffer's earlier research into noises.[63] This work was followed almost immediately by *Variations sur une flûte mexicaine* ("Variations for a Mexican Flute") of 1949 that employs sounds from a small, six-holed Mexican flute.

Schaeffer's inclusion of "exotic instruments" in his broad concept of "experimental music" and in his own music demonstrates his willingness to break down barriers between musics, to confound old binary oppositions between primitive and modern, a desire not unheard of in this historical moment in France. James Clifford has described the Musée de l'Homme and its first director's progressive humanism in terms that are quite similar to Schaeffer's own positions (though I have not been able to find any historical link between them). Clifford quotes and paraphrases Paul Rivet, director of the museum, from a 1937 passage that could just as easily have been written by Schaeffer, if we change "science" to "music": " 'Humanity is an indivisible whole, in space and time.' 'The science of man' no longer need be subdivided arbitrarily. 'It [is] high time to break down the barriers.' "[64] (Not just barriers, but old, deeply rooted binary oppositions between primitive and modern, premodern and modern.)

Before the *elektronische Musik/musique concrète* split, the two most prominent composers who worked in Schaeffer's studio in 1952 both expressed an interest in instruments from other cultures. Karlheinz Stockhausen (b. 1928), for example, said in a recent interview that

[in] 1952 I started working in the studio for *musique concrète*, of the French radio. Because I was very intrigued by the possibility to compose one's own sound. I was allowed to work in the studio of Pierre Schaeffer: I made artificial sounds, synthetic sounds, and I composed my first étude: *Étude concrète*. At the same time, I was extremely curious, and went to the Musée de l'Homme in Paris with a tape recorder and microphones, and I recorded all the different instruments of the ethnological department: Indonesian instruments, Japanese instruments, Chinese instruments; less European instruments because I knew them better, but even

piano sounds. . . . Then I analysed these sounds one by one, and wrote down the frequencies which I found at the dynamic level of the partials of the spectra, in order to know what the sound is made of, what the sound *is*, as a matter of fact; what is the difference between a lithophone sound [any instrument made of a series of resonant, tuned stone slabs] or, let's say, a Thai gong sound of a certain pitch. And very slowly I discovered the nature of sounds. The idea to analyse sounds gave me the idea to synthesize sounds. So then I was looking for synthesizers or the first electronic generators, and I superimposed vibrations in order to compose spectra: timbres. I do this now, still, after 43 years.[65]

And Pierre Boulez, who would soon repudiate *musique concrète*, as we saw, composed two works that year, the first of which, *Étude à un son*, made use of a *zanza*, as did Schaeffer in "Étude aux tourniquets." Vladimir Ussachevsky, upon hearing the work five years after its realization, wrote that "it remains a sort of 'tour de force' of planned transmutation of a single sound of an African drum into an austere linear landscape delineated by a sort of unsmiling musical logic."[66]

Schaeffer himself talks about being interested in African musics at the same time as *musique concrète*: "I was involved with the radio in Africa in the same period as I was doing *concrète*—I was doing both at the same time. I was deeply afraid that these vulnerable musical cultures—lacking notation, recording, cataloging, and with the approximative nature of their instruments—would be lost. I and my colleagues were beginning to collect African music."[67]

Schaeffer's thinking on nonwestern cultures was deeply influenced by the anthropologist Claude Lévi-Strauss, to whom he refers in writings and interviews. *Musique concrète* is a musical "science of the concrete." And when Boulez once disparagingly implied that Schaeffer was a mere bricoleur, the latter did not mind: "What did I try to do, in this context, in 1948? As Boulez said, extremely snidely . . . it was a case of 'bricolage.' I retain this term not as an insult but as something very interesting. After all, how did music originate? Through bricolage, with calabashes, with fibres, as in Africa. (I'm familiar with African instruments). Then people made violin strings out of the intestines of cats. And of course the tempered scale is a compromise and also a bricolage. And this bricolage, which is the development of music, is a process that is shaped by the human, the human ear, and not the machine, the mathematical system."[68]

Both the science of the concrete and the idea of the bricoleur are well-known parts of Lévi-Strauss's work. He famously proposed the concept of "bricolage" as a "primitive" cultural practice in *The Savage Mind*, first published in 1962; bricolage was the process of making culture, making knowledge through a "science of the concrete." The bricoleur makes what she needs with the materials at hand, the elements used are "preconstrained"; the scientist, on the other hand, is "always trying to make his way out of and go beyond the constraints imposed by a particular state of civilization."[69] Lévi-Strauss's clearest and most succinct characterization of "bricolage" can serve, he says, as a definition. In the process of bricolage, "it is always earlier ends which are called upon to play the part of means: the signified changes into the signifying and vice versa."[70]

In other words, the bricoleur begins with materials at hand and makes a structure out of them. The scientist, on the other hand, begins with an overall structure, a concept. "Mythical thought, that 'bricoleur,' builds up structures by fitting together events, or rather the remains of events, while science 'in operation' simply by virtue of coming into being, creates its means and results in the form of events, thanks to the structures which it is constantly elaborating and which are its hypotheses and theories."[71]

The bricoleur works in signs, the scientist with concepts. Concepts are creative, signs are re-creative, simply recycling, recombining existing meanings. Lévi-Strauss also included a discussion of art, arguing that there are three modes of art, the first two of which are the most important for my argument: Western art, which stresses the model, "primitive" art, the materials, and applied art, the user. But in the worlds of *musique concrète* and *elektronische Musik*, the last mode doesn't matter; the first two were locked in a deadly binary struggle.

It is clear that Schaeffer was attempting a musical bricolage, at least in retrospect; in a little book entitled *La Musique concrète*, published in 1967, he argues that *musique concrète* composition moves in the opposite direction of "ordinary" music (he means here acoustic classical music): "musique habituelle" ("ordinary music") begins as an abstract conception that is then worked/written out, and finally executed in performance; "musique nouvelle" (*musique concrète*) begins with mate-

TABLE 3.1
Pierre Schaeffer's schematization of the "ordinary" and "new" compositional processes.[72]

ORDINARY MUSIC ("abstract")	NEW MUSIC ("concrete")
PHASE I Conception (mental)	PHASE III Composition (material)
PHASE II Expression (working out on paper)	PHASE II Sketch (experimentation)
PHASE III Execution (instrumental) (from abstract to concrete)	PHASE I Material (fabrication) (from concrete to abstract)

rials, moves to a sketch or outline, and ends up as an abstract composition, as we see in table 3.1.

Thus, the *musique concrète* composer moves just as a bricoleur does: from materials at hand to a structure, whereas composers of "ordinary music"—just like Lévi-Strauss's scientists and engineers—begin with an abstract concept and move toward its material realization.

One of the underlying binaries contributing to the virulence of the debate was the oral nature of the bricoleur's work compared with writing in literate societies. Literacy has been a powerful trope of Western superiority for centuries, and it is no accident that Boulez and others grounded much of their rhetoric of superiority in the fact that their music was a kind of *écriture*, even when it was not notated, as in *elektronische Musik. Écriture* in contemporary French music circles has evolved into a complex term that describes not merely notation, or even attitude toward notation, but a whole attitude toward composition itself, closely linked to the idea of determinacy. For Boulez, *écriture* is an "affirmation of the autonomy of musical symbols and the primacy of thought over substance; it is a refusal to bow to the so-called 'natural' law of material and a decision to trust, rather, in the capacity of *écriture* to determine the consistency of material."[73] Crucial in this regard is Boulez's attitude toward timbre, which "is not approached through its 'natural' constituents, but through the *écriture* of which it is the product; it is a result of a certain arrangement of the initial, arbitrarily chosen material."[74] In other words, *écriture* precedes everything, even those musical parameters most resistant to notation, such as timbre.

For Boulez and his comrades, then, *musique concrète* wasn't simply an inferior music based on aesthetic grounds of little interest to most listeners, or even the lesser of musics in a revitalized postwar economy of musical prestige. Instead, for Boulez and the other detractors, *musique concrète* was akin to the music of primitives, or, perhaps worse from their perspective, civilized people who had "gone native." It was in the position of oral music rather than written; bricolage, not science; premodernity, not modernity. It is rather ironic that the terms of the debate, both explicitly and implicitly, are precisely along the lines of binary oppositions that Lévi-Strauss discussed so famously in *The Raw and the Cooked*.

Pierre Henry

I have spent some time describing Pierre Schaeffer's conceptions of *musique concrète*, and contemporary reactions to (or against) it, because as the prominent public figure and spokesperson for *musique concrète*, he directed the discourse about it at the time. His colleague from 1949, Pierre Henry, emerged as probably the more musical of the two, or at least the more prolific, as Schaeffer stopped composing in the early 1960s. Unlike Schaeffer and so many postwar composers, Henry never wholly subscribed to any empirical approach to making and studying music; rather, he always maintained that music communicates. Perhaps for these reasons, he has been relegated to the margins of the canon of twentieth-century music, since, as we have seen, the hegemonic discourses and practices valorized organization and the abstract. Henry had a falling-out with Schaeffer over this very issue: "Schaeffer wanted to create laws [about the nature of the sound object and reduced listening], while I sought expressivity above all," and so Henry disassociated himself from Schaeffer, forming his own studio in 1959.[75] Henry's interest in expressivity has, I think, also prompted a willingness to work with some popular musicians in the course of his career.

Let's examine in more detail Henry's position on musical signification. In a 1995 interview Henry said, "The source of a sound interests me because that's the adventure of mind's world. There are particular sounds that interest me because they have been cut in certain fashion, because they have a certain roughness, because perhaps there are these stories that have not been entirely excised. An analogy: Raymond Roussel wrote his books with mirrored images with coded words and I use coded sounds and shallow sounds and sounds that tell a story."[76] In other words, rather than worrying about or attempting to erase any semblance of signification attached to his source sounds, Henry's music attempts to retain it.

Elsewhere, Henry was more sweeping: "I've always considered music as a language, a form of communication, rather than an art. I work in solitude, and try to find ways of communicating, of making myself understood."[77] The issue of signification surfaces again and again in Henry's comments on his music. In a recent interview he said, "My sounds are sometimes ideograms. The sounds need to disclose an idea, a symbol. . . . I often very much like a psychological approach in my work, I want it to be a psychological action, with a dramatic or poetic construction or association of timbre or, in relation to painting, of colour."[78] Henry's use of the term *communication* refers to several things: expressivity, accessibility, and referentiality.

Henry's interest in communicating with his music, his interest in expressivity, separates him from Schaeffer, though the older composer had kind words for Henry later in his life. Schaeffer wrote, for example, that Henry triumphed over "the double problem of technique and the incorporation of extra-musical poetics" in his work *Coexistence* (from 1959, one of many ballets of Henry's music choreographed by Maurice Béjart).[79] A decade later, Schaeffer wrote that Henry's music "is expressive. It is neither particularly sentimental, nor particularly dramatic, but when one listens to the music of Pierre Henry, one feels something of being taken by anguish, fear, emotion, waiting, one is, one lives with the limits of the diagram, of what is audible, what can be bearable."[80]

Messe pour le temps présent

Messe pour le temps présent (1967) was cocomposed with Michel Colombier (a composer of film music and concert music) for the choreographer Maurice Béjart. Colombier's duty, as Henry put it thirty years later, was to "recreate the sound textures and violent atmospheres of certain American films."[81] The composition of the work was described by Michel Chion: "From April to June 1967, Pierre Henry worked with the composer Michel Colombier on the instrumental bases of four pieces: two jerks ('Too fortiche' and 'Jericho Jerk'), a 'Psyché Rock' and a slow foxtrot entitled 'Teen Tonic,' onto which he 'grafted' electronic effects and which were recorded by anonymous musicians, in a style intentionally like a provincial ball. And Pierre Henry remained faithful to this yelling style in the electronic effects that he manufactured to 'season' this music. He chose large electronic timbres, indicators, squares, like a very spicy condiment which he took approximately a month to carry out and mix."[82] Henry's method was, in a sense, akin to modern DJs, a fact not overlooked by Virgin Records, France in marketing the 1997 re-release of this album: "Pierre Henry then made, to some extent, the remix. He cut out, looped, added noises."[83]

Although contemporary information on the reception of this album is scant, it seems to have been heavily mythologized; at least, it has been in recent times. Michel Chion writes that "Pierre Henry became in 1968 a strange 'idol' after the release of the work."[84] A recent recording of remixes (about which more later) describes the original "Psyché Rock" track as having "made history as the veritable sound track of the psychedelic years."[85] *Le Monde* reported rather nostalgically in 1996 that "*Messe pour le temps présent* was at the top ten for weeks, at the same time as the miniskirt for the girls, long hair for the boys."[86] The album sold well in 1967, at 150,000 copies, and the album made the hit parade (another source claims 500,000 copies were sold).[87]

The original Philips release of *Messe* used a black-and-white photograph of Béjart's dancers, which was also used in the recent rerelease. But after the initial success of the original single, a subsequent release exploited the "full psychedelic explosion" of the work's reception in some quarters.[88] The cover of this issue featured psychedelic colors and design: a skull occupying the center of the image with a butterfly and partial rainbow in its brain; clouds and doves float by.

Messe consists of five movements, all with titles that speak (or attempt to speak) to the popular culture of the time, which is clearly influenced by American popular culture, since many of the words are in English: "Prologue," "Psyché rock," "Jericho jerk," "Teen tonic," and "Too fortiche." By today's remix standards, this is a fairly rudimentary effort, but Henry's music was composed by the arduous means of cutting and splicing analog tape; today's remixers work with digital equipment, which is much faster and easier to use. All of the tracks consist of a repeating rock groove (a drum kit and usually an electric bass, with the electric guitar also appearing now and then) over which Henry added various swoops and crashes. I suspect that the "instrumental base" that Henry credits Colombier with contributing is essentially this basic groove, which Henry loops and uses as a foundation. "Psyché rock" includes a sample from the famous "Louie, Louie," the R&B song by Richard Berry that has had one of the longest and most varied histories of any rock song.[89] (The presence of "Louie Louie" is so noticeable in "Psyché rock" that it has earned a place in "The complete[?] Louie Louie list" on the Internet, which purports to be a discography of all covers of the song.[90]) None of the tracks have any words. Rather than attempting to sound like a traditional mass, Henry's *Messe* sounds more like a secular ode to the present than anything else, as its title might indicate.

In 1996, at a festival of his music and Béjart's choreography, Henry recalled the genesis of *Messe*: "In 1967, there were not all these sounds, all these musics of the world. Maurice wanted jerks, the dance tunes that were in fashion. I sought them on American discs. It was the music of the film *The Wild Angels* of Roger Corman that inspired me. Made in 1966, it was the ancestor of *Easy Rider*, of films of motorcyclists, violent. There was in this film a color susceptible to being [represented] by sounds. I needed to be helped with the bass, the percussion. Michel Colombier is never cited as composer, arranger, but he succeeded in giving the beat I was looking for, the rocky grain, new to the ear. This music of variety has been the starting point of my research for ten years."[91]

Messe pour le temps présent has been discussed by a number of techno/electronica/noise music fans on the Internet but received little attention until it was rereleased in 1997, which immediately preceded the remix album in 1997 as part of Philips's commemoration of the work's thirtieth anniversary. Reactions to the rereleased *Messe* were enthusiastic; some listeners knew it from the original recording, which had become something of an underground favorite among collectors of vinyl. (The British popular music magazine *Melody Maker* reports that "Psyché rock" "has become firmly established as a back room staple at clubs").[92] One Internet listener wrote, in the summer of 1998, "Fantastic! This classic bit of funky electronic French stuff has been showing up in bits and pieces on various compilations over the past few years (most notably the cut 'Psyche Rock,' which has some sample history to it), but this is the full release of this amazing collaboration between electronic music pioneer Pierre Henry and Michel Colombier, and a soundtrack for a full length ballet of groovy electronic pieces. It's great all the way through, and many tracks have the same feel as the famous 'Psyche Rock.' Other tracks have a very spare electronic sound—there's odd bubbling sounds, cool funky beats, and some very groovy melodies. Wild stuff, and a great re-release in a beautiful package!"

And this from a British user, responding to the above: "This is one of my all-time favourite records. I picked it up at a charity shop about a year ago, expecting 'avant-garde' music, i.e. a lovely chromatic splurge and received a bit of a (welcome) shock. The 'Messe' basically consists of driving instrumental 'pop' music—drums, bass, organ and the odd bit of electric guitar, often quite manic. Then, over the top of this, and sometimes falling over the edge, there are weird electronic noises, not blips and bleeps, but rhythmic squawks, squeals and squarks. Sudden blasts of sound rather than ambient layers. Oh, and there's bells. Very emphatically, in places." Finally, a French fan writes that *Messe* "emotionally makes an astonishing music, unstructured, so strong, that I do not manage to do other things at the same time, but I have the impression that there is something behind it that seized me, that I do not understand."[93]

These (and other) listeners' enthusiasm—and flowery language—show their appreciation for Henry's technical achievements and his personal aesthetic, which does not eschew the possibility of communication. Even though fans occasionally talk about Henry's music in technical terms, they are less interested in Schaeffer's music, or for that matter any other early electronic musicians with the occasional exception of Iannis Xenakis (1922–2001) and Karlheinz Stockhausen. But even these better-known composers have yet to be honored by an album of remixes, as Henry has.[94] Today's DJs and techno musicians focus on Henry's music because they can hear that it was never strictly about formal issues. They can hear in it Henry's technical prowess and the music's accessibility and expressivity, and they are attracted to all of these qualities.

Spooky Tooth: Ceremony

The popular success of *Messe* resulted in a collaboration between Henry and the English rock group Spooky Tooth on a 1970 album entitled *Ceremony*. This album, subtitled *An Electronic Mass*, picks up on the religious overtones suggested by the title *Messe* but with a more overt experimental rock twist. Henry's contribution (he is listed as cosongwriter on all the tracks, with Spooky Tooth member Gary Wright, the only American in the group) is the addition of *musique concrète* sounds over the band's overly weighty songs. This does not seem to have been all that successful a release, though the French press was full of praise for a concert that took place in February of 1970. A couple of the articles, however, concluded by wondering about the youth of the audience; the reviewer for *Le Monde* thought that the audience liked Henry's *L'Apocalypse de Jean* (from 1968, on the first half of the concert) more than *Ceremony,* concluding "the public, very numerous, made a better greeting for *l'Apocalypse* than *Ceremony;* it is true that meanwhile the hair had lengthened and perhaps curtailed musical sensitivity."[95] Henry explains the album this way: "The reason for this was much more commercial than artistic. The great success of *La messe pour le temps présent* and *Les jerks electroniques* with Michel Colombier gave my editor at Philips the idea that I should work together with an English group to make a thematic album, based on the idea of the Mass. When this started, I didn't know these people at all, and I accepted for a number of reasons which would not interest me now."[96] Henry also said that the only condition for working on this project was to make the resulting work more integrated musically than *Messe* had been; Henry wanted this new project to be one in which "the electronic sounds, the aesthetic of the group and the general instrumentation form a homogeneous whole, where the effects are not applied on top of the themes."[97]

The result, though, still sounds rather more like a remix than a homogeneous work. Similar to *Messe,* Henry took the "instrumental bases" and remixed them; Michel Chion writes that Spooky Tooth gave Henry "carte blanche to work the tape over again, to add an electroacoustic [i.e., tape] part, like one harmonizes a given song."[98]

Ceremony consists of six "movements," or perhaps, "songs," with titles that vaguely resemble the proper of the Catholic mass (which consists of the Kyrie, Gloria, Credo, Sanctus, and Agnus Dei): "Confession," "Have Mercy" (which opens with a textual reference to the Kyrie with the words "Lord have mercy, Christ have mercy"), "Offering," "Hosanna," and "Prayer." Some of the melodies, which tend to recur frequently throughout a song/movement, are vaguely Gregorian chant–like, such as the main melody from "Confession."

The words, often sung over the progressive/metal guitar of Luther Grosvenor, are often difficult to understand; none of the words to "Confession" are intelligible, though I think letters "LSD" are audible. Henry's contributions are often in the background, though he does take some "solos" here and there.

Thirty years on, fans and reviewers don't much like the album; there are several derisive postings floating around the Internet about it (including some on a website devoted to the role of Satan in rock and roll). Henry himself said, rather cryptically, that "to me this enterprise was totally without any result for years."[99] But Henry is again working with a pop group; he did not name it in any interview, but it has proved to be the American band Violent Femmes, who collaborated with Henry on his 1998 album *Intérieur/Extérieur*. Henry in turn appears on the Violent Femmes' most recent album, *Freak Magnet* (2000).[100] Henry is described on their official website as "Violent Femmes' Favorite composer," and one of the band's members, drummer Guy Hoffman, concluded an interview thus:

> Question: What is the highlight of your stint with the Femmes?
> Answer: Celebrating my 40th birthday in Germany and visiting Pierre Henry at his home studio in Paris.[101]

The Violent Femmes website also includes a photo of the band with Henry in his studio.

Resurrections, Remixes, and Homages

If the rise of *musique concrète* and *elektronische Musik* brought anxieties about signification, and the place—and placement—of this new music in the histories of music, past and future, the digital transformation has brought its own unease over some of the same issues, particularly the latter.

While most techno musicians and DJs are not concerned with issues of structure and meaning to the extent that *musique concrète* and *elektronische Musik* musicians were, the nature of their tradition does matter to them. Many techno musicians seek forbears as a way of grounding themselves in a legitimate tradition, and so the rise of "electronica" musics in the last few years has also prompted a renewed interest in Henry and some of the other early electronic composers. Posts to various Usenet groups on the Internet—alt.music.techno, alt.music.ambient, rec.music.industrial, and others—occasionally inquire after some of these art music precursors, and a knowledgeable vernacular historian frequently answers.

Contemporary musicians have cultivated interest in Henry's (and other older electronic) musics for a variety of reasons, reasons that would be difficult to theorize adequately under the rubric of some kind of postmodern nostalgia or a pure aesthetic appreciation. Instead, it seems as though today's DJs and remixers seek out these earlier musics as a way of attempting, in part, to discover a musical past for themselves, or to join a preexisting tradition, effectively resuscitating a residual tradition (in Raymond Williams's conceptualization) of which they can be the contemporary heirs.[102] By actively linking themselves to a particular tradition or portion thereof and selecting heroes and forbears, contemporary popular musicians are able to construct an alternative history of popular music—not a history that begins with the blues and wends its way through R&B, Elvis Presley, Chuck Berry, Bob Dylan, the Beatles, the Rolling Stones, Bruce Springsteen, and others, but a tradition that has roots in studio experimentation, and perhaps even the romantic notion of the un(der)appreciated solitary genius.

This history, however, usually omits the African-American and gay musicians who are more demonstrably the real precursors of techno music, for it is mainly being championed by heterosexual suburban white men. For them, a lineage going back to the European avant-garde is more compelling than a more historically accurate one that traces their music to African Americans and gays.[103] As such, these latter groups are almost wholly exscripted as techno is championed as an intellectual music to be listened to, not danced to.

Still, the advocates of Pierre Henry and other members of the European avant-garde have found a substantial new fan base. Internet websites devoted to the history of techno music frequently pay homage to Schaeffer and Henry. Henry is often portrayed as the more important of the two, or even Schaeffer's predecessor, I think because Henry never stopped composing, and because his music is more accessible. A recent remix album (about which more below) established Henry as the "grandfather of techno" according to *Le Monde* and one Paris weekly; another called him the "father of all the technoids."[104] Daniel Smith, a Brooklyn-based clerk in an independent music store and part-time DJ, included the release of the complete works of Schaeffer in a list of five recommendations, and in his comments made Schaeffer sound like Henry's sidekick: "He used to work with Pierre Henry in the '40s, using sound cut-ups and early electronic instruments. It's great that people are finally catching on to the importance of this stuff."[105] The Ultimate Band List on the Internet includes an entry for Henry but not Schaeffer.[106] One website even begins the history of techno music with a discussion of Henry and makes no mention of Schaeffer at all.[107] *Mixmag* magazine, the leading magazine of electronic dance music in the United Kingdom, lists the original "Psyché Rock" as number 41 (of 50) on their list of "Mixmag Tunes of 1997." No other art music composer's music appears on this or any other *Mixmag* list.[108] The 1998 documentary *Modulations*, which bills itself as "the definitive history of electronic music," credits Pierre Henry as the father of *musique concrète*, though Henry, in one of his two brief appearances in the film, does mention Schaeffer.[109] An online guide called "The A–Z of Electronica" includes an entry on *musique concrète* that reads, "Avant-garde musical movement headed up by Frenchman Pierre Henry whose experiments in the Fifties with found sounds, turntables and motorized instruments prefigured many of electronic's [*sic*] working methods."[110] A recent article says that French DJs celebrate Henry as their master; one says, "Pierre Henry, it is trip hop made in the sixties."[111] A very favorable online record review concludes by saying that a recent composer possesses "the audacity and dramatic insight of the young Pierre Henry."[112]

Even vernacular histories of techno that do not attribute its origins to Henry nonetheless put him in good company. One Swiss website credits Stockhausen as the originator of techno, then goes on to say that "in the wake of Stockhausen, a broad side of contemporary music is passionate for electronic research. Varese, Berio in Italy, John Cage in the United States, Pierre Henry in France clear new fields of experimentation."[113] An Australian page states matter-of-factly, "in the 1950s and 60s, composers such as Karlheinz Stockhausen, John Cage and Pierre Henry were busily expanding the vocabulary of instrumental music."[114]

It is now common for musicians and bands to claim a Henry influence. The global popularity of techno has meant that Henry's music is traveling farther and farther. A recently formed Japanese band called Buffalo Daughter positions themselves this way, in the words of band member Sugar Yoshinaga: "We don't want to make just techno, drum 'n bass, or rock 'n roll. We are interested in every kind of music—we like techno, we like disco, we like rock 'n roll, electronic music, musique concrete . . . Pierre Henry, John Cage."[115] A German techno musician, when asked what bands influenced him, named, among art music composers, "Pendereckie, Varese, Pierre Henry."[116]

Métamorphose

Henry's newfound celebrity among techno musicians resulted in the release in 1997 of an album entitled *Métamorphose*, which features remixes by some of the most famous DJs in France and England. The most prominent participant is probably Fatboy Slim, a British DJ who frequently appears on the cover of British dance music magazines.[117] The other DJs are all reasonably well known by fans, and include William Orbit, Dimitri from Paris, Funki Porcini, Coldcut, Chris the French Kiss, and St. Germain.

Even before hearing the music, it is clear that the producers mean to invoke the birth of the postwar technological era. There is a Corbusier-like conglomeration of buildings on the cover (fig. 3.1) and on two inner pages, and fractal designs (geometric patterns that grow through the application of rules) adorn the two remaining untexted pages. One

FIGURE 3.1
Métamorphose, cover.

of these designs recalls the pavilion Le Corbusier designed for the 1958 Brussels World's Fair, for which Edgard Varèse (1885–1965) composed his classic *Poème électronique*.

In keeping with this paean to technology, the "Prologue" to *Méta-morphose*, by Chris the French Kiss, clearly reveals the fascination these musicians have not just for their musical forbears but also for the technology with which these earlier musicians worked. After about two minutes, out of the instrumental (re)mix we hear a slightly manipulated male voice saying "My voice should now be coming from a point between the two speakers." This repeats. Then we hear "Roger. Would you like us to change frequencies at this time?" This sample pokes fun at the "hi-fi" attitude, after the advent of, first, the long-playing record in the late 1940s, and then, a decade or so later, stereo. Old-fashioned analog sounds flit about, and it's clear that Chris the French Kiss is not just honoring or remixing Henry, but playing with our knowledge of recordings and recording technology, of music, new and old, as well as poking a bit of affectionate fun at Henry's sounds.

What Internet fans seem to like about *Métamorphose* is its variety, which they discuss in endless detail, haggling over styles and influences, such as this listener:

The Funki Porcini mix [of "Jericho jerk"] is a stretching interpretation of the original (read as samples of wacky synth noises circa 1968) its better than other Porcini stuff i've heard. This is not really my thing, but it is a solid jazz flavored jungle track, without being too wimpy.

The St Germain mix [of "Jericho jerk"]—how can i say enough about this guy? Brilliant. House with a LONG beat-less intro that sneaks nicely into the mix. same samples, more solos! solid jazz-house stuff.

Another listener proclaimed that *Métamorphose* had

all great trax.. i hate to say that the coldcut remix is PHAT! really nicely done, slow breakbeat acid jazzzy feel to it, it also has the original on the flip side which is nice . . . the track picture side is a slammer . . . also the william orbit mix is really sweet . . .

Coldcut Mix. Twisted beyond belief cut n' paste trip hop funkiness from the Cut with huge grungy bass and weirdo bell loops.

'St, Germain Mix'. St. Germain lay down a very live-sounding Jazz house remake with a fine organ solo over a crisp underground mix. Flip for Funk Porcini's hard-as-f**k techstep drum n' basser rework.

William Orbit Mix. Big metallic freaked out hard hop styled mixes that fall somewhere between Lionrock's clunky industrialized mayhem and Wall Of Sound's funky beat mastery.

Dimitri From Paris Mix'. Cooly Jazzy excursion from Dimitri on a mellow tip with some weird metallic noises to keep a hard element there.

These fans are obviously attuned to the wide variety of techno music styles, a preoccupation also thematized in the liner notes to the album. Each DJ brings his own dance music niche aesthetic to bear on Henry's music, and so we are treated to a veritable primer in late twentieth-century dance music styles, including techno, neoindustrial, cut-and-paste, house, funk, trip-hop, hard-step drum 'n' bass, hip-hop, ambient jungle, jungle, and ambient minimal.[118] Perhaps only this many styles could pay testament to Henry's importance to a generation of musicians working in an extraordinary range of today's dance musics, an importance due in no small part to Henry's refusal to take the formal path and choice instead to communicate.

MEN, MACHINES, AND MUSIC IN THE SPACE-AGE 1950S

If in France there was, by and large, optimism over technology in the postwar era, spending some time examining American ambivalence and anxiety over technology in the same era provides a useful comparison. To understand space-age pop music—jazz-influenced popular music of the 1950s and early 1960s that thematized the exotic, whether terrestrial or in space, and was intended to be played on hi-fis—it is necessary to discuss the historical and cultural factors that gave rise to it to hear how anxiety and ambivalence over technology are registered in this music.

Atomic Age, Space Age

This anxiety and ambivalence were not new; American ambivalence toward technology has a long history and has been well documented.[1] But the postwar era brought new machines to contend with, machines that were often used in the home. Lynn Spigel has written of the spate of articles and discussions in the popular press in the 1950s and the fears that technology was becoming out of control, that humans were becoming machines themselves, that people were losing their ties to nature.[2] The atomic bombs dropped on Hiroshima and Nagasaki in August of 1945 were only the most gruesome manifestations of the potential downside of science and technology.

This ambivalence and anxiety was one effect of a postwar obsession with the future and all that was associated with it: the atom, space, and science and technology more generally. Jules Henry has written of the "technological drivenness" of this era.[3]

As in France, the earliest manifestation of this obsession with science and technology in the United States was centered on the atom. Because of the horrors of the atomic bombs dropped on Hiroshima and Nagasaki, the whole world knew of the terrifying power of the atom; a tone of fear pervaded this era, as Paul Boyer writes.[4] So the U.S. government's desire to continue its research into atomic warfare and nuclear power needed a good deal of justification. The government launched what amounted to a massive public relations campaign in an attempt to make the atom palatable, the biggest such campaign since 1945.[5]

The U.S. Atomic Energy Commission produced educational pamphlets that were distributed nationally; *Understanding the Atom* booklets first appeared in 1952, and by the end of the 1950s over eight million copies were in print.[6] There were Boy Scout merit badges in atomic energy; dozens of songs; and images of the atom's orbit appeared on consumer goods, from electric shavers to clocks.[7]

Because of the complex science involved, most people didn't (or were told they couldn't) understand atomic power, which was often described in terms of magic, mystery, and wonder; in 1955, president Dwight D. Eisenhower started up the first commercial nuclear power plant in the nation by waving a "magic wand."[8] There was also a good deal of hyperbole about the conveniences nuclear energy would bring, hyperbole made possible in part because of the technological complexity of atomic power. Politicians, scientists, and journalists alike exaggerated the benefits of nuclear power, foreseeing a time when there would be power "too cheap to meter." Harold E. Stassen, Eisenhower's Special Assistant on Disarmament, wrote in a 1955 *Ladies' Home Journal* article that, in the near future, nuclear energy would create a world "in which there is no disease . . . where hunger is unknown . . . where food never rots and crops never spoil . . . where 'dirt' is an old-fashioned word, and routine household tasks are just a matter of pushing a few buttons . . . a world where no one stokes a furnace or curses the smog, where the air is everywhere as fresh as on a mountain top and the breeze from a factory as sweet as from a rose. . . . Imagine the world of the future . . . the world that nuclear energy can create for us."[9]

Promoting the peaceful use of nuclear power wasn't the sole

province of the federal government, however; the power of atomic energy, especially when described as it was by Stassen, gained influential converts. A Walt Disney television program entitled *Our Friend the Atom* had its premiere in 1956 (Disney published a book with the same title that same year).[10] Heinz Haber, Disneyland's new expert on "scientific development," said that the development of atomic power had been "almost a fairy tale," a point he illustrated by showing an updated cartoon of the Arabian Nights tale of the genie and the fisherman. In this newer version, the final image of the genie, duped by the fisherman in the original story into obeying the fisherman's wishes, is superimposed "onto reversed footage of an atomic explosion, so that the bomb appears to implode harmlessly back into the lamp."[11] This image of the "obedient atom" was one of the more common ones; a 1958 feature article in *National Geographic* entitled "You and the Obedient Atom" says that "these unimaginably tiny particles work like genii at man's bidding."[12]

The peaceful use of atomic power was one of the most salient scientific and technological issues of the early postwar era in the United States. Later, the possibility of space travel joined the atom as the most visible representation of the era's preoccupation with the future. Americans in the 1950s weren't blind to the potential horrors of linking atomic weapons with space travel, a possibility made clear in popular culture. In the film *The Day the Earth Stood Still*, from 1950, the extraterrestrial character Klaatu tells earthlings that "soon one of your nations will apply atomic energy to space ships. That will threaten the peace and security of other planets."[13] He recommended unilateral disarmament, but the popular choice of the day was that American possession of atomic weapons required that America go into outer space to maintain control. According to Brian Horrigan, control of space was seen as the moral high ground, synonymous with nuclear domination, a message that is apparent in nearly all treatments of the space theme in popular culture in the 1950s.[14]

The realization that rockets could carry nuclear warheads was cause for more anxiety, which, again, the federal government and space proponents sought to ameliorate through an advertising campaign. The visionaries of space realized the importance of sales promotion; Wernher von Braun, the German architect of the U.S. space program, also knew that popular public support was essential for a successful space program, particularly during peacetime.[15]

As with the promotion of the peaceful uses of the atom, the media helped. A 1951 Space Travel Symposium at the Hayden Planetarium in New York City had in attendance two journalists from *Collier's* magazine, then one of the most widely read magazines in America. One of the reporters was so excited that he convinced his managing editor that *Collier's* should host its own symposium with some of the same guests. This ultimately resulted in a series of eight features over two years, from 1952 to 1954, which one writer estimates was read by some twelve to fifteen million people.[16]

The *Collier's* series served as a basis for three Disney television films that spread the possibility of space travel even further in the public mind. One of the Disney animators told historian Randy Liebermann that he was given free rein by the normally tightfisted Disney to go ahead with the project, which was to complement Disneyland's "Tomorrowland," and the project ultimately cost about one million dollars, a huge amount of money to spend on a television program in that era.[17] Eisenhower was reportedly so impressed with the *Man in Space* episode that aired on March 9, 1955, and was seen by nearly one hundred million people that he called Disney and asked to borrow a copy of the film, which he later showed to Pentagon officials. (In 1955 the U.S. population was almost 166 million, which means that just over 60 percent of the population saw this show on its first airing).[18] Whether or not he was influenced by the film, on July 29 Eisenhower announced that, as part of American participation in the "International Geophysical Year" (1957–1958), the United States would attempt to launch an earth satellite.[19]

Even though the launch of Sputnik in October of 1957 was not a cause for worry in the Eisenhower administration since a U.S. satellite was scheduled to be launched soon afterward, Lyndon Johnson managed to kick up a fuss. As Senate majority leader Johnson convened hearings on the inadequacy of U.S. space efforts after the first effort to send up a satellite resulted in an exploded rocket on the launchpad on December 6, 1957. On January 31, 1958, the first American satellite went into orbit, and its chief designer, Wernher von Braun, became "an instant media hero."[20] By the spring of 1958 it was clear that the advertising and public relations campaign was working, for opinion polls showed that the public's attitude was turning into "space fever."[21]

The program cost a lot of money. One author estimates that in the four years of World War II the United States spent roughly $1 billion on research and development, but that by 1950, the federal government was spending $1 billion every year.[22] After Sputnik, the government was spending about $15 billion per year on research and development. To defend expenditures on this level, the program not only had to be justified, but also sold to the American public, men and women alike. Federal agencies devised the notion of spin-off technologies, goods that could be used by everyday folks in their homes (the benefits of spin-off technology are still touted, even on the National Aeronautics and Space Administration's Internet home page).[23] The ad campaigns not only helped to justify the massive expense of the space program, but also gave consumers the opportunity to purchase goods.

The planners of the space program saw it as a new source of national and nationalistic imagery, and purposely used language that would liken space to familiar American themes and images of exploration and discovery. Then House Speaker John McCormack said, in a hearing on space, that "in space exploration, and the scientific breakthrough it implies, we are beginning an era of discovery literally as far-reaching as the discovery of our own continent," saying that space would provide the country with a "new frontier"—"the greatest challenge to dynamic thought and deed that our pioneer spirit has ever received."[24] On May 25, 1961, president John F. Kennedy committed the nation to putting a man on the moon, a decision that was heralded by the media as nothing had been before. "Man is embarking on the supreme adventure; he is heading into the universe," wrote *Newsweek*.[25]

The American public was not simply fascinated by the atom and space; science and technology themselves were powerful notions in American consciousnesses in the 1950s and early 1960s. Michael L. Smith writes of a rise in what he calls "commodity scientism," a belief, negative or positive, in the ineffable qualities of science and technology. This ideology emerged as a result of the increasing prevalence of technology in American lives, at the same time that this technology was increasingly difficult to understand. This is, of course, related to Langdon Winner's "technological somnambulism," a term Winner uses to label the common mode in which most people experience technology, sleepwalking through it, not recognizing their own agency or role in developing and using it.[26]

The supposed incomprehensibility of science and technology afforded both government and industry an unparalleled opportunity to market science and technology to the American public, for it would help sell the nuclear weapons and space programs. Public displays of technology helped incorporate it into everyday life. The most striking examples were World's Fairs, and these spectacularized modes of display eventually became used by advertisers and the federal government alike. By the 1939 World's Fair, the main function of displays of technology was to instruct consumers to lump together personal and social progress with technology, and technology with new commodities.[27]

Smith argues that the best site at which to examine this phenomenon is in the marketing of automobiles, for they occupy an important role in American culture and are also the most expensive and technologically sophisticated machines anyone was likely to buy in this era. Smith argues that transitivity of power from car to driver was promoted through jargon and gadgetry: "Through a deliberately unfamiliar configuration of initials, number, and neologisms, jargon provided what motivational researchers called 'the illusion of rationality,' conveying 'inside-dopester' status to the consumer without requiring the slightest mechanical comprehension."[28] Neologisms pervaded the era, though not just those associated with technology. A television ad for the 1955 Chevrolet depicts a husband and wife in an older car; the husband puffs on a cigar, while his wife wears a gas mask. But the new Chevrolet, the ad tells us, has a "high level ventilating system" that brings in fresh air. And if the husband and wife bicker over the amount of air, there are separate air control knobs. "Ah, love is grand in a well-ventilated motoramic Chevrolet," proclaims the narrator.[29]

Commodity scientism permeated all aspects of American life, even domesticating the atom. In the mid-1960s, Connecticut Yankee Power, a public utility, produced a film called *Atom and Eve*, to help gain women's support for the state's first nuclear power plant; the film, Laura Nader writes, "indicated that a woman's desire for convenience and freedom can only be sated by the Atom."[30] One recent book on the era shows a 1955 picture of a woman cooking on an electric cooktop, and provides a caption, which appears to be the original: "Atomburgers coming right up!" General Electric, the ad's sponsor, claimed to have provided the power for these first hamburgers ever cooked with nuclear power, and in the background we see the nation's first nuclear-power plant.[31] The push-button technology, evident on the range in this ad (and mentioned earlier by Harold E. Stassen), was popular in this era, though it was underlain with anxiety about a nuclear war, since most of the prominent buttons in this era were the ones the public assumed that the U.S. president and Soviet premier had their fingers on.

Most scholars of the era agree that what best represents the domestication of nuclear technology was the famous "kitchen debate" between Soviet premier Nikita Khrushchev and vice president Richard Nixon in 1959. The two men were touring a model suburban home and eventually found themselves in the kitchen, the place where Nixon appeared to confront Khrushchev most effectively. "Isn't it better to talk about the relative merits of washing machines than the relative strengths of rockets?" Nixon asked. Khrushchev replied, "Isn't this the kind of competition you want?" continuing by stating angrily that the United States was engaging in both types of competition, clearly the case at the time.[32] This setting and argument epitomized complex American attitudes toward technology. The push-button conveniences of the modern suburban home, the center of which was the kitchen, best represented what America had in contrast with the Soviets, and the horrors of a nuclear war were relegated to the background. The prosperity, better emblematized by this kitchen than anything else, was worth defending, emphasizing the benefits of technology.[33]

Gender, Home Technology, and the Hi-Fi

The kitchen, however, was the woman's domain. Although many have written of the masculinization of technology in this era, it should be clear that, from the science and technology proponents' viewpoint, science and technology were supposed to benefit everyone.[34] If the federal government's plans for a massive expenditure of income tax dollars on nuclear energy and weapons and later the space race were to be justified, this technology thus had to be made acceptable to everyone, not just men. So women had their push-button and other kitchen and household appliances, potent symbols of American technology and technological superiority.

Women were also allocated important responsibilities. Kristina Zarlengo writes that for the first time, women in the atomic age were perceived as legitimate military targets, which meant that the suburban woman's job was not simply to cook and clean, but also to serve as a guardian of the home.[35] The head of the Federal Civil Defense Administration (FCDA) said that the home front of the cold war "actually exists in our homes, right now in our living rooms" and that failure to incorporate civil defense into the household would be like a " 'fifth column' action which undermines our national defense."[36] The FCDA portrayed homemaking as a serious, professional task entrusted to women; women and men would even share some more technical tasks.[37]

Nixon had also said that America was about the private sector, not the state, in contradistinction to the USSR. But "private" in 1950s America connoted the suburban home, the domain of women; given the centrality of the home in this era, women were thus important to American military might. And it was household technologies that revealed most significantly the breadth and benefits of American technological superiority. As a result, women in the homes were symbols of "serene goodness and capability, of attractiveness rather than sexiness, and control rather than decadence."[38] At the same time, however, wives and mothers also needed to be protected, and in this era there were some striking new radiation protection undergarments, such as lead brassieres and lead girdles.

The postwar rise of a consumer culture and commodity scientism was thematized in a number of musical pieces from the 1950s. In some ways these are paeans to the machine, as were some of the futurist works of the early part of the twentieth century, but instead of representing the factory or industrial might or heavy equipment such as the locomotive, these pieces from the 1950s and 1960s celebrate everyday technology that people had in the home.[39] An example is Dean Elliott and His Big Band's version of Cole Porter's "You're the Top," recorded in 1962, complete with every household appliance sound imaginable, and then some.[40]

Women had their own technology and their own responsibilities as guardians of the home. What did men have? Commodity scientism in the domestic scene for men is probably best represented by the hi-fi craze of the late 1940s and 1950s. Many of the first hi-fi enthusiasts were men who had learned about audio technology in the army during World War II. They continued their interest by becoming hi-fi hobbyists back home, a fad documented in a valuable article by Keir Keightley.[41]

Barbara Ehrenreich observed in *The Hearts of Men* that the hi-fi was a way for the man to reclaim some domestic space and authority in the home.[42] Coming home from a hard day at the office, the man, oppressed by his dull job, could relax with his own piece of space-age, futuristic technology and escape from not only work, but also the wife and kids. Or the bachelor could seduce his date with his fancy hi-fi by playing "mood music."[43] Either way, the hi-fi was his, unlike the television, which had proved to be far more disruptive to family life, as Lynn Spigel so vividly discusses.[44]

Hi-fis, however, do not simply occupy space in the living room; music can fill a room like nothing else—men and their hi-fis could colonize the entire living room and beyond. In this observation I am reminded of a remark by no less a figure than Immanuel Kant, who in his *Critique of Judgment* remarked that music "extends its influence (on the neighborhood) farther than people wish, and so, as it were, imposes itself on others and hence impairs the freedom of those outside of the musical party."[45] After noting that the visual arts don't do this, Kant goes further: "The situation here is almost the same as with the enjoyment produced by an odor that spreads far. Someone who pulls his perfumed handkerchief from his pocket gives all those next to him and around him a treat whether they want it or not, and compels them, if they want to breathe, to enjoy at the same time, which is also why this habit has gone out of fashion."[46] It is thus no accident that one of the main points of friction in hi-fi-equipped homes concerned volume, about which there was a good deal of contemporary discussion; volume was one of the main causes of what Keightley calls "spatial/spousal conflict."[47]

Hi-fis, however, were not only for men; some hi-fis were marketed specifically to women. These made use of the familiar push-button technology that women were accustomed to finding on their kitchen appliances. In other words, what was marketed toward, and consumed by, men, was not just hi-fi technology, but *complex* hi-fi technology. Not surprisingly, male hi-fi enthusiasts ridiculed the simpler equipment in its pretty box, and valued instead the complex hi-fi of separate components. One woman writer in the *New York Times* noted that "men have 'bulldozed' the opposite sex into the belief that they cannot possibly understand the workings of this complicated equipment."[48] Another woman wrote in *Harper's* that "Our equipment has become so complicated I can no longer try to play it."[49] According to Keightley, "The hi-fi fan's disdain for console sets and female control of high fidelity is here blended with a desire to view women as technically inept as three-year olds."[50] The point is, though, not that women were "untechnological," but that *complex* technology was defined as the proper domain of the man. The position that separate components are better than integrated ones is still held by today's audeophiles.

Space-Age Music

> Her hands began to saw the air, and a sort of Hindu version of the Lohengrin wedding music streamed out of the theremin, in eerie keening glissandos.
>
> —*Herman Wouk,* Marjorie Morningstar

What was played on men's hi-fis? One of the potential problems that male hi-fi buffs had to contend with was that music, especially classical music, could be seen as effeminate.[51] There was also a well-established association of the feminine with more "egghead" pursuits that were occasionally seen as sissified. For men of this era, tinkering with hi-fi sets was one way to avoid such contradictions. I suspect that many of these hi-fi sets were built to be built, not built to be used for playing music. Even today when speaking with audiophiles I often get the impression that they are more interested in equipment than music.

If the hi-fi was a way for men to reclaim domestic space, stereo was likewise about space, and it is significant that the decade of 1954–1964 witnessed the rise of the airy, open-ended nature of living space, with analogues in the altered perspective of the drawings of Saul Steinberg and the 3-D movies of the early 1950s.[52] The new suburban living rooms had hi-fi music composed especially for them. In the 1950s, Columbia introduced a series entitled *Music for Gracious Living* with titles such as *Foursome* (the cover of which depicts a living room sofa with card table and chairs) and *Do-It-Yourself* (whose cover shows dad and junior working on something at the basement tool bench while mom sits and demurely knits). These and other albums in other series often included tips on how to be a good host, including recommendations for which food to serve with which musical selection. [53]

Like homes and living rooms, hi-fis had their own music. This music was composed, orchestrated, and arranged to exploit high-fidelity capabilities, but also, by the advent of stereo in the late 1950s, music for hi-fis was also written to play with the sense of space available in that format. Recordings would therefore bounce sounds between speakers and spatialize sounds and sound effects in ways that were impossible before stereo. An article in *Hi-Fi/Stereo Review* says in 1960, "In the search for new material albums were made of sports car sounds, cracklings from outer space and ski lessons."[54]

Many recordings marketed to hi-fi aficionados, in the stereo era and before, emphasized the technology involved in recording, using neologisms and also opaque language. "It was almost effects set to music," according to a vice president of strategic marketing at RCA.[55]

Irwin Chusid, a New Jersey–based radio DJ who has done much to revive and repopularize space-age pop music, writes that "classic Space Age Pop albums often went to great lengths to explain technical recording minutiae. Waveform graphs were juxtaposed alongside mic[rophone] positioning charts, annotated with baffling references to the RIAA [Recording Industry Association of America] crossover curve, feedback cutters, and 500 cps. rolloffs. It was the record company's way of assuring the buyer: We know a lot of things you don't. Trust us—buy this record; it's a technical marvel. In some cases, arcane jargon lent an LP credibility otherwise lacking in the music. But, for the most part, it was obligatory hype, conferring status, and certain to be ignored."[56]

The back covers of many of these albums contained an immense amount of technical information. Rebecca Leydon writes of a compilation album released by Capitol Records in about 1957 entitled *Full Dimensional Sound: A Study in High Fidelity* that contained an accompanying booklet about hi-fi technology, explaining that this record will help listeners demonstrate "to themselves and to others the full range and capabilities of their sound reproducing systems."[57] Accordingly, each track on the album has a description about what to listen for. Les Baxter's "Quiet Village" (1951), an important work in exotica music (one of the styles/genres now usually grouped under the umbrella "lounge" or "space-age pop" that represents "exotic" others), is used to test the bass, as the liner notes say, "In spite of the sweeping effect on the entry of the highs, balance is maintained throughout with a nice dominance to the beating rhythm. The piano enters and still the overall level is held, for the dynamic range is not broad. The orchestra sounds much larger than it is. There are only nine strings—exotically colored by mutes—plus one bass, harp, piano and two percussion."[58]

Musically there were many styles available that exploited stereo sound, though some were marketed directly to the husband, the hi-fi owner, and sometimes to the bachelor, who was supposed to ply his date with "mood music." For the purposes of my argument here I am going to examine only those albums from the era that thematized space/science/technology/the future, in music, album iconography, and liner notes. This group, I should emphasize, was less a separate genre or subgenre of space-age pop music than a novelty sound that many groups and musicians exploited. Even the 101 Strings, never a trendsetting ensemble, recorded *Astro Sounds from Beyond the Year 2000* in 1969, after the popularity of this music had waned for the most part (though it got a bit of a jolt with the introduction of the Moog synthesizer in 1964, which spawned dozens more electronic pop works).[59]

One good place to begin is with a seminal recording from 1947, Harry Revel's *Music Out of the Moon.* This was an important album in its sound, but, like many of these albums, it pushed the technological enve-lope in ways that weren't strictly musical; *Music Out of the Moon* had the first color LP cover (see fig. 4.1), and was also the first in the genre to employ the theremin, an electric instrument invented in the 1920s by Leon Theremin.[60] This album, by conductor Les Baxter's account, sold

FIGURE 4.1.
Harry Revel: *Music Out of the Moon* (1947), cover.

very well.[61] (The theremin was also featured in Bernard Herrmann's music to the film *The Day the Earth Stood Still*, mentioned earlier).[62]

There are several key features that need to be discussed here: the music itself, and the cover artwork. I'll start with the music, which was ahead of the curve, virtually defining the space-age pop sound for more than a decade, including science-fiction film and television soundtracks. One track from this album, "Moon Moods," recently rereleased on a collection entitled *Space-Capades*, provides an example that uses all of what are now familiar devices: the use of underlying "Latin" rhythms; the choir that sings vocables, not words, emphasizing the otherworldliness or ineffability of the subject, a technique used in earthbound exotica pieces as well; the lush, full jazz orchestra backing, including a harp that gives the music the requisite heavenly sound; the electronic instrument that stands apart from the orchestra, as though the orchestra represents society as we know it; and the electronic instrument—the theremin in this case—signifying this ideological complex of science/technology/future at an uneasy distance.[63] The theremin solo, however, is preceded by an electric guitar solo, a good example of the ways that technology becomes normalized, since the electric guitar was only about ten years old at the time of this recording,[64] but it sounds unremarkable in a piece with a theremin in it. "Moon Moods" is particularly interesting in the ebullience of the choir and orchestra and the theremin interjections.

It is worth spending more time with this seminal and semiotically rich work; the musical structure (schematically represented here as table 4.1) reveals a minidrama that encapsulates the argument I am

EXAMPLE 4.1.
Harry Revel: "Moon Moods," main chorus.

TABLE 4.1.
Harry Revel: *Music Out of the Moon* (1947), "Moon Moods," structure.

Structure	Measures	Music
Intro, unmetered	—	organ trills, harp, chorus (male and female) upward swoop
Intro, metered	4	rhythm section plays "Latin" rhythms
Chorus A1 (AABC)	16	men's choir, stepwise downward motion; "Latin rhythms"
Chorus A2 (AABC)	16	repeat of Chorus A1 with slight variations
Chorus B1 (DDEF)	16	electric guitar solo
Transition	4	"Latin" rhythms and harp return; men's choir melody seems about to repeat on organ, which sounds first pitch, accented
Chorus A3 (AABC, transition)	16+4	first theremin solo; spare accompaniment with "Latin" rhythms, leads directly to—
Inter-	8	choir, which takes over from theremin
ruption	4	percussion, dominated by cow-bell, continuing "Latin rhythms"
Chorus A4 (AABC)	16	choir, men and women, with instrumental doublings
Chorus A5 (AABC)	16	theremin plays AA, trombone plays BC; accompaniment not as spare as before
Chorus B2 (DDEF)	16	choir, men only, alternating parts with xylophone
Chorus A6	16+2	theremin plays AAB, piano plays C; theremin fades for 2 bars
Outro	4	piano solo

making here about anxiety and ambivalence over science, technology, and the future.

Revel's piece begins in a fairly commonplace way: "moon" is evoked with the organ trills and harp; the choir enters on an upward swoop, as if dramatizing the upward flight to the moon. "Latin" rhythms begin in the rhythm section, in case it is not already clear that we are dealing with an *elsewhere* and an *other*, though at least familiar ones so far. The men of the choir then sing a straightforward melody (example 4.1, above) as if depicting the exploring men, checking that the moon is safe for the womenfolk. Just to make this clear, this chorus is repeated with only minor variations.

An electric guitar solo enters playing its own tune, chorus B1, though the form is the same as the earlier chorus; the use, however, of two separate choruses is noteworthy and has implications I will note shortly. After this chorus, there is a short transition to chorus A3. During this transition, the "Latin" rhythms return to remind us of the otherness, the elsewhereness that is the theme of the song, and the harp returns to invoke the heavens. The organ sounds one loud, accented note, the same pitch and register as the men's melody, so it seems we are about to go back to that melody, which would make sense after the new melody of the electric guitar. Instead, the entire choir and virtually all the instruments drop out except for a spare accompaniment of "Latin" rhythms in percussion. The theremin enters, sounding the choir's by-now familiar melody, which it plays in its entirety, but then adds four more stepwise chromatic ascending notes until this line is snatched away by the choir, singing something dramatically new: downward minor triads in a sequence that descends chromatically by a semitone, the only time this music is heard in the piece.

This reclamation of the spotlight is followed by four bars of percussion dominated by the cowbell, which allows listeners only a moment to regroup before the chorus A3 begins, sounding the familiar melody of the choir, which is this time joined by women. The presence of women here is interesting since they haven't been heard from before except in the intro. It's as if, while the women had to be protected from the moon at first, there is at the same time something about the moon that is being constructed as feminine, since the theremin solo is juxtaposed with the women singers' first entrance into the body of the piece.

The men's choir's main melody appears again (chorus A4), this time sung by both men and women in a relatively unchanged way. Then the theremin plays the same melody but only the first half; the trombone interrupts it to conclude chorus A5. The theremin might have been allowed by the chorus to sound their melody, but the instruments are putting up a fight. Emboldened by the trombone, the men apparently decide to battle as well and take chorus B2, singing the melody of another instrument, the electric guitar solo from B1, as if to indicate that they know how to deal with *that* kind of electric instrument, as well as an "old-fashioned" machine, the xylophone, which takes over some of the choir's phrases. But the theremin returns in chorus A6 and this time manages to play three quarters of the choir's primary melody before the piano takes it back, though the theremin puts up a valiant effort, nonetheless dying a slow death over two bars, after which the piano, the quintessential acoustic instrument, concludes the piece alone.

I'm describing this as a kind of drama because it is. It can be read as capturing—even forecasting—the attitudes toward the technology of the era, attitudes that were somewhat playful and hopeful while at the same time concerned and anxious. The theremin is permitted an entire chorus, but only once, after which it loses more and more ground to the other musicians before just fading away. This kind of story, in which technology loses out to humans, is only a fantasy, however, for even in the late 1940s when this was recorded, the specter of technology loomed large.

That specter was caught up in male concerns and anxieties over gender relations, the subject to which I now turn. The cover of Revel's album (see fig. 4.1), featuring a barely covered woman reclining on a bed, is by no means atypical; a great many space-age pop albums from this period featured nude or scantily clad women. There is one difference between this cover—and Revel's music—and later iconography, and that is that all later representations of women equate them with space aliens, or with space itself, the woman floating out in it; "human"—i.e., male—scale and perspective are represented by rockets or other forms of space travel technology (see fig. 4.2).

There are other examples, but I have been unable to locate copies to reproduce here (there are more, however, at the website for this book). The most striking is perhaps Revel's *Music from Out of Space* (1953), which depicts a tastefully nude woman in a dramatic gesture in a field of planets and their orbits.

At any rate, Revel's earlier artwork is transitional. The equation of man with technology and woman with space that occurred just after Revel's *Music Out of the Moon* makes sense if we recall the earlier discussion of domestic space and technology. If in the 1950s and early 1960s science and technology could be seen as patriotic, albeit with a strong undertone of anxiety of what the atom could do, this complex

FIGURE 4.2.
Esquivel: *Other Worlds Other Sounds* (1958), cover.

ideology of science/technology/patriotism/anxiety was frequently best represented in the form of a sexualized woman who is "otherized" as an alien, or set apart from men and technology in other ways.

Images and discourses linking a beautiful woman to the bomb abounded in the 1950s and early 1960s, popularizing the idea of the voluptuous "bombshell."[65] Kristina Zarlengo writes of an obscure model by the name of Linda Christians who appeared in *Life* magazine in September of 1945, after the bombs were dropped on Hiroshima and Nagasaki. The editorial, entitled "Anatomic Bomb: Hollywood Starlet Linda Christians Brings New Atomic Age to Hollywood," employed telling language to describe Christians's beauty. One of the photographs depicted her in an "unexplosive moment"; in another she was "explosive."[66] Elaine Tyler May includes a reprint of an illustration from a government civil defense pamphlet showing "dangerous radioactive rays as sexually flirtatious women."[67]

Also, recall some of the discourse used to describe the atomic age, and, later, the space age: discourses of discovery and domination, which have been used by the West for centuries in colonial and other contexts, feminizing the land as part of the ideological mission, as Anne McClintock and many others have pointed out.[68] This historical moment was

FIGURE 4.3.
Andre Montero and Warren Baker: *Music for Heavenly Bodies* (1958 or 1959), cover.

profoundly ambivalent about the atom—anxious and optimistic both—and this very ambivalence is present in myriad ways in the historical record: sometimes the atom is a threat to domestic tranquility, sometimes it is a protector; sometimes the voluptuous woman who adorns so many of these space-age album covers is a threat to domestic tranquility, sometimes she is a mate. These images also vouched for the male hi-fi owner's heterosexuality.

Nowhere is the intertwined nature of science/technology/future and woman, and the ambivalence toward this complex, better exemplified than in an album from 1958 or 1959 entitled *Music for Heavenly Bodies*, which features a fairly obscure orchestra and arranger, Andre Montero and Warren Baker, and a cover with a nude woman reclining on the Milky Way, a suggestive placement indeed (see fig. 4.3).

The performance is as polished as the best of this music. The liner notes begin by enunciating this very connection between space and woman: "Heavenly Bodies, whether it [*sic*] be the type that whirl about us in space, or those that have the glitter of Monroe, Mansfield or Bardot, have always had a magnetic attraction for man. The cosmos, infinite galaxies, lunar bodies suspended in space, glimmering stars light years away from the Earth . . . all of these are both stimulating and staggering to the imagination."[69]

The track entitled "Holiday on Saturn" runs the gamut of space-age pop/lounge/exotica styles, and includes a variety of "Latin" rhythms, including a bolero, and melodies that are quite like those of the exotica type—that is, sometimes disjunct, sometimes chromatic, sometimes using the famous augmented second that signifies the Middle East to Western ears. But what is truly remarkable is the entry of the "electro-theremin," an adaptation of Theremin's instrument, played by Paul Tanner.[70] This is clearly what the piece has been heading toward, and when the solo concludes, nothing musically significant occurs before the end of the work, which is marked by a loud gong.[71] It is interesting that this work does not present the theremin as a threat or problem, as did Revel's "Moon Moods"; the celebration of heavenly bodies is the main theme here.

While most liner notes from the albums of this period did not make explicit the connection between woman and the ideological complex of science/technology/future, several distinct discursive strategies appear on most liner notes: there was usually a sense of humor, occasionally tinged with a little cynicism about space and the future; there was usually a more serious mode in which sincere interest in space and the future appeared; and, as we have seen, there was usually something about recording technology or the electronic musical instrument.

A few comments on each point. It is important to note that, even though the allure and anxiety over technology and the future were real, many of these albums coped by making fun of it, perhaps attempting to skewer some of the more hyperbolic predictions we encountered earlier. For example, the liner notes to Les Baxter's *Space Escapade* (1957) begin by saying, "Even today, in an era of science and satellites, the mystery of the universe has lost none of its magical appeal. We can close our eyes and dream of the future, wondering whether a starlit planet might soon replace a tropical island, the Riviera, or a distant mountain lodge as the ideal spot for a romantic holiday. Or, with the aid of the music in this album, we can drift into the future's lovemist with Les Baxter and make a spaceliner escapade by earthlight, tongue safely fastened in cheek."[72] Note how these comments virtually equate distant places on earth with (more) distant places in the universe. And, given the contemporary feminization of space, there is an introduction of an element of romance that was made explicit by the cover art, which portrays a space-age cocktail party: three scantily clad women with anten-

FIGURE 4.4.
Bobby Christian and His Orchestra: *Strings for a Space Age* (1959), cover.

nae cavort with two men in spacesuits, the shadow of a rocket in the background. Most are toasting each other with brandy snifters.[73]

Again, note that the men are the spacemen, the explorers, but this time, the women, rather than being represented in a different scale than the men, appear as the same size, but they are exoticized by antennae coming out of their heads and their lack of spacesuits and helmets.[74]

While some of these albums' words and sounds may seem laughable today (which is part of their appeal for some collectors), many musicians had a genuine interest in attempting to capture in sound the feeling of space and space technology, as the above quotation indicates; even the notes to *Music for Heavenly Bodies* includes a passage about the electro-theremin's ability to convey the "awe-inspiring feeling of asteroids and comets."[75] Other liner notes contain similar language. For example, Bobby Christian's *Strings for a Space Age* (1959) attempts to "radiate some of the same energy an artificial satellite generates as it is projected into space." The album's second side musically chronicles the flight of a satellite, indicated by titles: "The Call, Preparation," "Count-Down, Flight into Orbit & Empyrean," "Re-Entry," and "Finale"; the tale is announced on the album's cover (see fig. 4.4): "A Story in High Fidelity Sound." The notes tell us, "By the time the music dies away, the

FIGURE 4.5.
Les Baxter: *Ports of Pleasure* (1957), cover.

listener has a very clear trajectory that parallels that described by a missile orbited into space and pulled back to earth."[76] Despite this apparent serious and educational mission, however, the cover art features a very familiar visual combination of a rocket and a beautiful woman who is represented as apart from the rocket ship, part of space itself.

The ways that all these different sounds from different (sub)styles and/or (sub)genres were used points to how interchangeable all of these categories were. *Exotic* could mean Hawaiian, "Latin," Indian, Middle Eastern—it was a single musical sign system to which electronic instruments such as the theremin were added to signify "space." And "space/technology" seemed to be a natural extension of this, for Others were others, and you have to travel to get to them, or they to you, either by jet or spaceship.[77] The notion of *woman* was included in the iconography in part because of her historical association in the West with nature and her more recent association with the bomb and space. Remove the electro-theremin and Montero and Baker's "Holiday on Saturn" could just as easily have been entitled "Holiday in Bali," "Holiday in Hawaii, "Holiday in Tahiti," "Holiday in the Bahamas," "Holiday in Thailand," or . . . As such, a major musician like Les Baxter could release an album entitled *Space Escapade* in 1957, with a massive rocket/phallus in the background, the same year as *Ports of Pleasure* (see fig. 4.5), with a beautiful exotic woman on the cover and phallic symbols in the background. Either way, in all of this music, beautiful women were part of the picture, always exotic, always threatening, and always tempting.

The promise and potential peril of the atom and space were thus domesticated in such sounds and images; the bomb might represent an unimaginable threat, but the beautiful scantily clad woman was at least a familiar one. And both bomb and bombshell had their tempting and dangerous qualities.

Music, the Future, and Science Fiction

While most of the space-age pop albums were in the vein I have been discussing, some recordings addressed space and the future more directly, and articulated the linked themes of anxiety and hope more directly as well. One of the most important sites for this music was music for science fiction films, which afforded composers thematic opportunities to use electronic and/or "spacey" sounding instruments. The most important of these is the remarkable music by Louis and Bebe Barron for the 1956 film *Forbidden Planet*.[78] The plot revolves around an expedition to a distant planet to discover what happened to the human colony that had landed there twenty years earlier but had never been heard from again. The earth explorers find one man and his daughter, the last of the humans; the father tells the recent arrivals that 200,000 years earlier, this planet was host to an extremely advanced race called the Krel, now extinct, but whose technology survives. The planet is being ravaged by some mysterious beast that destroyed all the other humans except this father and daughter, and, sure enough, it attacks the spaceship. There are some casualties, but the captain of the ship finally learns that it is not a beast, but, astonishingly, the father's id that is causing all the trouble.

The plot raises many of the issues we have encountered with respect to technology and the future in the 1950s. Space travel takes one into the unknown and can be deadly; contact with advanced technology is trouble, sometimes psychological trouble. And even having advanced technology cannot prevent one's civilization from disappearing.

The Barrons' music for this film is entirely electronically generated (instead of the more usual and predictable practice of representing space creatures with electronic music and earthlings with acoustic music). A recent rerelease of the soundtrack includes notes by the Barrons that are worth quoting at length:

> We design and construct electronic circuits which function electronically in a manner remarkably similar to the way that lower life-forms function psychologically. There is a comprehensive mathematical science explaining it, called "Cybernetics," which is concerned with the Control and Communication in the Animal and Machine. . . .
>
> In scoring FORBIDDEN PLANET—as in all of our work—we created individual cybernetic circuits for particular themes and leit motifs [*sic*], rather than using standard sound generators. Actually, each circuit has a characteristic activity pattern as well as a "voice."
>
> Most remarkable is that the sounds which emanate from these electronic nervous systems seem to convey strong emotional meaning to listeners.
>
> We were delighted to hear people tell us that the Tonalities in FORBIDDEN PLANET remind them of what their dreams sound like.
>
> There were no synthesizers or traditions of electronic music when we scored this film, and therefore we were free to explore "terra incognito" [*sic*] with all its surprises and adventures.[79]

A related album, *Man in Space with Sounds,* released in 1962 (but reportedly recorded in the early 1950s) to accompany the Seattle World's Fair, features music by Attilio "Art" Mineo, commissioned to compose music that fair-goers would hear inside the Bubbleator, a huge, 150-person elevator constructed of a sphere of clear plastic that transported people inside the World of Tomorrow exhibit. The Bubbleator was operated by a man in a shiny silver suit "right out of a Buck Rogers comic strip," according to the liner notes to the CD rerelease.[80] *Life* magazine included a photograph of the Bubbleator in an issue from May 1964 with the following caption: "BUBBLEATOR. Visitors ride a spherical, oddly named elevator into a maze of cubes containing pictures of the hope and havoc of space and the atom. 'First floor,' chants the pilot, 'threats and thresholds, frustrations and fulfillments, challenges and opportunities.' "[81] The original LP of *Man in*

Space with Sounds is a rare collector's item that I have seen for sale for as much as $75.

Man in Space with Sounds features tracks of pseudo-classical music in a late-Romantic style with inflections of Igor Stravinsky and Béla Bartók. There were also electronic interjections, all meant to be the music of the future. While the World of Tomorrow exhibit was designed, as so many such exhibits were in the 1950s and 1960s, to show how much easier life would be in the future, Mineo's music is not a paean to the future at all, but rather registers contemporary attitudes of ambivalence and anxiety. It is edgy, tense music that leaves no doubt in the listener's mind that, for Mineo at least, the future might not be all that it is promised to be; at the very least, the future was frightening. It is interesting that, while the orchestral music is in styles reasonably familiar from both the nineteenth- and early twentieth-century classical repertoires as well as science-fiction film music and thus isn't relentlessly gloomy, the electronic portions are always threatening, as though Mineo is saying that we know how to cope with the horrors of the past represented by the acoustic music, but the potential horrors of the future are another matter altogether.

Consider the track entitled "Man Seeks the Future." The announcer precedes the music with these words: "If there is one theme which dominates our tour in space, it is man's eternal search for a brighter future. Twenty centuries of achievement are just the prelude. We look to a new century in which science will scale the heights of creative imagination." Then strings enter, playing a chromatic pattern, followed by a kind of warped horn call and Stravinskyesque birdsongs in the winds. Soon after this, an electronic clanging starts softly and in the distance, and seems to get louder, come closer, as if the encroaching future is a kind of demented robot programmed to seek and destroy. But it recedes, the strings retaining their edgy timbre. The sound recurs a couple of times, however, never taking over the orchestral music, but never retreating with any finality, either, perfectly conveying the dual meanings of science, technology, and the future in this era: always promising, and always perilous, offering, at best, "threats and thresholds, frustrations and fulfillments, challenge and opportunities."[82]

TECHNOSTALGIA

If you have seen television, magazines, or newspapers, visited websites, or heard music, you are probably aware that we are in the midst of a 1950s and early 1960s revival. There was a 1950s revival before, in the 1970s, when, for example, *Happy Days* was the number one television program in the 1976–77 season. That nostalgia was precipitated for different reasons than today's, due mainly to the turbulence of the 1960s followed by the disillusionment with the government following the Watergate scandal.[1] Today's nostalgia, if it can be called that at all, is more abstract, consisting mainly of the reuse of 1950s–early 1960s graphic arts styles (as we see in the cover artwork for this book), some dress styles, and, of course, some musical sounds as in films such as *Pulp Fiction* (1994), which featured a good deal of 1950s popular music. Today there are some more overt reuses of the 1950s and '60s than in the previous wave of fifties nostalgia, such as the film *Pleasantville* (1998) and the two Austin Powers movies, *International Man of Mystery* (1997) and *The Spy Who Shagged Me* (1999), or Matt Groening's television program *Futurama*, which pokes fun at some of the fifties' and sixties' (and other) attitudes toward the future; or the series of lesbian detective novels by Mabel Maney set in the 1950s that insert lesbian detectives into the past while always poking affectionate fun at that era.

That the music and the graphic design that accompanied recordings in the 1950s have been revived by collectors and musicians today in part registers a new ambivalence and anxiety over today's digital technology. At the same time, these resurrections mark a disillusionment with technology, for they are often manifest as a kind of nostalgia for past visions of the future, a future that never arrived. This disillusionment, however, is often obscured by cynicism, humor, affection, and disappointment, sometimes all together in a complicated mix, sometimes dominated by just one or two of these qualities.

In this chapter I will generally discuss two main ways that sounds from the 1950s and early 1960s are registered today. One concerns the resurgence of interest in the space-age music of the past, music that often purported to be about space or the future. There was a veritable explosion of this music in the late 1950s and early 1960s, some of which was quite popular in its time but which was eclipsed fairly quickly by rock and roll. But for certain aficionados, those old vinyl albums are forgotten no more, and can now sell for as much as $100. And some of today's musicians sample these earlier recordings for use in their own music. The other way 1950s and early 1960s music has reappeared today is through the reuse of early electronic analog technology, mainly synthesizers such as those by Robert Moog, the Farfisa company, Chamberlin, and others, in part because some musicians prefer the sounds of these older instruments, and in part because these older instruments have fewer automated features than today's instruments and thus allow musicians a greater degree of control. These and other old synthesizers can now sell for more money than they cost when they were new.[2]

Space-Age Pop Revival

Chris Morris writes in *Billboard* of a seminal moment in which the two leading figures of two opposing musics—the jungle "savage," as Elvis Presley was seen by his detractors, and the main musical represensor of the jungle "noble savage," Les Baxter—went head-to-head on *The Milton Berle Show* on June 5, 1956.[3] In that moment, of course, Elvis and rock and roll were on the ascendant, while Baxter, and space-age pop/exotica/lounge music in general were on the way out, blown off the stage, blown out of the sixties, seventies, and eighties. But nobody thought that forty years later Baxter—and lounge—would be back.

A couple of summers ago I had occasion to find myself in the middle of a horde of teenagers at a summer camp. Most were clothed in the post-grunge mode inflected by hip hop that at that time was the norm in most urban American areas. But in this throng I spotted a young man of about fifteen, wearing penny loafers, clean khaki pants, a blue Oxford shirt, and a burgundy bathrobe, sipping bug juice out of a plastic martini glass.

Lounge culture was back.

That is, this young man represented the revival of 1950s and 1960s attitudes and musics currently lumped under the label "lounge," but which comprise "cocktail culture," and in music, "exotica," and "space-age pop," or "space-age bachelor pad."

Why space-age pop? Why now? It seems clear that what now appears to be the fringe popular culture of the 1950s and early 1960s seems to be repeating, not as farce but as camp. The resurgence of interest in space-age pop needs to be understood and explained by examining several different social, generational, and musical trends, all of which are bound up with one another, as they usually are.[4]

First, and perhaps most obviously, in a consumer culture there is always the desire, both manufactured and real, for something new.[5] Radio DJ and space-age-pop champion/revivalist Irwin Chusid writes that

> these recordings are an antidote to everything you're sick of in contemporary music. Had it up to your adenoids with attitudinal rock posturing? Feel besieged by bombastic Boltonism? Does country sound like the same old same old? Have earth-destabilizing dance beats and in-yo'-face hip-hop sneers induced migraines? Tired of the latest incarnation of punk, Bon Jovi soundalikes, and British twit-rock? Bored with self-pitying singer-songwriters and rich, pampered balladeers?
>
> Welcome back to the Space Age.[6]

In addition to its seeming novelty, collectors and music lovers frequently talk about the quality of the music itself. As one person who posted to the exotica mailing list on the Internet writes, "It's the social aspect of hanging out with a group of friends listening to music that in comparison to the often jagged, discordant, repetitive, formula sound of much rock music today is amazingly fresh, well-crafted and highly melodic. And the funny thing is these people who like this stuff are amongst the most learned musically cognizant people around, whose record collections span several eras and several genres."[7]

Space-age pop fans often talk about the well-crafted music in appreciative ways such as this; they are attentive to arrangements, to artistry in a fairly old-fashioned (or even classical) sense. Fans admire the artistry of the music. As one reviewer writes, "Rock is jam driven, riff driven. Lounge is carefully plotted, carefully arranged with afore thought [*sic*]."[8]

Irwin Chusid frequently discusses the quality of the music: "In the rock era, music has been more about exuberance. This music is about perfection. It's very meticulous, played with precision and skill."[9] Elsewhere, Chusid writes that "popular as this music was in the 1950s and 60s, it was reviled at the time by hipsters. Why? Here's a good place to start: it was meticulous: the artists and producers were perfectionists. This aesthetic flies in the face of rock 'n' roll, which values energy and spontaneity over technique."[10] And Dickie Davenport, a former punk rock musician who now works as a DJ spinning space-age pop, says that the music of Esquivel, one of the most prominent space-age pop musicians, is "genius work, brilliantly arranged."[11]

But the music often seems to be a secondary interest.[12] The exotica FAQ site on the Internet addresses this question:

Q: Many people still regard music in those styles as "obviously awful." Do Exotica fans REALLY enjoy this music or is it all some ironic put-on?
A: Fans of Exotica are well aware that these genres were reviled as "easy listening" or "plastic" by the rock 'n' roll generation; for some collectors, the perverse kitsch appeal was the starting point. However most would say that the more time you spend with this music, the more your appreciation grows for its energy, inventiveness, and musicianship, and for the creativity of the arrangements—despite the somewhat misguided concepts that may have been explored.
Also, the original intent to create "commercial" music for a particular market can no longer be regarded as something sinister—by now it must be seen as a fascinating anthropological window into the spirit of an earlier time.[13]

Collecting, therefore, is the main attraction for many, for collecting is as much a part of the experience as the music itself, or "hanging out," as the earlier quotation pointed out. Byron Werner, credited with coining the term "space-age bachelor pad," writes that "working together, these collectors can establish a database of forgotten music of the past."[14] For example, an exotica Internet list user argued for the importance of acquiring vintage vinyl by saying "Old records are the only repository of a lot of vital, compelling musical and cultural history. Dismiss it as sentimental, provincial museum fare if you must, but don't blame me if in [the year] 2,010 you're listening to an endless loop of Bob Marley at any of the 90,000 McDonald's in Honolulu. Diving into this area of record collecting means both endless home entertainment and a fascinating journey filled with strange, wonderful, and often hilarious correspondences with kind, kindred souls and scads of truly creative people."

Much of this music and the cover art are appreciated for its kitschiness. But it is still an affectionate appreciation; kitsch is part of the larger bundle of reasons this music has been revived. Take the most recent issue of one of the many zines that have sprung up to cover this music: *Cool and Strange Music!* derives its title from the seminal volumes of *Incredibly Strange Music* that played a great role in starting this revival, along with Joseph Lanza's *Elevator Music*.[15] *Cool and Strange Music!* proclaims itself on the cover to be "America's Wackiest Music Magazine!!" and written underneath the title in smaller letters are these words: "Dedicated to Unusual Sounds • REFRESHINGLY ODD." All of these lines, including the title, are written using "wacky" type fonts.

Each issue of the zine is filled with reviews of cool and strange music; pictures of album covers such as those I have reproduced in this book; special features and interviews with major space-age pop musicians; articles on record stores where this music can be found; and more. And there are dozens of 1950s and 1960s photographs, in ads and in the magazine proper, used to evoke the era. There is the occasional graphic that also brings back the 1950s; the current issue has a line drawing of the Seattle Space Needle with a World Wide Web address for it. The editorial address of the magazine includes, following the country (USA) the following words: "Planet Earth." Such a magazine may sound like it appeals to a tiny clientele, but it is available at Tower Records, among other places; the editor, Dana Countryman, tells me that its circulation is roughly 3,200 copies.[16]

And Jack Diamond of Jack Diamond Music in California, who was instrumental in rereleasing Attilio Mineo's *Man in Space with Sounds* in 1998, tells me that it's sold over 3,000 copies.[17] These numbers are not huge, but still more than one might expect, given that the album is mainly distributed by Diamond himself at his website (though amazon.com also carries it).

Will Straw, who has written an important study of record collecting as of this writing and notes its links to older notions of oppositionality and rock music, believes that to collect the obscure and the formerly unhip is to "refuse the mainstream," or to exhibit a "transgressive anti-conventionalism."[18] Refusing the mainstream is what rock was all about for many fans, and so today's collectors of the marginal can participate in that position.[19]

Relevant to the space-age pop revival, Straw notes that the last couple of decades have witnessed the rise of "boy-dominated trash fandoms" interested in the obscure and out-of-the-way, such as space-age pop.[20] Vernacular scholarship is evident here, as we have seen. By privileging the illicit or abject, trash fandoms run the risk of an "amorality which valorizes transgression irrespective of its content or purpose." "Indeed," Straw writes, "in the current easy listening revival, the most prominent dynamics are those which diverge from the more respectable and populist anti-rockism which was one of this revival's original impulses. In place of that impulse, one finds an ongoing move to rehabilitate ever more scandalous currents. . . . Here, as in trash fandoms more generally, collecting is refigured as anthropology, an expedition into the natural wilderness of discarded styles and eccentric musical deformations. Indeed, within the easy listening revival, the civilised sound of tinkling Martini glasses is counterbalanced by the image of intrepid explorers marching from one thrift store to another."[21]

There are plenty of examples of the "anthropological" nature of record collecting, beginning with the quotation from the exotica mailing list FAQ quoted earlier. Another prominent example comes from Byron Werner, who advocates what he calls "vinyl anthropology."[22] And the first volume of *Incredibly Strange Music*, published in 1993, informed would-be collectors of these obscure and unhip musics, using striking imagery to describe the role of the collector. "In search of amazing endangered records . . . we interviewed not just original musical innovators . . . but trailblazing *collectors* who, without benefit of discography or reference guide, went out into backwater flea markets and thrift stores to search through that which society discarded. Experiencing the thrill and adventure of the hunt, they made their selections and then listened for hours to ferret out exceptional recordings."[23] Note how the explorer/hunter/adventurer language is reserved for the collectors, not the composers and musicians. This discourse is continued in the introduction to the second volume, which editors V. Vale and

Andrea Juno say "continues the exploration of the territory" of volume 1. "Readers (and travelers)," they say, are welcome to become collectors.[24] Such language echoes in part the music and imagery of the 1950s that these collectors prefer, for much of this music is engaged in space exploration, the future, or, in the exotica strain of the music that I have only mentioned in passing (Les Baxter's "Quiet Village" and *Ports of Pleasure*), the primitive other here on planet Earth.[25]

The adventurer/explorer trope points to the gendered nature not only of the collector, but also the gendered nature of the music itself. As Straw notes, the majority of record collectors generally are men, which is no less true for collectors of space-age pop. In some music genres, the male gender bias is difficult to explain, but in space-age pop it is not so difficult since this was music marketed to men in the first place.[26]

It is also interesting to note that, because this revival by people born after this music's heyday seems so odd, most fans and collectors in this little culture have a theory about why they like this music. Many acknowledge it as a form of rebellion. Young Americans well know that they are supposed to rebel against their parents and their parents' values, and what better way to do it than with the music their parents reviled in the 1950s and 1960s? A website devoted to promoting a new guidebook to lounge music and culture includes a section entitled "Why Lounge? Why Now?" and lists first the issue of rebellion: "Lounge is the current generation's rebel music. As rock was the antithesis of lounge in the 60's, so Lounge is the antithesis of rock in the 90's. Lounge is apolitical, fun, incomparably danceable, and surprisingly sophisticated."[27]

Rock mattered in the sixties because it was seen as a necessary—for some, formative—part of the rebellion of that era. But in our own time, nostalgia for the sixties and the commodification of 1960s brands of political radicalism and musics have led in part to a kind of cynicism that expresses itself, in part, by listening to prerock (or nonrock) popular musics, opting out of rebellion to antiestablishment politics and instead being alternatively rebellious by seeking community and embracing the formerly uncool; one poster to the exotica Internet list wrote in the summer of 1997 that Bob Dylan and Van Morrison "represent practically everything that I personally happen to be against." Today's exotica fan thus rebels against her parents' generation by listening to her grandparents' music. "It's the first time I've identified with my grandparents over the same kind of music," says one listener.[28] Rock in the 1960s worked because it was perceived as authentically linked to the real feelings and aspirations of a generation, because it was made and listened to by real youths with real concerns.[29] Today's space-age pop listeners have real concerns too, but they're tired of this 1960s brand of (now) overcommodified authenticity.[30] If John Lennon and Yoko Ono can be used to sell Apple computers, then what's left of the 1960s that's not for sale?[31]

The revival of this music is, in some sense, about consumption, it's about today's listeners not buying, not wanting to buy, what the increasingly consolidated music industry tries to sell them. Perhaps as the industry—all industries—get better at targeting demographic groups and niche marketing, listeners are getting more desperate to escape and confound the marketers. The industry tries to locate the cool, then sell it, or it tries to fabricate the cool and then sell it. Exotica/lounge/space-age pop is about the uncool, the unhip, the cheesy, the passé, and it's about being a smart consumer who has distinction, not a dumb, hapless consumer who buys the latest Spice Girls recording because it's the latest Spice Girls recording (or because it's on the front rack in the record store).

There are other reasons for the revival of this music. Irwin Chusid, in the liner notes to the compilation album *Cocktail Mix*, says that "if you long for the days when smokers had rights and exercised them freely—*in public;* when alcohol was imbibed without finger-wagging by the FDA; before fat-free became a national fixation—in short, for the days when people enjoyed themselves *without guilt*, then *Cocktail Mix* is just the tonic."[32] Similarly, in an *Esquire* cover story, Randall Rothenberg—himself an acknowledged fan and champion of these musics—writes that "life is very difficult today in many ways, especially sexually. The list of noes is huge. Inhibiting. Unnatural. That's why a lot of this has to do with the formality of another time. In a world where sex roles have broken down, unhappily and uncomfortably, this whole Lounge thing allows for a more stylized and predictable relationship between men and women."[33]

Buying, having, and listening to these records is a way, apparently, for male collectors to listen their way back to a time when, they believe, a man's home was his castle, his hi-fi occupied the center stage in the family home, his wife didn't work outside the home. And she dutifully kept his home clean for him, and served a hot dinner at 5:30 P.M. sharp when he came home from work. So, in a sense, this revival is in part about the male anxiety over what has happened to the authority of the male in the late twentieth century, which, as we have seen, was intimately connected to questions about domestic space and technology in the 1950s. Now the wife works, the husband probably has more domestic responsibilities than he'd like, and high-quality hi-fis have gotten too expensive, swamped by the junk in the national-chain electronics stores.

Some collectors, then, collect these records as a way of dealing with social anxieties such as AIDS, the changing gender roles that some men perceive as threatening, identity politics, and more. These and other contemporary American phenomena have played a role in male collectors' fascination for the past. Reviving this music is a way for men today to wish that things were as they are perceived to have been in the 1950s: men were free to be playboys, swingers, and, if married, their lives were not complicated by working spouses. More than one proponent of this music mentions "the way things were" (though as Stephanie Coontz has pointed out, they weren't).[34]

The revival of space-age pop is a way to come to grips with another anxiety of the variety that is the subject of this chapter. Collecting this music is one way of voicing our own era's disillusionment with the promises of technology, by reviving music that seemed on the surface to be optimistic about science and the future, but whose sound often belied that optimism. "We used to believe it was part of a future that was going to happen, that this was how we were going to live," said a contributor to a BBC radio program about space-age pop culture that aired in 1996.[35]

This complex of ambivalence, playful cynicism, affection for past visions of the future is entering more mainstream popular culture, and not just in terms of some retro graphic designs. I mentioned a few films at the opening of this chapter, but would like to examine briefly here Matt Groening's cartoon television series *Futurama* (the title is taken from a popular ride at the 1939 World's Fair in New York), which, among other things, pokes fun at past visions of the future. In Groening's future, technology is a mixed blessing. *Futurama* features doors that slide open, as on *Star Trek*, but they don't always work; technology has also preserved Richard Nixon's talking head in a jar. Groening says that his future is much like the present: "Traditionally, you have either the overly optimistic world's fair/chamber of commerce/*The Jetsons* point of view or you have a dark, drippy, cyberpunk, creepy future à la *Blade Runner* or *Brazil.* I'm trying to offer an alternative that's more like the way things are right now, which is a mix of the wonderful and the horrible. I'm reacting in part to the liberal optimism of *Star Trek* and *Star Wars.* There's going to be some pretty great entertainment and a lot of very compelling advertising in the future and in *Futurama.* But the No. 1 TV show will be *The Mass Hypnosis Hour.*"[36]

Groening's view of the future pokes fun at the very idea of future and speaks again to the kinds of anxieties over the future, our place in it, and technology's place in it. Groening says, "There are certain conceptions of the future which I think are more interesting than others. I love the look of the 1940s and '50s and early '60s."[37]

Jean-Jacques Perrey, whose music has also been swept up as part of this revival,[38] speculated about the present moment's disillusionment with technology in past views of the future in a recent interview:

> Technology has developed faster than the general consciousness; spiritual and moral values have *not* been preserved. Like Dr. Frankenstein, man has been surpassed by his own creation and technology. People feel a crippling *desensitization.*
>
> The human soul has lost its sense of magic; people have lost their sense of humor and everything is now banalized—instead of "joie de vivre" people feel "mal de vivre." So *the future is not what it was,* because humanity did not correctly manage its inheritance, Planet Earth. Now everyone is increasingly worried, anxiety-ridden, preoccupied and under pressure—and this generates sadness, intolerance, and violence.[39]

Perrey has influenced a revivalist group I would like to consider here, but in order to do so it is necessary first to spend some time on Perrey himself. Unlike his colleagues in the 1950s, Perrey made the occasionally humorous and/or cynical nature of space-age pop his primary mode, even as he recognized that the future could be anxiety producing. Perrey (born Jean Leroy in France in 1929) is perhaps one of the most interesting and durable of all these space-age pop musicians. Perrey moved to the United States in 1960 and held a variety of jobs, including that of sales rep for the Ondioline, an electronic keyboard invented in 1938 by Georges Jenny in France.[40] He appeared on television occasionally and wrote and cowrote many television and radio jingles.[41]

But, unlike his *musique concrète* colleagues in France, Perrey insisted that a sense of humor was important in music. His reaction to the anxiety brought by new technologies was neither to agonize over it, as did his colleagues back in France, nor treat it musically, but, rather, to make light of it. "I sincerely think that *humor* will help save humanity from the swamp into which it is sinking," he has said. "Today we can't afford to be pessimistic, so let's try and keep a sense of humor bolted onto our hearts, soul and spirit! Let's shove pessimism aside for better days . . . when we will be in better shape to handle it!"[42] Elsewhere Perrey described his music as "recreational," and again discussed the need for humor: "The world is becoming so sad, that this sadness is showing through the heart of art . . . and I want to contribute to try changing these facts."[43]

In 1966 Perrey collaborated with Gershon Kingsley on an album entitled *The In Sound from Way Out!* that continues the space-age pop fascination with the future (its subtitle is *Electronic Pop Music of the Future Created by Perrey-Kingsley*), but with a humorous twist, registered of course in the music itself, but also in such titles as "The Little Man from Mars," "Barnyard in Orbit," "Spooks in Space," and others.

The liner notes to *The In Sound from Way Out!* clearly attempt to position it against the more serious and pessimistic music of avant-garde electronic composers in Europe, as well as these composers' "mood music" counterparts in America, such as those discussed earlier—Les Baxter, Attilio Mineo, Andre Montero—and many others:

> Here are a dozen electronic pop tunes. They are the electrifying good-time music of the coming age, the switched-on dance music that will soon be it. This is the lively answer to the question that puzzles—and who knows, even frightens—people who have heard the serious electronic compositions of recent years and wonder, is it the music of the future? As for that avant-garde wing, we say more power to it. But there are other things in the future, such as pleasure. And so presented here is the electronic "Au Go Go" that might be heard soon from the juke boxes at the interplanetary way stations where space ships make their rest stops. The idiom is strange and yet familiar; here a touch of rock, there a touch of bosa [sic] nova, a whiff of the blues in one piece and a whiff of Tchaikowsky in another. But these atoms of pop music are exploded into fresh patterns. They outline a strange new

sound world, yet one in which we can feel at home. The future is upon us, they say, and the future is fun.[44]

The rather embarrassing attempt to be hip here shows up in the music, which today too often sounds trite, despite the evident expertise and inventiveness of Perrey and Kingsley.

The notes continue, offering biographical information on the two musicians, but half of the notes are about the process of making the music, putting this album squarely within the 1950s and early 1960s hi-fi tradition in the notes' attention to the details of recording.

Perrey and Kingsley's music nonetheless bespeaks the same contemporary attitudes toward technology as their more serious counterparts; many songs make fun of the space race and the future, and the humor in these tracks enters not just through the tunes themselves, which are often catchy bordering on trite, but Perrey's acknowledged use of *musique concrète* techniques that introduce familiar swoops and interjections which, in this context, add another level of wryness, directed at what Perrey and Kingsley believe to be an overly serious fascination for space and the future.

Stereolab

Some of the collectors and revivalists of space-age pop are musicians, and they resurrect it in ways other than simply collecting it, which many do. They bring back the sounds, the styles, the instruments, graphics, modes of presentation in liner notes, or some combination thereof, trends that are increasingly visible in other cultural arenas such as styles employed in graphic design in many media, from television and magazine ads to Internet websites. And they have their own anxieties with more recent early technology.

Stereolab, a British band with a French woman lead singer, taps into the 1950s and '60s in particularly clever and provocative ways. Band leader Tim Gane notes that he first got interested in space-age pop/hi-fi era music because of the record jackets.[45] Elsewhere Gane has said, "I like the designs [of the space-age pop albums], the general ways the records are put over. I like the idea of people listening to a record and being aware of what went into it, the mechanics of it. Musically, I like a lot of it. It mixed together a lot of things that hadn't been put together before, it mixed avant garde ideas with pop, big band stuff with organs.

FIGURE 5.1.
Stereolab: *The Groop Played "Space Age Batchelor Pad Music,"* cover.

They weren't doing it to be avant garde musicians, they were just doing it to achieve a purpose, a somewhat cynical purpose: a strange conglomeration of ideas that wouldn't have come out any other way. The fact that they were trying to make an overtly stereophonic record opened doors to mixing and all sorts of stuff that came later. There's all sorts of stuff you can pick up and use later."[46]

And picking up and using stuff is what Stereolab is all about. The name of the band refers to the Vanguard record label's line from the 1950s that featured recordings meant to test one's hi-fi. Everything about Stereolab reflects this interest in the space-age pop music/hi-fi age of the 1950s and early 1960s: the instruments, the cover art, the fonts used on the albums and liner notes. The cover to *The Groop Played "Space Age Batchelor Pad Music"* demonstrates this infatuation clearly (see fig. 5.1).

It's all there: the invocation of "science" with the sound waves, the atom's orbit, the graph paper, even the simple use of only a few colors. And the album title clearly refers to space-age pop from the past. Another title, *Switched On Stereolab* (1992), refers to Walter (now Wendy) Carlos's legendary *Switched On Bach* of 1969, which has recently been rereleased.[47]

Stereolab's 1993 album *Transient Random-Noise Bursts with Announcements*—a jargon-laden title that recalls the heady hi-fi days—features a track entitled "Jenny Ondioline," referring to Georges Jenny's instrument, popularized mainly by Jean-Jacques Perrey. The track doesn't actually feature an Ondioline but is instead an homage to Perrey, if only in the title; there is, however, a sound sample, credited in the liner notes to a recording entitled *Channel Recognition Phasing and Balance*, about which I have been able to discover nothing, but, judging from the title, it must be one of the many hi-fi era test albums. The cover of the album features a greatly manipulated photographic image of a turntable hovering above a disc; the liner notes contain blurry photos of old electronic equipment.

Transient Random-Noise Bursts with Announcements features a back cover much like the space-age pop that it emulates. There is a good deal of technospeak about the audio qualities of the recording. Each track is listed along with information about what audio effects listeners could use to test their speakers. For "Jenny Ondioline" the accompanying technical information reads: "Music and background noise tests, for confirming secure tracking of a pickup that has been set up with the aid of other tests and the acceptability of equipment noise."[48]

Not unexpectedly, the band also seems interested in 1950s and 1960s views of the future. Gane says that "in the '50s and '60s, when they were writing music, they had to imagine what music would sound like in the future, they had to imagine what music would sound like from another world . . . it was about their imagination trying to think of what it would sound like, so you'd throw away the rules, and they'd try to create music which would be nothing like what was going on at the time. Much of this music was pretty cynical, but despite that, so many amazing things were happening for the first time, which opened doors to people later on to explore those things—mixtures of electronics, of orchestrations, different dynamics."[49] Gane notes the cynicism of this space-age pop music, but he is looking, with his own knowledge of what happened, to the future of the 1950s. It's really the kind of anxiety over technology and the future that I have been examining in this chapter. I think the cynicism is more Gane's, but it is a cynicism also marked by a desire for that future that never arrived.[50]

Régis Debray writes that "the most recent layer of signs reaches us through the older ones, in a perpetual re-inscribing of the archives, such that the new takes effect in, by, and on the old."[51] But when the new and the old are mixed together in the same song, or over the course of an album, there is a kind of chronoschizophrenic quality; the resulting sound is a jumble of electronic and acoustic sounds and styles from several decades. Some timbres are from 1970s machines, some from the 1980s, but the unifying bass and drums could only be 1990s, techno-influenced. In terms of affect, however, Stereolab's songs are not that far from the semi-ironic, affectionate, playful treatment that the space age pop revival conveys.

In addition to evoking the space-age pop and hi-fi era with iconography and (faux) technical information, Stereolab also uses a good deal of early analog electronic instruments. Interestingly, however, Gane's explanation does not touch on his interest in the recordings of the past. Rather, he explains, "We use the older effects because they're more direct, more extreme, and they're more like plasticine; you can shape them into loads of things. Modern effects sound blander to me and are less human, more characterless. The older effects have a strong sound straightaway."[52] The "plasticine" features of the older equipment mean that the human operator has more control, for the machines don't do very much. In other words, the issue of agency resurfaces here.

Gane is not alone in his assertion that more control over machines is better. The sophisticated digital hardware, and software that can replace some hardware, have caused some musicians to worry about what is happening to their control over their own sounds, their own music. The well-known composer and producer Brian Eno, long an advocate of music technology, has growing doubts.[53] In a recent *Wired* article, Eno described working with some extremely advanced studio technology, concluding that it was "a horribly unmusical experience."[54] Eno says that he is "struck by the insidious, computer-driven tendency to take things out of the domain of muscular activity and put them into the domain of mental activity. This transfer is not paying off. Sure, muscles are unreliable, but they represent several million years of accumulated finesse. Musicians enjoy drawing on that finesse (and audiences respond to its exercise), so when muscular activity is rendered useless, the creative process is frustrated. No wonder artists who can afford the best of anything keep buying 'retro' electronics and instruments, and revert to retro media."[55] Robert Moog, inventor of the Moog synthesizer, made much the same point in a recent radio interview, saying that the older equipment invites a physicality, and offers a tactility that are pleasurable and unavailable with most newer instruments having buttons instead of knobs, which is why he thinks there is a demand for it again.[56]

The software developer's urge to maximize options emanates from what Eno views to be a faulty notion, that "more options" correlates with "greater freedom" for the user. For Eno, it's the reverse: more options block intuitive work, take up too much of the brain's function that should be left to respond with "attention and sensitivity to the changing texture of the moment."[57]

People in the larger computing world share these concerns. In a thoughtful essay for the online magazine *Salon*, software developer Ellen Ullman wrote of her decision to remove Microsoft Windows from her system and switch to UNIX, a far simpler operating system. While Windows wants to do everything for you, UNIX, she says, "always presumes that you know what you're doing. You're the human being, after all, and it is a mere operating system."[58]

There are periodic moments of nostalgia in any literate culture with access to cultural forms of the past. Yet the space-age pop music revival is not nostalgic as much as it is a complicated mix of irony, affection, cynicism, and genuine aesthetic appreciation, which shows up not just in fans' love of the music but contemporary musicians' homage to their space-age pop forebears. In its darkest form, it is a way of combating what Leo Marx has called a "surge of technological pessimism," brought about by memories of recent failures of technology.[59]

While Will Straw's thoughtful article on record collecting helps us, in some ways, to understand today's fans' passion for this older music, there is something deeper at work, I think, and by way of conclusion I would like to turn to an essay by anthropologist Grant McCracken that can be used to shed more light on the space-age pop revival. McCracken, unlike most influential theorists of things and commodities, is interested in use-value, in function rather than exchange, a position I find congenial, though some might find McCracken's work on this subject a bit idiosyncratic.[60]

McCracken seeks to theorize what he calls "displaced meaning," the meaning or set of meanings that a particular culture displaces in order to harbor and preserve them. This happens when cultures place their ideals elsewhere, available to be recalled at a moment's notice, but safe from whatever dangers their real world presents. The strategy of displaced meaning helps give these ideals a kind of "empirical demonstration"; they seem practicable when distant, so that the gap between the real and the ideal can be understood in terms of local problems.[61]

Almost anything can be chosen as the locus of displacement, but the most common strategy is to identify a "golden age," a strategy we have seen in this chapter. This tactic, although the most common, faces difficulties, for in a literate society there is always plenty of evidence to contradict what this golden age was supposedly about. So these golden ages are largely fictitious, in which "social life is imagined to have conformed perfectly to cultural ideals."[62] There are two other strategies: the future, and a distant space. The future works because, unlike the golden age, it is less bound by actual facts.

These three strategies are particularly striking in the context of this chapter, for the space-age pop music revival combines all three. It is a revival of a music from the past that was about the future, frequently coupled with ideologies of exoticism exemplified both in the overlap of space-age pop and exotica music styles and album iconography, in which women could both represent an earthbound exotic other as well as an exotic other representing the triumph and terror signified by the bomb.

It is one thing to displace meanings, but how are they reclaimed? This is one of the functions of goods. But if an attempt is made to uncover meanings, one has to be careful not to damage them or expose them to the harsh light of the present. As McCracken notes, "Recovery must be accompanied in such a way that displaced meaning is brought into the 'here and now' without having to take up all of the responsibilities of full residence. When displaced meaning is recovered from its temporal or spatial location, it must not be exposed to the possibility of disproof. In other words, access must not be allowed to undo the work of displacement."[63]

Goods serve as bridges in two ways: before they are owned, and after. When a good is not owned but coveted, it can still connect the would-be owner to the displaced meanings through the individual's anticipation of purchase and the meanings she will acquire. Coveting helps the individual rehearse the ways of life and social situations that ownership of that good will provide.[64] Coveting and desiring goods allows the individual access to the displaced meanings, even to own them in some sense. However, goods do this without subjecting the displaced meanings to the real world; the goods "[make] displaced meaning accessible without also making it vulnerable to empirical test or compromising its diplomatic status."[65]

Owning can threaten to delete or compromise the displaced meaning, however. The only way out of a cycle of desire/purchase/desire more is to collect. McCracken sees collecting as the refuge of the wealthy, though since not only the wealthy collect, I would say it is a broader strategy. Scarce, rare items have to be hunted down, not simply bought—the record collector is a "vinyl anthropologist," an intrepid explorer. The scarcity of goods allows displaced meanings to reside more powerfully, and, as we have seen with respect to the collectors of old space-age pop albums, much of the meaning resides in the act of collecting itself.

McCracken is really talking about inanimate objects here; at one point he excludes spoken language and music, for their meanings are not "concrete and enduring," which means they are unable to transcend the here and now. This, of course, makes sense in some ways, for old out-of-fashion music sounds old and out of fashion. But what is striking about space-age pop collectors and revival bands is the extent to which they argue on behalf of space-age pop music's transcendent qualities. I have never studied a popular music whose qualities of composition and arranging are discussed with such frequency, or in terms of such approbation, even though it is by no means the case that everyone collects the albums for their music.

In a more recent book, McCracken touches on the space-age pop revival, and here he does not invoke the idea of displaced meanings. Rather, he posits what he calls "temporal cultures," that is, constructions of the past, usually in the convenient package of the decade, that provide ways by which people in the present can impose order on an increasingly disorderly, plenitudinous, world.[66] McCracken also writes that temporal cultures provide those caught up in them with ways of dealing with difference. Plenitude, that contemporary condition that gives its name to entitle McCracken's recent book, produces difference at the same time that it provides us with ways of managing difference. "This is handy," writes McCracken. "Here's diversity that helps us survive diversity. Here is plenitude that forgives plenitude. Here is a way to accomplish commonality even in the face of our present explosive . . . heterogeneity."[67]

It is no accident that, at the same time as the rise of electronica musics generally, there was renewed interest in space-age pop, especially by young middle-class white people. If the rise of identity politics meant that "real" people of color might not want to engage with young whites in favor of emphasizing their essential identities (and thus seeming to demonize essentialized identities of young whites), then whites who had a complicated interest in racialized others—whether a genuine, nonprurient interest or a more illicit one that took pleasure in tribalized images and sounds—could turn to this music of the past, which made light of such differences, turning all of us into "sames" as space becomes the elsewhere, the home of others, marked by an even more fundamental division, gender.

The space-age pop revival is a complicated kind of displacement into the temporal culture of the 1950s, which holds displaced meanings of a better present in which there would be no nuclear war and technology would be cheap and simplify our lives. This set of meanings is overlain by our "golden age" displaced meanings of the late twentieth/early twenty-first century in a complex sign system that could only happen in this era of the overabundance of cultural forms of all kinds, this plenitude. The meanings of this sign system are enhanced by the community-making aspects of collecting and the Internet, which allows these fans to find each other, and the ever-decreasing costs of computers and software that allow people to publish their own zines (such as *Cool and Strange Music!*) on a huge variety of subjects. And these same meanings are further amplified by the fact that these old LPs are not simply objects, but objects that have stored on them affect-making sounds which mask their own displacement through the immediacy of the music. Then the music itself is shunted aside in favor of campy album covers and crazy liner notes, or, if it is talked about, it is in terms of its quality, as though it were nothing other than a pure aesthetic object that has withstood the test of time.

And the collectors are believers. "Some people describe this as the soundtrack to the life I'd like to lead," says one fan.[68] Nicholas "The Millionaire" Cudahy, a member of the first and still most important revival band, Combustible Edison, says that, yes, in some ways this music is escapist, "but in other ways brings the element of escapism into your daily life," as though living with these displaced meanings reclaims them while still keeping them safely at arm's length.[69] Many fans and collectors really do think that, as one wrote on the exotica Internet list, "I know I've been born 30 years too late."

SPACE

A RIDDLE

WRAPPED

IN A MYSTERY

Globalization as we currently discuss it and theorize it
cannot be conceived without taking into consideration digital technologies that have speeded up the movement of information. It is for
this reason that Manuel Castells prefers to label this era both global and
informational, not simply one or the other, as much of this book makes
clear.[1] This chapter, therefore, takes off from Castells to examine the
ways that music moves around the world, and the consequences that
this movement can sometimes have, with respect to a specific case of
the German band Enigma and their appropriation of a song by aboriginal musicians in Taiwan.

Globalization/"Glocalization"

Much has been made in the last few years of the new globalized,
transnational world that we all live in, a world with flows of
"technoscapes," "ideoscapes," "ethnoscapes," "mediascapes," and "finan-
scapes" that Arjun Appadurai has so influentially labeled and theorized.[2] To this list I would add, or tease out, another, an "infoscape,"
which to some extent is the atmosphere in which the others exist, made
possible by the computer, the Internet, and other digital technologies.[3]

With the rise of these recent "scapes," however, and terms such as
transnational, or *global economy,* it is important to wonder just how
new this new global economy is, for claims about the "new" global
economy are almost never historically informed. There is a good deal of

evidence that in terms of overseas investment we aren't really any more global than we were at the height of the imperial era, that is to say, early in this century. Doug Henwood has written that in terms of exports as a share of the gross domestic product, the United Kingdom—the biggest imperial power among developed nations—was only a little more globalized in 1992 than in 1913; Mexico exported more than twice as much in 1929 as in 1992; today, the United Kingdom exports almost twice as much as Japan, which most people think is the biggest exporter. The United States economy is more internationalized now than it was at the turn of the century, but it nonetheless exports far less than the United Kingdom and Japan and is in fact closer to Mexico in these terms.[4]

If we step further back in history we can discover that people—and thus their culture, and more specifically, for my purposes here, their music—have always interacted. Historian Jerry H. Bentley asserts that "cross-cultural encounters have been a regular feature of world history since the earliest days of the human species' existence."[5] Asian, African, and European peoples regularly traveled and interacted, he argues, via trade routes that crossed the Eurasian landmass; religions such as Buddhism, Christianity, and Islam influenced people far from their points of origin.[6]

Bentley distinguishes three main periods of travel and intercultural exchange beginning with the Roman and the Han empires (he begins in this moment because of the scarcity of historical sources before). He first identifies the era of the ancient silk roads, which he dates as roughly 400–200 B.C., as the first major period of intercultural contact. The next major period began around the sixth century, with cross-cultural exchange fostered by the foundation of large imperial states such as the Tang, Abbasid, and Carolingian empires, and which relied on the cooperation of nomadic peoples who provided transportation links between settled regions. In this period, there was also more frequent sea travel across the Indian Ocean. This second era blended into the third, the last pre-Columbian one, from roughly A.D. 1000 to 1350; long distance trade increased dramatically over both sea and land, and was also marked by the rise of nomadic peoples into political power and expansion, namely the Turks and the Mongols. The bubonic plague in the later fourteenth century disrupted trade until the fifteenth, leading to a fourth and more studied colonial expansion of European powers.[7]

Immanuel Wallerstein has written of a period a little later than this, the expansion of European empires after Columbus's "discovery," and coined the term the "modern world-system" to describe the establishment of regular contact around most parts of the world. For Wallerstein, modernity *is* this rise of capitalism and world trade that began in the sixteenth century. This expansion, he tells us, wasn't just a geographic (that is, colonial) expansion, but was also economic, accompanied by demographic growth, increased agricultural productivity, and what he calls the first industrial revolution. It was also, he notes, the period in which regular trade between Europe and the rest of the inhabited world was established.[8]

At one level, then, while some of the foregoing may resonate with today's headlines, it's old news. Today's globalization is less something new than a continuation of global processes that have been in place since the late fifteenth century, and which themselves were preceded by precapitalist forms of cross-cultural exchange. To think in binary terms—as if we are now in a moment of "globalization" that renders the past as a monolithic moment of "preglobalization"—doesn't get us very far.

And yet, of course, some things are different today. Today's globalization, as people in the so-called developed countries are experiencing it, would not be happening without digital and other technologies, which mean that the exchange of information is faster, travels farther, and that there's thus more of it. The main difference, though, I would argue, isn't merely the speed of dissemination, or even the seeming glut of forms and signs, but rather, the fact that there are more and more signs from elsewhere coming to the developed countries. What we are in the midst of today isn't simply a globalization in which forms flow everywhere, but rather a moment in which forms from elsewhere are coming to the West with increasing frequency; it was this increase in recordings from other places to European and American metropoles that prompted the invention of the "world music" term a decade ago.[9] As Stuart Hall writes, "our lives have been transformed by the struggle of the margins to come into representation."[10] It is thus a bit Euro- and Americocentric to think that the world is newly globalized, since Western forms have been globalized for decades, through colonialism, imperialism, and the movement, as Wallerstein writes, from economic cores to peripheries (and the extraction of materials to the core).

So why is the term *globalization* so frequently used if it describes processes that have been ongoing since the beginning of recorded history? The term obfuscates, as Henwood, Timothy Brennan, and others have argued.[11] The hype surrounding the new global economy covers up, to a certain extent, the fact that capitalism is as exploitative as it ever was—perhaps more so—and is constantly seeking new people around the world to use as cheap labor, which, according to Wallerstein, has been the impetus behind global expansion for centuries.[12] The term also helps preserve an old binary opposition that is increasingly waning, the binary between "global" and "local," which has been much theorized lately.[13]

Perhaps a better term than *globalization* is the term *glocalization*, a word that originated in Japanese business in the late 1980s and was quickly picked up by American businesses.[14] Glocalization emphasizes the extent to which the local and the global are no longer distinct— indeed, never were—but are inextricably intertwined, with one infiltrating and implicating the other. Indeed, it may now be difficult or impossible to speak of the "one" and the "other."[15] Older forms and problems of globalization continue but are increasingly compromised, challenged, and augmented by this newer phenomenon of glocalization.

Beginnings

Now let me turn to the specific musical case of this chapter. In May 1988, the cultural ministries of the French and Taiwanese governments brought about thirty Taiwanese residents of different ethnic groups to France to give some concerts. These musicians ultimately performed in Switzerland, France, Germany, the Netherlands, and Italy for a month, earning a stipend of fifteen dollars per person per day. Unbeknownst to the musicians, some of their concerts were recorded, and the following year, the Ministère de la Culture et de la Francophonie/Alliance Française issued a CD recording called *Polyphonies vocales des aborigènes de Taïwan* that contained some music from these concerts. A Taiwanese ethnomusicologist, Hsu Ying-Chou, says that the musicians signed a contract before the tour, and that the Chinese government approved the French recording.[16] Pierre Bois, of the Maison des Cultures du Monde, told me that the musicians did in fact know they were being recorded, and that the Chinese Folk Arts Foundation was in regular contact with the musicians, whom he assumes were paid for an earlier recording.[17] That is, this CD also included music recorded a decade earlier by a Taiwanese ethnomusicologist and was accompanied by liner notes by two Taiwanese ethnomusicologists, one who had made the original field recordings, the other who had issued them in Taiwan.

In the meantime, Michael Cretu, a Rumanian émigré to Germany (also known as "Curly M.C.") and his band Enigma were busy scoring a colossal international hit with their album *MCMXC A.D.* This recording came out of nowhere to sell seven million copies worldwide, which made it the most successful German production abroad ever; the single from the album, "Sadeness Pt. 1" (after the Marquis de Sade) became the fastest-selling single in German recording history. *MCMXC A.D.* went to number 1 in several European countries, including the United Kingdom, and peaked at number 6 with a run of 150 weeks on *Billboard* magazine's Billboard 200 charts in the United States. The gimmick (or combination of gimmicks) that proved so salable was Cretu's combination of sampled Gregorian chants mixed with a dance beat resulting in a kind of sped-up New Age litany.[18]

A few years later, in 1992, Michael Cretu sat in the studio he built with the proceeds from *MCMXC A.D.* on the island of Ibiza off the coast of Spain. Cretu, in the words of one fan, took "3 years [to] work his way through hundreds of CD's of native song, sampling, cataloguing and synchronising many sounds before he began his songwriting process."[19] Cretu himself said that "I'm always looking for traces of old and forgotten cultures and I'm listening to hundreds of records and tapes."[20] Encountering *Polyphonies vocales des aborigènes de Taïwan,* Cretu found what he wanted in the first track, a song called "Jubilant Drinking Song." Cretu's publishing company, Mambo Musik, paid 30,000 francs (about $5,300) to license the vocals from the Maison des Cultures du Monde; half of this money went to the Chinese Folk Arts Foundation. The resulting single—the most successful single from Enigma's second album, *The Cross of Changes*—is called "Return to Innocence," and it went to number 2 in Europe, number 3 in U.K., and number 4 in the United States. The album *The Cross of Changes* went to number 2 in Europe, number 1 in the United Kingdom, number 9 in the United States, and number 2 in Australia in 1993. Because of Enigma's earlier success, 1.4 million advance orders were made for this album, which ultimately sold 5 million copies and was on *Billboard*'s Top 100 Chart for thirty-two straight weeks.

Two years later, Kuo Ying-nan, a seventy-six-year-old betel nut farmer and musician in Taiwan, of Ami ethnic ancestry, received a phone call from a friend in Taipei. " 'Hey! Your voice is on the radio!' And sure enough," said Kuo, "it was me."[21] "I was really surprised," he said, "but I recognized our voices immediately."[22] Kuo and his wife Kuo Shin-chu were two of the musicians who had toured Europe in 1988, and were also on the earlier recordings collected on the *Polyphonies vocales* recording.[23]

Now, cut to Atlanta, Georgia, in 1996, where the International Olympic Committee was selecting music to showcase at the games their city was to host that summer. They commissioned ex–Grateful Dead drummer Mickey Hart, a leader in the "world music" genre, as winner of the first Grammy award for that music in 1991, and Hart duly composed "A Call to Nations," a work that featured many different kinds of drumming, as well as Tibetan Buddhist chanting and other sounds, demonstrating the notion that we're all one world. Other composers were commissioned, and, relevant to this discussion, previously recorded works were also made official songs of the Olympics. Enigma's "Return to Innocence" was named one of these. It thus appeared on a collection featuring official Olympics music, and was used by CNN and NBC in advertisements for their coverage of the Olympics, though I have been unable to locate this album.[24] (Some press reports say this Olympics exposure is how Kuo learned of the use of his voice).[25] Gill Blake, assistant producer of the project that produced the promotional video for the Olympics, wrote, "We listened to several pieces we felt had something spiritual and timeless about them. It was then purely a matter of making a subjective choice. . . . In addition, 'Return to Innocence' seemed to work in conjunction with the ideas expressed in the video of fair play, peace, unity, etc."[26]

On July 1, 1996, just before the beginning of the Olympics, Magic Stone Music, a record label in Taipei, issued a press release that said that they were representing the Kuos in a lawsuit against EMI (the parent company of Virgin, Enigma's record company), and that they were also producing a new album by them, an album of their traditional music mixed with pop sounds.[27] On July 26, 1996 it was announced that the president of the International Olympic Committee, Juan Antonio Samaranch, had decided to send an official thank-you to the Ami couple, following a report to the committee by Wu Ching-Kuo of Taiwan.[28] The Kuos' attorney claimed that the original use of their voices was illegal, and thus all subsequent uses are also.[29] Their attorney also said that this was not just an intellectual property case, but that the Kuos' human rights had been violated: the musicians "think EMI is ignoring the human rights of the Ami people."[30] "Minority peoples around the world have been treated unfairly over and over in this way," Magic Stone said in their press conference. "In the 17th century, people cheated the aborigines out of their land, but why are the basic rights of aboriginal peoples still being ignored today?"[31]

At some point (a date has not been mentioned) Enigma was reported to have sent a check for $2,000 (another report said 15,000 francs, which is almost $3,000) to Hsu Tsang Houei, who had made the original field recordings in 1978.[32] Professor Hsu deposited the check in an Ami community trust fund. Some reports said that this money was sent to Kuo himself. One account said that Enigma suggested the possibility of further collaborations with Kuo. The Taiwanese government said that the higher figure was paid by the Maison des Cultures du Monde, which was responding to a letter from Hsu Tsang Houei, and that the money was paid to the Chinese Folk Arts Foundation, which had brought the singers from Taiwan to Europe in the first place. To date, however, the money appears to have remained in the hands of the foundation and has not been paid out to the Kuos or anyone else.[33]

As far as I can tell, this threatened lawsuit went nowhere for nearly two years. I sent a few faxes to Magic Stone inquiring about its status but received no reply; in the last of these I volunteered my professional services as a musicologist, but still nothing. Finally, in March 1998, two press reports clarified matters. The lawsuit had indeed stalled, because the Kuos "representatives" were told by the (presumable) defendants in the suit that it could cost about $1 million to bring suit. Attorneys willing to take on the suit pro bono could not be found until, finally, a Chinese-American intellectual property lawyer agreed to take the case.[34]

This lawyer, Emil Chang of Oppenheimer Wolff and Donnelly in San Jose, California, posted a plea to the Internet newsgroup alt.music. enigma-dcd-etc in June 1998 headed "HELP STOP EXPLOITING ABORIGINAL CUTLURES! ABORIGINES SUE FOR JUSTICE AND RECOGNITION: JUSTICE FOR THE KUOS!"[35] Chang included more explicit information about the suit that demonstrates the chain of ownership in today's multinational music world, for the suit was filed against a variety of music production and recording companies, including EMI and Sony. The basis of the suit was copyright infringement and "for failure to attribute the plaintiffs as the original creators and performers of their work."

In the middle of the suit, Emil Chang left the firm and the case was taken over by E. Patrick Ellisen, who told me early in 1999 that the judge was anxious that the case be settled out of court before the scheduled court date of midsummer 1999.[36] But mediation in the spring of 1999 failed to produce results, and Ellisen expected to go to court. The failure of this mediation meant that another lawsuit was filed, against various licensees of EMI, since "Return to Innocence" appeared on many compilation albums, as well as in films, television programs, and television advertisements. Ellisen's office also considered another lawsuit, against EMI in France, and against Maison des Cultures du Monde, that was not filed.[37] Ellisen and his staff faced an uphill battle, for most traditional music is not copyrighted, so it is easy for defendants in such cases to claim that the material wasn't copyrighted, or that any usage of it constitutes fair use. For this reason, Robin Lee, director of Taiwan's Association of Recording Copyright Owners, said that Kuo had no legal case: "The original authors of traditional folk chants have long been dead. And since performers are not authors, they have no copyrights."[38] Lee is wrong, though, for it isn't true that folk music can't be copyrighted; it has become standard for folk musicians to list the music as traditional, but the "arrangement" of it as copyrighted. So listings such as "All music traditional, arranged by x" are now common. The defendants' attorneys also claimed that the Kuos knew that they were signing away rights to the concert recordings made in France in 1988, as Pierre Bois of the Maison des Cultures du Monde maintained.

Finally, in June of 1999, the parties reached an out-of-court settlement, most of which is confidential. What is known is that the Kuos will be given written credit on all future releases of the "Return to Innocence" song, and would receive a platinum copy of *The Cross of Changes* album. Additionally, the Kuos would be able to establish a foundation to preserve their tribe's culture, particularly its music, an act that Ellisen says was "not to be construed as implying there was any money" in the settlement terms. For its part, Virgin Records America thanked the Kuos "for the important contribution that their arrangement and performance of the vocal chant 'Jubilant Drinking Song' made to the song 'Return to Innocence.' "[39] The careful use of the word "arrangement" here indicates that Virgin never altered its position on the Kuos' music—it is an "arrangement," that is, a version of a work for which they do not hold the copyright.

While the lawsuit was in progress, an established Taiwanese pop band called Xin Baodao Kangle Dui (or New Formosa Band) released an album on which they sing in two local dialects: Minnan, also known as Taiwanese, and Kejia, also known as Hakka.[40] The first track is described by a Taiwanese fan as an "Enigma-like song reminding a person most strongly of 'Return to Innocence'. The only thing is that it's done in a mix of Kejia and Taiwanese. It definitely bewildered me the first time I played it."[41] Think of this: a Taiwanese group singing music in local languages in the style of Enigma's song that had extensively sampled music by an Ami couple singing in their native language. New Formosa Band's song is compiled and remixed on a later release, and advertised as a dance tune with world music rhythms, entitled, in English, "Song for Joyous Gathering." The band also added a new member on this compilation album: an Aboriginal musician from Taiwan. Bobby Chen, a pop star in Taiwan, has recorded yet another version of this song.[42]

Twists

That's the story as clearly and as simply as I can put it, though there are some interesting twists. Enigma's fans responded to the claims by the Kuos that they had not been consulted or recompensed, and I am going to turn now to discussing fans' reactions to this case, for they, too, are no less a part of this "infoscape" surrounding the case of the Kuos and Enigma. The press release mentioned above provoked some angry responses from fans on the Enigma Internet mailing list; a few posters were concerned about the incident, but for the most part Enigma's fans were angry that someone was, in effect, questioning their hero's creativity. The most vociferous (and most loudly agreed with) statement was this:

Wow, foreign greed, tis but strange since most greed comes from the States.

Now I've raved about this before, but I'm sad to say "screw this guy". He took his cut, and now that his voice is famous people are getting him to cash in on it. There should be definately a statute of limitations on stuff like this, espically if the suits come _after_ the song is a big hit. I shall participate in my very small "one man boycott" (OHHH AHHH :)). And be sure not to help these people profit in any way. But not that it matters to anyone.

Still, why didn't they sue 3 years ago eh? Ya gotta wonder …

PS Enigma is still the best _where-ever_ and _how-ever_ they get the samples!!!

And so forth. The gist of this and most subsequent posts was that the Kuos had been paid (though, as I indicated, it isn't clear if they actually received any money) and that they had no right to ask for anything else.

Another post by this same user, slightly mollified by a calm call for fairness, wrote back, saying that

anything he [Kuo] deserves should not have anything to do with Enigma and/or its management. Let the people they bought it from deal with this guy. Also, you have to wonder if it had been some other band and/or the song made little money would anyone care? The only thing left that would make this perfectly _American_ is if this guy claimed some sort of racism or something. eheh :) Seriously though, I think the original party who sold to Enigma should have to be responsible if anyone is going to take the fall. I mean if this original anthro guy made this recording and such then it is kinda public domain stuff. Enigma basically paid the society for their "efforts" and that's about all that was neccessary. Now if the guy's original recording had a bunch of dance beats and other vocals then we'd have a problem ;)

This user's view seems to be that the original recording was of raw material in the public domain, but if the original recording had been refined by the addition of "dance beats and other vocals," that would indicate that their music had been produced in a studio, and thus copyrighted.

After this flurry of responses, lawyer Emil Chang's later posting, quoted above, generated some rather nasty responses. Most Enigma fans (the vast majority of whom subscribe to the mailing list and do not frequent the newsgroup that Chang posted to) were not sympathetic. Most argued that, even though the Kuos contributed something, "Return to Innocence" simply did not exist before Michael Cretu worked his magic. One person wrote, "As so far as 'Recognition' goes, an almost 80-year old Taiwanese singer is not credited on each and every copy of Enigma2's album because Michael Cretu **is** the creator of RTI ["Return to Innocence"]. Period."

It is clear that Enigma's fans are heavily invested in their highly romantic perceptions of Michael Cretu's genius; they view Cretu as a supremely gifted maker of meanings and speak of him in heroic terms. Their denunciations of, and impatience for, the Kuos' lawsuit makes this clear: they don't like Cretu's claim to genius and originality questioned at all. Or, if they admit that Cretu took somebody else's music, he is described as refining it, turning some raw material into art.[43] Here's one post to the Enigma mailing list during discussions of the Kuos' lawsuit: "OK, so Cretu probably realized that he could afford (and it would be well worth) a hell of a lot more than $2000 for the recording he made. But look; who else do you know who can take a two thousand dollar recording and make it into a multi-million dollar recording? Do you see that Andy guy who sang part of the chorus complaining? Let's not forget that even though the dude from Taiwan has a great voice, it was Cretu creativity that made the real music happen."

Clearly invoking Romantic ideas of the genius as a person driven to work, and working in isolation, the Enigma FAQ on the Internet describes Cretu working alone in the studio at all hours, sorting through hundreds of CDs to sample: "He is a self-confessed night owl, and also a workaholic, this being seen by the fact that the production phase for *The Cross of Changes* took 7 months with the computer log of his sound bridge often stating that recording sessions from 10pm to 11am occurred. During this whole period he rarely saw the sun."[44]

One of the ways Westerners appropriate other music is to construct the original makers of that appropriated music as anonymous. Anthropologist Sally Price was told by a French art dealer that "If the artist isn't anonymous, the artist isn't primitive."[45] Cretu positions Kuo as anonymous and timeless in order to advocate his "return to innocence," a return to spiritualized past. But when the makers of the original sounds talk back, Cretu's originality is called into question.

Kuo and his wife are assumed to be "primitives," but they're inconveniently privy to the rest of the world via the various "scapes" mentioned earlier. At the same time, though, there's a refusal by Cretu's fans to recognize this. The Kuos' music is constructed as "pure," primitive, and thus infantilized by Enigma, but by attempting to get credit and remuneration Kuo is behaving too much as a contemporary, worldly person: the subaltern speaks.

Enigma contributes to perceptions of their originality and the "primitive" and/or ancient nature of their music iconographically. The cover art on the single is faux "native" art, the Persian mystic poet Jalal ad-Din Muhammad Din ar-Rumi (1207–1273) is quoted, and more. Enigma also uses a typeface on the cover of the "Return to Innocence" single that that looks as though it was made by a manual typewriter, as though Enigma is just a small band who make and sell their own recordings, inviting a degree of credibility with listeners.

One last wrinkle concerns the reticence of Michael Cretu and the people behind Enigma. They claim, through their manager, that they want to avoid cheap imitations of their music, that is, people who take the samples in an attempt to make music like Enigma's, and so they rarely disclose where their samples come from, unless, as we saw, they are forced to.[46] The keeper of the Enigma FAQ on the Internet, Gavin Stok, met with Enigma's unnamed manager, who works in a firm called Mambo Musik based in Munich, and asked him about Enigma's sampling problems. The manager claimed that license agreements state that they don't have to credit some samples. It became clear in the course of this interview that Mambo Musik was more worried about other musicians who track down Enigma's samples in order to make cheap imitations of Enigma. Here are Stok's words: "Their major concern is of commercial rip-off artists who steal the samples and try to quickly release a song to 'cash in' on the popularity of the first single from a new album. Evidence of this was apparent with the release of *MCMXC A.D.* and Mambo does not want to see it happen again."[47]

This is quite an interesting statement. On the one hand, Mambo Musik adheres to the letter of the law, listing sampled musicians only when required to do so; on the other hand, by not crediting other musicians, they are thus making it much harder for people to find those samples. In practices such as these, Mambo is asserting a kind of de facto ownership over Enigma's samples in these cases. Simon Frith writes that "Samplers have adopted the long established pop rule of thumb about 'folk music'—a song is in public domain if its author is unlikely to sue you. And so sample records make extensive use of sounds lifted from obscure old tracks and from so-called (far away) 'world' music; lifted, it seems, without needing clearance."[48]

Without attribution in the liner notes (except in the first European pressing of the album), several people came forward with very different statements about the origins of the sampled music in "Return to Innocence." Ellie Weinert wrote in *Billboard* that "the archaic-sounding vocals on 'Return to Innocence' are not sung in any particular language but represent a sequence of vowels."[49] A later *Billboard* article referred to the "Indonesian voices" on the album.[50] An online review by a Norwegian Enigma fan, keeper of one of the Enigma web pages on the Internet, said that "this track cleverly blends the joik (Lapp chant) with modern rhythms and song structure. The joik is used as the chorus. This track gives me a feeling of pleasure and happiness, and some of the reason is that Enigma has turned to the ancient Nordic musical culture, the Lapps living in the northern parts of Norway, Sweden, Finland and Russia."[51] (I should point out that the preferred term for "Lapp" is now *Saami*). A Finnish Internet user also thought that the music was joik.

But the song is perhaps most frequently heard as Native American. The video that accompanied the song uses images of "Indians in some tropical jungle," as one fan writes.[52] In a class discussion, a student presented this sampled music as Native American, and it has been used as a Native American song on television and in films. One Enigma fan, who claimed to be "part Native American," heard the song as Native American. And "Return to Innocence" appears in the Jonathan Taylor Thomas/Chevy Chase film *Man of the House*, a 1995 Disney movie about a boy and a man attempting to bond while in the Indian Guides together.

This scramble for attribution provides one example of what this glocalized/informationalized world is bringing. Information may be moving about, but it is not always true or accurate. The Internet is essentially a giant word-of-mouth network, which means that ascertaining "truth" can problematic, difficult, or impossible. Anyone who paid attention to the Pierre Salinger fiasco (in which the former White House press secretary claimed that a U.S. Navy missile brought down TWA flight 800 over Long Island, based on "proof" obtained on the Internet) knows what I mean. Salinger clearly approached Internet-disseminated texts as journalistic sources (i.e., more conventional texts) only to discover that he had made a rather large mistake.[53] For ethnographers and fellow travelers like myself, this is less of a problem, since we are interested less in "truth" than in (re)presentations of truth. But we are also information gatherers, and more than once I have felt stymied by the absence of information—or, just as frequently, the welter of contradictory information—about a particular musician, recording, incident, or what have you.

This is not to say that ours is the Misinformation Age, but that the rapid movement of information around the planet does result in mistakes, and, sometimes, bizarre forms of relativization. As an example of the latter, take Microsoft's Encarta encyclopedia CD-ROM. The most recent edition (as of this writing, 1999) was issued in nine versions, each of which was aimed at a particular regional/linguistic market. In the American version, Alexander Graham Bell invented the telephone; in the Italian version, it was invented by a little-known candlemaker named Antonio Meucci five years earlier. In the American Encarta, Thomas Alva Edison invented the lightbulb at the same time as the Briton Joseph Swan, who is credited in the British Encarta as having been first. While such a strategy identifies Microsoft as more of a marketing corporation than one concerned with accurately representing knowledge, its Encarta staff insists it is attempting to be responsive to different viewpoints. "We're not changing facts," says the editor of the U.K. edition, "we're changing emphasis."[54] But because these changes in "emphasis" can travel beyond their intended audience, others can learn of them, as the spate of publication about this new Encarta illustrates.[55]

Music

Now let's move to a discussion of the music itself. The song on the original recording of Ami music that Enigma sampled is the first of "Two Weeding and Paddyfield Songs" (called by the couples' lawyer Emil Chang "Jubilant Drinking Song" and on a later album, "Elders Drinking Song"—the title changes with the use) with the following text:

> Friends, we need this hard work, we the people of the land
> Let us not despise it!
> Friends, we will undertake this difficult task with joy,
> So that we may live off the fruits of our labours.
> Friends, have no fear of the difficulties, nor the burning sun,
> For we are only doing our duty![56]

Enigma doesn't manipulate the Ami song at all, save for the addition of a little reverberation. The fact that Enigma leaves this music largely unchanged points to their usage of it as a kind of artifact, not something used merely to be ripped apart and scattered throughout their track, as do many musicians. The Ami music we hear in "Return to Innocence" is clearly used not as "material" or as "local color" but rather as a largely intact sign of the ethnic/exotic unspoiled by technology, or even modernity. This use of identifiably "ethnic" music samples is part of a growing trend in popular musics, dance musics in particular, even giving rise to a new genre name: "ethnotechno."[57] Some of Enigma's fans credit Cretu with spawning this new genre with "Return to Innocence."

Enigma's song is four minutes and sixteen seconds in length, and samples the Kuos' voices for over two minutes of this time. Cretu effectively takes the Kuos' pentatonic melody and undergirds it with lush, synthesized, diatonic harmonies. The song concludes with a wash in the dominant seventh that takes us to the tonic in minor, which then segues directly into the next track, entitled "I Love You . . . I'll Kill You." The stop-and-start quality of the original Ami music is echoed by the drum track in the Enigma song, an effect that compels listeners' attention. This also announces the song as a song without a practical function, that is, dance, for you couldn't dance to it easily with the drum track starting and stopping as it does. Cretu is making another kind of point with this song, away from dance and physical pleasure toward something more introspective. The beat isn't fodder for discotheque music here, but is recoded by Cretu as something primal and timeless, in keeping with the partly "spiritual" orientation of the album, and the band's style and image more generally.

What Enigma fans seem to like about the song is its homogeneity, its consistency, and its refusal to make the Kuos' music markedly distinct from the music by Enigma. Enigma experts and fans have commented on the simple formal structure of the song—the Norwegian web page owner mentioned above calls it their most traditional song—a verse-chorus arrangement, with the Ami music serving as the chorus. Some fans like this simplicity, but others find it too simple or traditional. Other fans believe it to be conservative because the vocals are too intelligible, in other words, too much like what they derisively call "pop music."

The similar version by the New Formosa Band, however, sounds like pop music. It's called "Song of Joyous Gathering" and makes use of a folk song from an indigenous tribe in Taiwan and sung or spoken in several dialects, a folk dialect as well as the Minnan and Kejia dialects. The main similarities with Enigma's song concern the use of the folk music as a chorus, though the New Formosa Band sings the chorus themselves; it isn't sampled. The message of unity is made partly in this way, but in other ways as well. The song is almost a study in the possi-

FIGURE 6.1.
Difang: *Circle of Life,* cover.

bilities of harmonious, egalitarian combinations and juxtapositions. First, the two singers alternate between the Minnan and Kejia dialects; second, the folk song is sung first in Minnan and then in the folk dialect, making the earlier idea of juxtaposing languages even more local; the folk song is mixed with the music of verse three; finally, the folk song itself is harmonized in thirds for the first two bars.

The New Formosa Band has recently released a collection that introduces a new member of the band. The track on the collection that they highlight is the one I have just analyzed, but this time, in a new guise. It's a remix of the earlier version, but, despite that, it's described as a dance tune with world music rhythms; and "world music" is written in English. (There is virtually no English anywhere else, save production and copyright information, and descriptions of two other songs, one as "Acid Jazz," and the other as "Techno.") This remix version cuts a few parts of the original out, but the main difference is the addition of a drum track that sounds much more hip hop influenced than the earlier version.

The primary significance of the New Formosa Band's music, for my purposes here, is that it demonstrates the ways in which musics are increasingly caught up in the global flow of sounds, images, ideas, and ideologies made possible by digital technology. Even though this Taiwanese band doesn't expressly address Enigma's appropriation of Ami music, they nonetheless critique the blockbuster German band by asserting both a native perspective and working with an indigenous performer, and by scrupulously sharing the spotlight in the song.

Since the onset of this controversy, Difang (Kuo Ying-nan's Ami name) released the promised recording on Magic Stone in 1998. *Circle of Life* (the title is in English) shows Kuo on the cover (see fig. 6.1) and features many traditional songs sung by the Kuos. This album topped the charts in both Taiwan and Japan.

The songs on *Circle of Life* were mixed in the studio with drum machines and synthesizers and sound much like Enigma's "Return to Innocence." But the difference, of course, is that all of this was done with the Kuos' knowledge, permission, and cooperation. And as a way of further critiquing Enigma's treatment of them, the penultimate track is a version of the song that Enigma sampled, which is far less intrusive. The final track is the original version of their song without any added studio sounds at all.

The Ami music in *Circle of Life* was recorded in a studio in Taipei. The resulting tapes were then sent to the Belgian musician and producer Dan Lacksman, who produced the album *Deep Forest*. The resulting band of the same name is Enigma's main competitor in the realm of ethnotechno/New Age pop.[58] Lacksman also released his own ethnotechno album in 1996 entitled *Pangea*. He was reportedly recruited via the Internet, and has said that *Circle of Life* represents a crossover between traditional and contemporary music.[59] Lacksman's contribution helps explain the contemporary electronic sound of the album, which may also explain its popularity in Japan, where it was one of the top-selling world music albums.

But Lacksman's presence on *Circle of Life* also helps illustrate the circle of musical sounds possible under new regimes of glocalization. Lacksman, who credits only one sample on all of *Pangea* (presumably because that's the only one the copyright holders were likely to hear), occupies a different structural relationship within the music industry for *Circle of Life*, but at the same time lends his prestige to it, for the words "Deep Forest" (in English) appear on a cardboard slip on the cover.

The cover was reportedly designed by a Japanese magazine that had sent people to visit Kuo for an interview: "They were so touched by the Ami singers' songs that they volunteered to do the photography and design work for the record."[60] Kuo thus appears alone on the cover—a true world music star—surrounded by a sea of green grass that situates him and his music in the realm of the "natural," thus justifying Lacksman's refinement of this natural musical resource. Photographs inside, and even the picture on the CD itself, continue this theme. The Kuos and the other singers are photographed in their natural habitat, completely exoticized.

This self-exoticization is abetted by the liner notes, which begin in the form of a fable (in fact, the first line is "This is a fable").[61] Continuing:

> There was a great eagle, circling in the sky for several generations. Its eyes gazed relentlessly on a flock of people on the ground who had, for many generations, been worshiping the eagle. They night and day, ceaselessly, sung the legends of the eagle. Because of this the eagle was immortal.
>
> But with the passage of time, little by little, the great eagle was no longer able to hear the singing of these ballads. They were being replaced by a catastrophic flood of love stories and wild, violent cryings. The large eagle lost its direction of flight. From then on, the eagle disappeared.
>
> Fortunately, there are still people on the ground who remember those songs, those brave legends—the honesty and purity passed down for generations. Like prophets, they continued to sing and pass them on. But the ignorant have viewed it as a new sound, causing at first apprehension and fear. Later, they blindly followed, plagiarizing. The value of those singing (and passing on) the songs was overlooked.[62]

The notes then continue to tell Kuo Ying-nan's story, and also relate the story of Enigma's appropriation of their song, though only obliquely mentioning the lawsuit by referring to "an explosion of international controversy over the authorship and rights of native peoples' music."

While it may seem as though the opening of the liner notes perpetuate an old notion of the natural primitive, writing the notes thus has another, clever, aspect, for this style allows Enigma to be accused of plagiarism, a charge that, in the absence of a settlement of the lawsuit, could not be straightforwardly made at the time of the release of the recording. The musical-rhetorical strategy employed by Cretu in "Return to Innocence" to convey feelings of mysticism and timelessness has been used against him to advance the Kuos' and other Ami viewpoints.

The Enigma and Kuo story is illustrative of older "globalizations" competing with this newer "glocalization," facilitated mainly by new digital technologies of communication and the dissemination of (mis)information in the "infoscape."

Enigma's success with "Return to Innocence" and the entire *Cross of Changes* album has awakened the music industry to the potential of "indigenous cultures," to whose members royalties are almost never paid. This, to recall Wallerstein, is definitely cheap labor. Roger Lee, senior marketing director of Sony Music Taiwan, persuaded Sony's huge worldwide hit band, Deep Forest, to sample music from the Ami, as they did on their 1995 album *Boheme*, which won the Grammy award for best world music album in 1995.[63] (This album is also popular with Enigma fans, judging by the response to the Enigma Internet mailing list). According to Lee, "This era has revealed the infinite business potential of indigenous culture. We shouldn't just passively go with the flow of the predominant cultural mechanism. Mainstream needs to be countered by non-mainstream, and any non-mainstream influence may turn out to be tomorrow's mainstream."[64] The kind of appropriation Lee is advocating has roots, of course, in much older ones, as I have pointed out, and such a statement points to the kinds of old and continuing problems currently occurring under the rubric of *globalization.*

The term *globalization* can hide old forms of exploitation dressed up in contemporary business language like Lee's. Capitalism in this global/informational economy is finding new ways of splitting sonic signifiers from their signifieds and from their makers, in a process Steven Feld has called "schizophonia."[65] This newer phenomenon of "glocalization" helps us understand the ways that there may be at the same time new forms of resistance to this process. Digitized sounds move to the centers in ways they didn't before, but, for the first time, the original makers of these musical signs are finding ways of bringing them home.

MUSIC
AT HOME,
POLITICS
AFAR

On October 21, 1996, the Packard Bell computer company unveiled its sixty-second television ad that shows real/retouched—hyperreal—people waiting in line at a forbidding big city bank. They wait and wait and wait, hardly moving in this impossible queue. The weather is dark, moody, awful, postnuclear. We see a young woman age suddenly. No one talks to anyone. Storm troopers march and intimidate. A bureaucrat inside the bank lets out an evil laugh. A little girl peeks, frightened, out from behind a copy of *Paradise Lost*. The scene is a postapocalyptic vision of modernity gone terribly wrong. Then, after exactly three-quarters of the ad has elapsed, it cuts to a cartoon house, inside of which is a bright (real) study with a shiny new Packard Bell computer sitting alone on a table. "Wouldn't you rather be at home?" a suave male voice asks. Indeed (fig. 7.1 shows eight still photos from this ad).[1]

This ad illustrates some of the changes in contemporary America: public spaces are increasingly thought to be uninhabitable, intolerant and intolerable, even monstrous; being in public is like being in prison, or in a police state. And even if our home lives are problematic or unreal—indicated by the idealized cartoon house in a cartoon green valley—there is one pleasant, real reality, brought to you by Packard Bell computers. The music used in the ad is electronically generated, save for a male voice that wails wordless vocals above the mix. But when

FIGURE 7.1.
Stills from Packard Bell television ad.

we pan to the idyllic cottage in the country, the music shifts, brightening up, changing from a minor mode to major, and a chorus joins the single voice. The musical message is that in public, you're alone, but when you're alone with your computer, you're not alone at all.

Packard Bell's ad is part of an American public culture that is waning; more and more people are seeking the solitary pleasures of their home computers, where they can now conduct all sorts of household business, such as banking, or information gathering. And musicking. But in this Packard Bell ad, while there are people in the postapocalyptic untechnological "before," in the bright, shiny, and technological "after" there is only the computer alone sitting on a desk; there is no person in front of it. I will discuss below that what the computer and the retreat from the public seem to be resulting in are new configurations of identity, as individuals who are separate from groups at the same time make affiliations with delocalized groups or causes. The ways the musicians who are the subject of this chapter represent themselves in their albums, on the Internet, and other media also shed light on their self-conceptions. I want to examine here the retreat into a personal world of musicking and the concomitant contraction of a certain public cultural space, and what this has meant for music and musicians in musics called techno, ethnotechno, ambient, tribal, and electronica—musics made solely by computers, samplers, and drum machines.

Before going further, however, a brief word is necessary on the use of the term *public*. For a word that does as much cultural work as this one does in contemporary American life, the various contrasting and conflicting uses of it have interestingly never been teased out. This isn't my task here, though; instead, I would like to examine a few variations and how the insights they offer bear on this chapter.

Nowadays it is practically impossible in academic circles to use the word *public* without invoking—intentionally or not—the work of the German philosopher Jürgen Habermas. Over the years, Habermas has provided clear-cut characterizations of what he means by "public sphere": "The bourgeois public sphere may be conceived above all as the sphere of private people come together as a public."[2] Elsewhere he writes, "We mean first of all a realm of our social life in which something approaching public opinion can be formed."[3] Habermas is interested in the space in which the "public" hashes over the crucial issues of a democratic polity; for him, the public sphere is the space of an idealized democratic process. All well and good, but this formulation isn't without problems; most importantly, as Nancy Fraser and others have argued, Habermas's formulation is highly gendered, and exclusive.[4] Habermas never really asks what for Fraser and others is the crucial question: public sphere for whom?

Another public that might shed some light on the issues here is the term *public culture* as outlined by Arjun Appadurai and Carol Breckenridge in the inaugural issue of the journal of that title. For them,

public culture designates an "arena . . . in which . . . emergent cosmo-
politan cultural forms . . . shape each other."[5] It is "realm" in Habermas's words; "arena" in Appadurai and Breckenridge's. Yet all these
scholars are less interested in processes than results, or the forms that
result from processes. I am interested in these, too, but at the same
time neither formulation of these "publics" refers to what I mean by
the word here, which is more of a street sense of the term. I use the
word *street* on purpose, for I am using *public* to refer more than anything else to the "modernism in the streets" written about so vividly by
Marshall Berman in *All That Is Solid Melts into Air*.[6] This is an urban
phenomenon, to be sure, a "primal scene" as Berman describes it,
made possible by the construction of wide boulevards in Paris in the
second half of the nineteenth century and chronicled by Baudelaire. In
this new Paris of the 1860s and 1870s, for the first time, everyone
could see everyone else, and at the same time be unnoticed in this new
flux of people. So my use of the term "public" here refers to space
more than anything else, in keeping with Berman and others who
study the ever-changing geography of urban areas such as Mike Davis
and Edward W. Soja.[7]

Electronica, Technology, and the Self

The decreasing cost of technology to the average consumer has resulted
in the last decade in entirely new kinds of musics that rely heavily on
personal computers, synthesizers, drum machines, and other electronic
gear. These new musics can be performed "live," in public, but they are
just as frequently never heard live at all, the musician sitting alone in his
(it is usually a he) studio cranking out tunes. These new technologies
aren't solely used in these relatively marginal musics, however; I think it
is safe to say that there is virtually no contemporary music that does
not make use of some kind of electronic technology, whether or not listeners can discern it. Before the advent of recording technology and
radio, people made their own music most of the time, but what is radi-
cally different today is that it is now possible to create entire worlds of
sound all by yourself with your computer; it is no longer necessary to
be with other people. Music as social activity is becoming a thing of the
past for many of these musicians. It may well be, however, that one of
the reasons that sampling has itself become a kind of art form is that it
provides aural glimpses of the social, metonymized into fragments of

acoustic musicking, but in their new contexts of electronically generated music, these glimpses are historical.

It is common in the various electronic dance music little cultures to
hide or obscure the names of the musicians; insiders know, but this
naming practice is a ploy to ensure that these musics are not co-opted
into the mainstream. If you're an A&R (artist and repertoire) rep from
a major label and an outsider to the scene, it's very hard to track down
the people who make this music.[8] So many of these bands use names
that cover up their membership; many change their names frequently;
many use different names simultaneously; some change their name for
every album; many use different names for the different kinds of music
they make. The two bands that I'll talk about in detail here are called
Muslimgauze and Banco de Gaia, two groups that are pretty far from
the attention that has been given to more mainstream electronica
bands such as the Chemical Brothers, the Prodigy, Underworld, Aphex
Twin, Orbital, and others. Like some of these better known groups,
Muslimgauze and Banco de Gaia are also not "bands" at all, but individuals, for each band involves only one person.

This use of names that hide rather than reveal—or celebrate—the
individual musician is partly what I want to point out: that in this
moment in which public culture seems to be waning, it is not necessarily waning in favor of a new or heightened individual. Just as that
Packard Bell ad showcased the computer alone, not a fictionalized
"everyuser," so these bands draw attention to themselves not as individuals, but as hidden, mysterious creators. I have never seen an album in
these electronic genres that shows a recognizable picture of the musician, and I have never seen an album that uses the musician's real name
anywhere in it, except occasionally in the copyright fine print (even this
only happens when the band is reasonably well known and wants to
protect itself from being sampled or remixed without permission).
Some of these musicians have websites and give interviews, but even if
these include pictures, as they occasionally do, the pictures are so
abstract and/or obscure that it is often difficult or impossible to tell
much about what the person actually looks like. For example, *The Wire*,
the British new music monthly, featured Muslimgauze's Bryn Jones in
an interview and published a self-fashioned photograph of Jones
obscuring his face in a way that is reminiscent of a Muslim woman's
veil, obscuring all of his face save his eyes, and a bit of his nose and fore-
head (see fig. 7.2).[9]

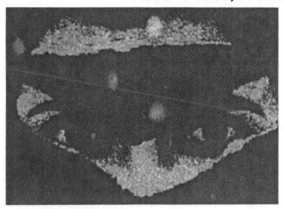

FIGURE 7.2.
Self-collage by Bryn Jones of Muslimgauze.

Like Bryn Jones, Banco de Gaia's Toby Marks conceals his identity, though not quite to the same degree; his former website on the Internet (now gone) offered a few photographs that were reasonably clear, though still highly manipulated—fuzzy, colored, hazy. At the same time, though, perhaps the most extensive part of his website was a series of pages devoted to a quiz about his biography; he provides many paired statements that you can click on to proceed to the next pair, but there's only one answer that tells you when you're right:

In 1995 I released my second album on Planet Dog Records.
Yes, you made it—it's all true![10]

Of course, all the pairs before this one can't be true. And for this one entry, there are ten that tell you you're wrong, and fourteen others that pose paired statements only, without giving any clue to the correct answer. So for the most part, we never know what's true (though some of the multiple-choice answers given are improbable and we can occasionally surmise what's *not* true). For example:

In 1989 I completed my training and got my first job on a building site.	In 1989 I gave up carpentry after an unfortunate gardening accident.

Both could be true or untrue, and we are never told which.
So while Marks has fun with his biography, it appears that he is thus

partly hiding behind the name of the band, which he claims in interviews is the title of an obscure Giacomo Puccini opera about an accountant that contains long passages in the libretto about accountancy. In one interview Marks said that

> it's a very little known fact . . . that Puccini actually wanted to be an accountant, but he wasn't very good at math, so he had to learn to be a musician, to be a composer instead.
> *[Interviewer]: That's strange. That's kind of backwards. You usually expect it to be the other way around.*
> You'd be surprised how many frustrated accountants there are [. . .] and I should know.
> *You're a frustrated accountant too?*
> Yeah. I really do want to be an accountant.
> *You're kidding me, right?*
> Yeah, I might be.
> *Don't mess with me like that.*[11]

As a diligent musicologist, I should point out that there is no obscure or unfinished opera by Puccini called *Banco de Gaia*; this is a fabrication as well.

On the Banco de Gaia website, there was this "information": "Banco de Gaia was a 16th century Spanish missionary in South America who came across a small tribe in the jungle somewhere. Whilst trying to convert them to Christianity he learned a lot about their own spiritual system and they ended up being known as the 'Gaians', practising a mixture of Virgin Mary worship and pagan earth magic."[12] Near as I can tell, this isn't true either.

It will help to illuminate this practice of problematizing the self—either through concealment or obfuscation—among these fringe techno/ambient bands if I contrast it to another genre, and I do this not only by way of comparison, but to point out also that there is a good deal of overlap between all these electronic musics that incorporate world music influences, though the practices around them can be quite different. People on the Internet newsgroups alt.music.ambient, alt.music.techno, and others argue all the time about what makes their music different from other genres. The biggest split among these musics occurs between New Age music and everything else, mainly because New Age music is now a mainstream genre that works through the normal channels in the music industry, but, like all musics, has its margins, and these are blurred with ambient, techno, and other electronica. New Age music has a chart in *Billboard*; it has a Grammy award; it has stars who can make fortunes (though they don't sell as much as musicians in the rock category).

But one of the biggest differences between New Age musicians and other musicians who make electronic musics is that New Age musicians usually foreground themselves as selves. They almost always include pictures of themselves on the material accompanying their recordings; they use their real names, or perhaps just their first names (such as Yanni or Enya) but there is never any doubt as to who they are. Yanni and Enya are big stars, but even the New Age musicians on the margins never let you forget who they are. So, for example, Tobias de la Sarno goes by the name "Tobias" only, but if you open up the booklet accompanying his CD entitled *Rainforest Rhapsody in the Key of Bali*, you find his full name listed as the producer.

It seems to be the case that if one of these groups wants to try to enter the mainstream, they will hit on a name and exploit it. One prominent example in this genre is Deep Forest, which in its first album, *Deep Forest*, wasn't named as a band at all. But with the astonishing international success of this recording (which sold at least 2.5 million copies worldwide since its release in 1993), the two Belgian producers who had made the album decided to go by the band name Deep Forest on their next album.[13]

While there are active electronica dance music little cultures in many urban areas, the electronica musicians I am concerned with here tend not to participate, even though their music and practices have various features in common with more public electronic dance music little cultures. The fans of ambient and techno musics are more dispersed. But one of the more interesting features of this music is that its reliance on technology means that, in addition to the musicians themselves being competent with computers, their fans are as well. There is a vast amount of information on these musics available on the Internet; in fact, Yahoo's guide to music genres has more entries for electronica than any other genre save rock and pop (first), and classical (second). There is usually comparatively little on individual musicians, except for the most famous of these, but the newsgroups devoted to these musics are legion, and they are extremely active. A good deal of arcane technical information also floats around—information about equipment, how-to guides, and more.

But I should also note that while there are many conversations about this music, there are few places where the fans of musicians who don't, or seldom, appear live can gather together. This is largely though not exclusively postconcert and postsocial music, if in using the word *social* I am permitted to refer to face-to-face (or "f2f" as these Internet users write) interactions in both the production of the music and its consumption; conversations about it occur primarily on the Internet, not face-to-face. Information is spread mainly through the Internet and zines rather than the public space of concerts or clubs, or, for that matter, the mainstream media. So this music, in its sound and use of samples, and in its reception, is largely delocalized, deterritorialized, though the Internet unites musicians and fans.[14]

One-Cause Wonders

Even as these musicians question or even attempt to efface their identities, they redirect what one could call their identity function in other ways. A few of these electronica musicians take on overt political causes, and it is to this that I now want to turn my attention. Despite the great differences in approach, presentation, discourse, and, to a lesser extent, music, it's interesting that the techno/ambient crowd tends to be more overtly political than the New Agers—or at least, it wields more conventional signifiers of the political. I have found a number of bands devoting entire albums to political causes, such as Muslimgauze, which was formed to project an Islamic point of view to counterbalance what its sole member Bryn Jones saw as a news media dominated by pro-Israel coverage. Banco de Gaia's *Last Train to Lhasa* (1995) includes in the notes a plea to help get China out of Tibet.

Even so, these musicians' ideas of the political are by no means conventional or common. Some of the statements of these musicians, as well as their music, are enough to leave one breathless.

Muslimgauze

Muslimgauze, for example, was formed in direct opposition to Israel after that country's invasion of Lebanon in June of 1982. The band's sole member, Englishman Bryn Jones, possesses a fair amount of knowledge about the political situation in the Middle East, but he has never been there and says he has no ambition to go, is not a Muslim, and doesn't know Arabic. Moreover, it is not clear how his politics are received by any Middle Eastern people, or Muslims in general; Jones gets no feedback from any Palestinian, Islamic, or Arabic sources, and says that "we [sic] don't look for it, it's not important." (Muslimgauze is virtually never discussed on any Islamic/Middle Eastern/political newsgroups on the Internet.) Jones does say that he gets "abuse" from Jews and other supporters of Israel.[15]

Jones's rhetoric is marked by an incredible passion and vehemence equaled only by its inflexibility. When asked by a *Village Voice* interviewer about the October 1994 bombing of a Tel Aviv bus by Hamas that had been criticized by Edward Said as "criminal" and "stupid," Jones replied: "They're doing what they think is right. They're fighting for the people. I don't think you can criticize them from the outside." Continuing, the interviewer asked,

> *Didn't you find the attack at the very least counterproductive?*
> I don't think so. Those people have got absolutely nothing. They're working from zero. They can't vote.
> *There must be other forms of resistance.*
> There isn't.[16]

In another interview, when asked if he had "complete animosity toward the state of Israel" and if he would "exempt certain Israelis that [he] might consider good people," he replied, "I wouldn't talk to any of them, the whole people are disgusting so no, I wouldn't."[17]

Jones's music strikes the listener as being as compromising as his rhetoric is uncompromising. There's little about it that could be considered a political polemic; though some fans occasionally describe it as aggressive or angry, it is unclear if they are hearing this in the music or reacting to Jones's rhetoric and packaging. The only sign of his political position is in the artwork accompanying the recordings, and in album and song titles. His first LP was called *Kabul* (1983), forming a critique of Russia's invasion of Afghanistan. Other albums have been more explicit: *Hajj* (1986), referring to the major Islamic pilgrimage to Mecca; *The Rape of Palestine* (1988); *United States of Islam* (1991); *Vote Hezbollah* (1993); and *Betrayal* (1993) featured a photo of Yasser Arafat shaking hands with Yitzhak Rabin in 1993. These are just the album titles; song titles convey more comments, as does the cover art. For example, the cover to *Hamas Arc* (1993) shows Iranian women shooting handguns (see fig. 7.3).

These titles and cover art do not make specific political points,

FIGURE 7.3.
Muslimgauze: *Hamas Arc,* cover.

however. They invoke violence in the Middle East, violence involving Muslims, but beyond that, Jones leaves specificity to his discourse about the music.

For Jones, who never plays live, all these politics are largely distinct from the music. "The music can be listened to without an appreciation of its political origin," says Jones, "but I hope that after listening the person then asks why it's called what it is and from this finds out more about the subject. It's up to them. Go out and discover."[18] Elsewhere, in an answer to a request to sum up Muslimgauze, he said, "Every piece of music is influenced by a particular fact, be it Palestine, Iran, or Afghanistan, the whole Middle East is an influence to Muslimgauze. From the political situations I am influenced to create music, endless music."[19]

Some fans of Muslimgauze seem a bit put off by Jones's political views. For some, it gets in the way of the music. One wrote to the newsgroup rec.music.industrial that "unfortunately, the stratifying political propaganda that the group puts out will always keep me at arms length from embracing the music." Others seem to feel that Jones's output is becoming derivative; he is too prolific, and his music is beginning to sound the same. Sometimes, the discourse of art is invoked to critique

Jones's music; an e-zine reviewer of one album wrote that "I hate politics, and I think art should not demean itself by letting itself be used for political manipulation."[20]

Muslimgauze, however overtly political it is in one respect, nonetheless samples music and sounds from all over the place, but seemingly without any overriding aesthetic or rationale, as one interview indicates:

> *You have a strong rhythmic base to your music and a heavy emphasis on percussion, does that come from some aspect of Islam?*
> No, it's just what interests me, percussion sounds working with other sounds as well, it's whatever interests me really. We don't aim to be pigeonholed into any musical category, that's one thing that I hope Muslimgauze can't be, you know, put into a specific box; we do this or that or the other. Personally, when people ask me what it's like, I can't really explain.[21]

Banco de Gaia

Like Muslimgauze, Banco de Gaia, another English "band," is the work of one person, Toby Marks, of Leamington Spa, England, who formed it in 1992. One important difference between Muslimgauze and Banco de Gaia is that Banco de Gaia occasionally appears live, and so is closer to the dance music roots of electronica than Muslimgauze. This is partly an accident of geography; Leamington Spa is not exactly an urban center teeming with dance clubs, but it is fairly near what has become one of the most active and influential clubs in England, Whirl-y-Gig, the brainchild of DJ Monkey Pilot. The success of Whirl-y-Gig brought Marks and other musicians to national prominence, and since so many of these bands sample "ethnic" musics, they were ultimately noticed by Peter Gabriel, who created a Whirl-y-Gig tent at the WOMAD (World of Music and Dance) festival in 1995.

Still, Marks thinks of himself as providing music to listen to, not dance to: "I generally write albums, I don't really think in terms of 12's [LPs] and singles and DJ's; I write for albums that I envisage people sitting at home and listening to, with maybe the odd DJ playing the odd track, but on the whole not writing dancefloor music. So the idea of actually trying to release something which was aimed specifically at DJ's and at the dancefloor appealed to me quite a lot."[22]

Banco de Gaia, like Muslimgauze, depends on DJ remixes to turn its music into dance music. Oliver Lieb and Speedy J, "hardly the usual suspects in the area of global ambiance," writes one interviewer, were brought in to make dance versions of "Kincajou," a track from *Last Train to Lhasa*.[23] Explains Marks, "It was deliberately aimed more at the dancefloor than what I normally do, the idea was to emphasize the more techno side of it, the more dance friendly side of it."[24] He recalls that hiring DJs to make dance remixes of his music was probably his record label's idea, but he supported it.[25]

Marks, in the one instance I have known him to take a political position at all, advocates a single megacause, as does Bryn Jones. "The one thing I find difficult is there's so many causes and so many fights in the world, that sometimes it feels very strange just to be highlighting one above all the others. But, one thing at a time—this album's called *Last Train to Lhasa*, so it was the obvious thing to mention."[26] Marks has made it clear that he decries the Chinese occupation of Tibet and its treatment of Tibetans, and speaks in strong terms about it. "The Chinese have been very brutal about the way they've gained control of Tibet: torturing, killing, destroying the culture. This goes on everywhere, even our countries have done it. In this day and age there's no reason this should be allowed to happen, the rest of the world can stop it. They won't, though, because China is such a big trade market, which is a perfect example of the way governments work these days. Countries would have to take a moral stance that China has no right to invade Tibet, but they won't because they don't want to lose all those wonderful trading dollars from China. Governments have become big banks, or corporations." But Marks's political views are as reluctant as Jones's are vehement. In answer to the question following the one I've just quoted, he says, "I'm not into political music, I don't have slogans chanted over the top of my music or anything."[27]

So Marks explains the album's title, *Last Train to Lhasa*, this way:

[W]hen I was putting this album together I wasn't writing a concept album, it wasn't supposed to be about Tibet or anything in particular, apart from the track *Last Train to Lhasa*, which was very loosely inspired by the thought that it would be shit if they built a railway, that would really do it, that would really finish it off, 'cause at the time I had no idea there was going to be a railway, it was just theoretical.

So then I'd written all the tracks and the album needed a title, and someone said, "Oh, Last Train to Lhasa, that'd make a good name for an album," and I thought, yeah, okay, that'll do. It was no more than that. Then I started thinking about it . . . well, if you're gonna call it this, maybe I could do something useful here, 'cause people read sleeve notes, and it is in effect an advertising space, so why not write something on there just highlighting what's going on in Tibet, and what it's all about, and who to contact if people wanna do something about it.

Unfortunately, what's happened, in retrospect, and I should have realised it, is a lot of people approached the album as a concept album about Tibet. I saw one review where it was saying "this is a really nice album, but I really can't see what this is supposed to have to do with Tibet. I'm disappointed, I thought it'd be more obvious." I never said it was about Tibet! Don't tell me I've failed on that score![28]

Yet inside the liner notes to the CD there is a photograph of the Potala, the Dalai Lama's historical main residence in Lhasa; the note accompanying the CD booklet gives a brief history of the Chinese invasion and genocide in Tibet, and concludes with information on how to contact the International Campaign for Tibet. The newer Banco de Gaia website for a time featured a series of pages called "Why Bother? Reflections on Tibet," with film clips of Chinese soldiers beating Tibetans, but these pages have been removed.[29]

Like Muslimgauze, Banco de Gaia's cover art is one of the important sites of political articulation. The cover of *Last Train to Lhasa* features a photograph of a locomotive with a red star, behind which is the Potala and the Himalayas; Tibetan people, some of whom are monks, appear near the train (see fig. 7.4).

It is not unrelated that New Age and other mainstream electronica musicians such as Deep Forest by and large eschew the kind of politics and advocacy I have been discussing here. New Age musicians tend to construct their identities as modern, bourgeois subjects, even hyper-subjects; they are creative individuals who seem to want their creativity recognized. Anything that might seem to be political might compromise their artistic autonomy and prevent their achieving a wider audience or major hit. New Age musicians, when they identify themselves with a particular cause at all, tend to espouse cuddly ones, the we're-all-

Banco de Gaia

Last Train to Lhasa

FIGURE 7.4.
Banco de Gaia: *Last Train to Lhasa,* cover.

one-big-happy-world kinds of causes—for example, Alain Eskinasi's recent *Many Worlds, One Tribe.* He appears (along with several unnamed "natives") on the front cover (see fig. 7.5), and there are three more pictures of him inside the CD booklet and on the back page. There may be many worlds and one tribe, but only one person in this tribe has power of representation here.[30] This cover also illustrates a difference from fringe electronica such as Muslimgauze and Banco de Gaia, who never appear in a recognizable fashion in or on their albums, which is rarely the case with New Age musicians.

Sampling: Aesthetics and Practices

Like Bryn Jones and most of the people who make this kind of music, Toby Marks has clear views about sampling as a practice and art, and possesses a high modernist idea of how to treat sampled material—as extremely aestheticized bits of sound (that is, snippets of sound for sound's sake). Marks's descriptions of what he's doing can be at odds with the effects: "There's about three ways to go about it. First, you can get it cleared by the rights holder of the original piece you sampled. That can be a complete nightmare, and be quite a bit more expensive.

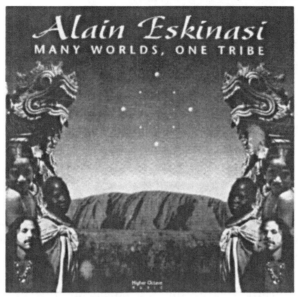

FIGURE 7.5.
Alain Eskinasi: *Many Worlds, One Tribe,* cover.

The second way is you distort the sample to such an extent that it's not recognizable. As far as I understand it, under UK law, that's legitimate. If its not recognizable as the original, then you're clear and your piece is considered a new artistic work. The third way is to use really obscure samples, which probably no one is ever going to know where it's [*sic*] come from." Marks goes on to say that "a lot of my samples come from all over the world, and I don't want to rip people off and not give them any credit. For instance: I find a Chinese sample which is lovely, but I can't track down where it came from—I'm going to use it any way."[31] This "for instance" is an example of ripping someone off and not giving them credit, not his unwillingness to do so.

Yet I would maintain that there is a difference between a modern, aesthetic idea of the sample, and a different, newer, technological idea. Jones and Marks view their samples not just as raw material, but as fetishized, reified, digitized bits. Modernist composers, no matter how much they hid their appropriated musics, both with their discourse and their musical procedures, nonetheless tended to choose music to which they had some sort of connection, or to which they wanted to attach some kind of meaning. So the Russian Igor Stravinsky (1882–1971) took Russian folk music; Hungarian Béla Bartók

(1882–1945) took Eastern European folk music, and American Charles Ives (1874–1954) American music; and more.[32] Later composers, after World War II, didn't necessarily possess an ethnic or national connection to the music they appropriated, but they nonetheless tended to establish long-term relationships to it, whether Olivier Messiaen (1908–1992) and his "Hindoo Rhythms," which pervade his *Technique of My Musical Language* of 1957, or Henry Cowell (1897–1965) and his lifelong study of musics from many parts of the world.[33] It was meanings they were after, and they both found and constructed them in these other musics. It wasn't until the late 1960s that the kind of pastiches now common arose, and even these would be put to a larger idea, much like the New Age musicians discussed earlier. Karlheinz Stockhausen's (b. 1928) *Hymnen* (1966–67), for example, pulls together national anthems from all over the world; and *Telemusik* (1966), he tells us, is an attempt to realize an "old and ever-recurrent dream: to go a step further towards writing, not 'my' music, but a music of the whole world, of all lands and races."[34]

In hip hop, the popular music that first used samplers as musical instruments and not just shortcuts or cost-cutting devices, sampled material to this day tends to be used either as homage to musical forbears, such as Parliament/George Clinton, and James Brown, and/or they're used as a way to establish a kind of musical community; hip hop musicians sample music of their own past, music they like, music from their parents' record collections.[35] As Prince Be of P.M. Dawn told an interviewer, "I love listening to records, I love feeling vibes from other people, I love being influenced by everything. I guess that's why music takes the turns that it does because there are no boundaries in who we want and who we listen to; we can take a Sly Stone sample, we can take a Joni Mitchell sample, we can take a James Brown sample, we can take a Cal Tjader sample. It doesn't really make a difference, it's just all vibes and how everything feels and how everything emotes itself, you know."[36]

Or this from De La Soul's Posdnuos: 'We don't exclude anything from playing a part in our music. I think it's crazy how a lot of rappers are just doing the same thing over and over—Parliament/Funkadelic/James Brown—and all that. I bought Steely Dan's *Aja* when it first came out, and 'Peg' was a song I always loved, so when it came down to making my own music, that was definitely a song I wanted to use. . . . It doesn't make any difference whether a sample is from James

Brown, Cheech and Chong, Lee Dorsey, or a TV theme; if there's something that catches my ear, I'll use it."[37]

Some African-American musicians view sampling as a more political act, as does Public Enemy's Chuck D: "Our music is filled with bites, bits of information from the real world, a world that's rarely exposed. Our songs are almost like headline news. We bring things to the table of discussion that are not usually discussed, or at least not from that perspective."[38] No matter the discourse, or the result, almost all hip hop sampling practices are involved with making meanings, meanings that make sense to the musicians and to their fans.

But these ethnic, national, or political, and community connections—meanings—are largely gone with these electronica musicians who are the subject of this chapter; affect—as Fredric Jameson famously diagnosed—seems to have waned.[39] These musicians can digitally manipulate the music they sample as well and as complexly as art music composers, but their manipulations don't necessarily have anything to do with their discourse and their messages about the music. Toby Marks samples and manipulates both Chinese and Tibetan musics (among others) in the tracks on *Last Train to Lhasa*, and doesn't seem to notice that it might be possible to interpret his use of Tibetan music as not unrelated to Chinese treatment of Tibet and Tibetans. Marks has said that "people need to see that it's just other traditions which I'm taking."[40] Yet, this "taking," as I and many others have written, isn't completely distinct from the European colonial project generally, and the Chinese imperial project in particular that Marks is supposedly critiquing.[41]

Marks says that he gets his samples from all over:

I don't have any particular method of even finding them. I just sort of come across things, like when I'm traveling I've heard people play and recorded a bit, I've picked up tapes, heard things here and there. It's something that I can't be to [sic] specific about for obvious reasons.
Do you usually have samples you want to use first, or musical ideas?
It various [sic]. Sometimes I'll just come across something I think is amazing and I might be able to imagine a tune built around it. Other times I stockpile stuff and when I'm working on a tune if I need a male Arabic vocal to fit a section I'll see if I have anything which would be suitable. But it tends to vary. Sometimes a sample

will suggest the whole tune to me, but not very often unfortunately. It would be far too easy if that happened all the time![42]

Note the kinds of categories Marks uses: "male Arabic vocal," for example. It is clear that he possesses a very different idea about what
music is: it's something that can be sampled, and neatly categorized.

Once he has his samples, Marks's use of them is completely and arbitrarily free; he manipulates them any way he wishes: "[I]t's pretty rare
to [sample] something straight. Usually I'll find a starting point, I'll fil-
ter it, reverse it, slow it down or something so that it's different from the
original. On one of my songs, 'Amber,' the vocal is actually backwards.
It actually sounded more natural backwards. It was from this really
weird language. I just slowed it down a bit, reversed it, and thought:
'that sounds fucking gorgeous!' Played forward it sounds fucked up;
played backwards it sounds like someone is singing it. It's weird."[43] Natural *to whom*? Weird language *to whom*? I played this vocal backwards
(that is to say, as it originally sounded) and it didn't sound much different (or any more recognizable); neither did Marks's synthesized music.

Again, this discourse is far different from similar practices in more
mainstream musics. Steven Feld writes in a recent article that one of the
four primary narratives through which Western digital sampling practices operates is a discourse that always professes admiration for the
appropriated music. "Everyone—no matter how exoticizing, how
patronizing, how romanticizing, how essentializing in their rhetoric or
packaging—declares their fundamental respect, even deep affection for
the original music and its makers."[44] This is true in the more mainstream genres such as New Age, and pop and rock, where declarations
of love, appreciation, and professions of small-worldness are de rigeur.
But on the fringes, which is where these and most electronica musicians work, musicians' attitudes toward the samples tend to be more
circumspect, and more informationalized—conceived of as bits of
information as much as sound. In other words, New Age/mainstream
musicians haven't abandoned meanings, signification; their samples
are there to do some work, whereas for electronica musicians, samples
are more likely to be thought of as raw material, incidental to the piece.

Another more tentative reason for the New Age/mainstream discourse may be that this music can become popular enough so that
people whose music has been sampled will demand their fair share, as
is happening with increasing frequency. Very small labels and bands

out of the mainstream, on the other hand, can sample with relative impunity. I have yet to see any sample copyright clearance information on any of these albums, or even any discussion on the albums of what the samples might be. When samples and influences are discussed it is in the most general terms, such as "ethnic percussion" or "Chinese vocals," or, as we saw above, "male Arabic vocal."

What's Up?

Now that I have outlined some of the ideas and musical practices and political stances of these two musicians, let's move to a discussion of how we can understand them in a larger cultural framework. There are several interrelated issues: one is the lack of a public projection of self, while at the same time the public connection with political causes; another concerns attitudes toward sampling; and the last concerns a postmodern theoretical concern with the "objectal form" (as Jameson calls it) of contemporary cultural production at the expense of the practices in which such forms are made and caught up.

Digitization of the Self and the World

In the face of the increasing penetration of extremely sophisticated technology into everyone's everyday lives, we in the so-called developed countries are in the midst of a transition into some kind of new historical moment, but one in which, at the same time, older ideologies and practices haven't been eclipsed. They're still available, but not in an across-the-board, monolithic way, just as these new technologies and postsocial worlds don't necessarily affect everyone. Not everyone owns or can afford the kind of music-making technologies I have been talking about, for example.

This new era we are in, or moving toward, has been vividly examined by psychologist Raymond Barglow, whose reports of the dreams of his patients, who work in the computer industry in Silicon Valley, are quite startling: "Image of a head—it might be of a cat, or human—and behind it is suspended a computer keyboard. The keys are being depressed, you can see them going up and down like the keys on a player piano, but no one is there operating them. Attached to the head is a network of wires and tiny lights as if it were a Christmas tree—a light near an ear, another on the nose, one on the mouth, etc. As the keys depress and release, the lights wink on and off to some banal programmed music."[45] Barglow draws on this and other cases to argue that the Western ideal of the unified subject is increasingly problematic.

Taking off from Barglow and others, it is possible to make a case for an increasingly separate, digitized, contemporary culture in which everything, every "plane of life" is more particularized and detached than ever before. Sociologist Manuel Castells writes in a recent study of technology and its relationship to contemporary culture that recent social movements tend to be "fragmented, localistic, single-issue oriented, and ephemeral, either retrenched in their inner worlds, or flaring up for just an instant around a media symbol. In such a world of uncontrolled, confusing change, people tend to regroup around primary identities: religious, ethnic, territorial, national."[46] But in the absence of religion—which, after all, many Western Europeans and Americans have abandoned—alignment with megacauses can serve some of the same functions.

Castells identifies the central dynamic of the late twentieth century as the increasing distance between globalization and identity, between what he calls "the net and the self." It seems to me that in this late modern or postmodern era of computers, of zeros and ones, this process of splitting, fracturing is becoming highlighted and emphasized and at the same time more particularized, so that new kinds of juxtapositions and combinations are possible, resulting in even greater contradictions and paradoxes than we saw in modernity. This same process is the digital process.

Digitization is busily colonizing everything, turning everything into information that can be disseminated instantly if one is affluent enough to own or have access to the proper technology. Paul Virilio writes that information "nowadays [is] outstripping the notions of mass and energy"; then, with the advent of "tele-action"—that is, telecommunications transport of data—"information comes to the fore as an entirely separate form of energy: *sound and image* energy, the energy of long-distance touch and contact."[47] This is information as the digitized bit, which has the power to imperialize everything and everywhere, while at the same time it interferes with our sense of where everywhere is.

Despite these newer, smaller, looser bifurcations and splits, at the same time, it is beginning to be possible to posit a new larger binary opposition between Castells's "the net and the self," where the net isn't only the Internet, but the network of communications, trade, and information that more and more of us inhabit.

If we return to an examination of Jones and Marks and their music, it's clear that they seem to want to be political and nonpolitical at the same time. Rather than pursuing a local politics, they advocate faraway causes (and it may not be a coincidence that these two British subjects have chosen to protest imperialist regimes). The samples in their music may or may not have anything to do with their rhetoric about the music. They make a kind of music related to electronic dance musics and the English dance club scene, but Marks seems to owe his fame not to his few live appearances but his CD sales, and Jones doesn't appear live at all, so CD sales seem to comprise his main income. And both "bands" make music for albums, not dances, and their music is later remixed by DJ/producers to make it danceable.

It is also possible to make an argument that electronica musicians such as Marks and Jones eschew the club scene in favor of a more aestheticized musicking. This is Sarah Thornton's argument in *Club Cultures*, in which she writes that ambient musicians attempt to aestheticize the music and make a bid for it as art by distinguishing it as a music to be listened to rather than danced to.[48] This would not be unrelated to these musicians' adoption of a starving-poet-in-the-garret mode of production, one of the deepest Western cultural myths about artistic production.

So there seem to be many contradictions and paradoxes, but the point is that, from a more digital and digitized perspective, these aren't contradictions and paradoxes at all; contemporary life for these and many other people simply operates in new structures that are not necessarily unified or contiguous.

Sampling

Nothing better exemplifies musically the split between the microself and the espousal of macrocauses than the use of samples in this music. Andrew Goodwin has labeled the kind of sampling practices I have been examining here as "postmodern," in which samples are juxtaposed sounds in a web of texts that deny any evaluation of them, leaving the listener only a patchwork of fragmentary references that render impossible any definitive hearing or interpretation.[49] I should point out, though, that one cannot know if interpretations are prevented without talking to interpreters, and, as usual, it is an ethnographic perspective that is almost always lacking in such discussions. Some people do make meanings out of this music, and for these musicians themselves, while nonetheless hearing their samples more as information than affective signifiers, it appears to be also the case that affect isn't entirely absent, either, as I will illustrate in a moment.

For these fans, this music isn't necessarily postmodern in the Jamesonian sense of depthlessness, or mere pastiche; they don't often hear the samples as decontextualized or aestheticized, but as things that contribute to the meaning and coherence of the songs.[50] For the listeners to the bands on the fringes such as Muslimgauze and Banco de Gaia, fans' discourse is harder to come by, and also tends to speak more to the aestheticized nature of the music and sampling. Fans tend to speak in fairly technical terms, though there are some at the same time who say simply that they love the music. Early in 1997, one wrote in to the Enigma mailing list (which often considers Enigma-like music) that "the title song of this album [*Last Train to Lhasa*] is a very attractive track, at 12 minutes it has a well-made buildup starting initially with the sound of a steam train. This forms the rhythm frame to which the percussion and drums add. Later on a Tibetan chant is used to good effect as the singing part." These Enigma fans almost always note that Banco de Gaia's music is "a bit more techno" or "a bit more ambient" than Enigma, but that they still like it. And I should note that they speak of Enigma's (and other more mainstream acts') music in extremely emotional terms.

Outside of the Enigma mailing list, however, fans speak mainly in technical terms. One fan wrote into rec.music.ambient in March 1996, "*Izlamaphobia* [Muslimgauze's 1995 album] is 30 or so (still shortish) rythmic ejaculations, most of which don't bother with the mundane concepts of introduction or theme development, dropping you in abruptly to some nerve-crushing loop space, with no linear beginning, middle or end. Most of the cust are in the three minute range (with some as long as 8 or 9 minutes (and some only 1.5 minute specks), which ordinarily bothers me, as ususally sound needs some chronic space to develop its groove. However, the music here is so nasty and aggressive and intense, the lengths are just fine."[51] And so forth.

The fans of Banco de Gaia and Muslimgauze are clearly more concerned with technical issues than the fans of related but more mainstream musics, but at the same time it is evident that they possess an aesthetic and are able to make affective connections with this music.

Postmodernism, or, Benjamin Defended against His Devotees

So far so good. Everything I have written about this music, the musicians, and their fans seems to jibe pretty well with the postmodern world described by Fredric Jameson and others. Cultural production in this historical moment—at least on the margins I have been examining—is nothing but a sea of floating signifiers, ungrounded in anything real, much less original or authentic; all forms are pastiches, blank parodies, statues without eyeballs; affect has waned; a new depthlessness seems to be the order of the day.[52] And I have used some of these terms in the discussion thus far.

But concentrating on what these new cultural forms are like, or on sampling as not so much a practice per se but as a practice that results in musical objects, seems to me to be too focused on these forms as objects or products, rather than as always already incomplete results of an ongoing process. In discussions of mechanical, and now, electronic and digital (re)productions of cultural forms, Walter Benjamin's 1936 essay "The Work of Art in the Age of Mechanical Reproduction" is almost always employed.[53] Given the high visibility of this article, it is probably not necessary to outline his argument here beyond saying that, for Benjamin, the increasing mechanical reproduction of artworks signaled the end of the "aura" of the artwork—that which made it original, unique, authentic. Benjamin lamented this end, but at the same time was aware of the liberatory possibilities raised by mechanical reproduction, partly because this would make artworks available to the masses as never before.

I find this essay cited with growing frequency, to the extent that I think we are at present in the midst of a decade-long Benjamin renaissance. And yet, I think Benjamin's argument is actually quite limited in helping us understand the materials I've presented here, or popular culture in general. It's clear from Benjamin that he is talking about visual art; and I would thus argue that his conception of aura simply does not apply to popular musics, and never did, and that extensions of his argument into the realm of the popular are ignorant of audiences, reception, and ethnographic perspectives generally, perspectives that Benjamin himself did not seek out either.

Yet Benjamin is invariably invoked in discussions of popular music and technology—there is undeniably a specter of aura haunting popular music studies. Benjamin turns up in Andrew Goodwin's "Sample and Hold," for example (and if I seem to be picking on Goodwin here it is only because his arguments are better than most).[54] Goodwin writes that "*everyone* may purchase an 'original,' " even though I would counter that this was never an issue for musicians or fans except some collectors of old vinyl recordings—again the lack of an ethnographic perspective causes problems.[55] Goodwin accounts for the attendance at live concerts as a way to soak up the aura of live performers, but I would say that this might be the only time this term should apply, and that, more importantly, it may be the communal aspect of going to concerts, and the cultural capital acquired in doing so, that provide the more compelling motivation. Besides, people go to sporting events and attend speaking engagements of public figures for the same reason; if this is aura, it is not restricted to art. Goodwin is also right to tackle "the postmodernists" who insist on viewing sampling as a new and depthless practice without noticing how much it is tied to earlier ways of musicking, and without paying enough attention to actual music.

I am sure that some would argue that the distinction I am making between popular culture and art is too facile, too binarized, and is ignoring what some have viewed as a crucial feature of postmodern cultural production generally, that there is an increasing communication across the "great divide" of high and low in terms of cultural production.[56] There is a little crossing down (more like "slumming"), I think, and there are some subgroups that listen a little more adventurously than they might have in the past (particularly those groups with high amounts of educational capital). And a subset of the electronic dance music fandom prefers to find its forebears with western European art music composers rather than African-American and gay musicians who are more clearly their immediate forebears. Nonetheless I would argue that, ethnographically speaking, this great divide is still with us; the same audiences go to pretty much the same concerts, and the consumption of cultural forms is as linked to cultural capital as it ever was, as Pierre Bourdieu so memorably taught us.[57]

In rejecting the Benjaminesque aura in considerations of popular music (and popular culture in general), I am not jettisoning ethnographic concerns of authenticity, originality, or creativity, which are often discussed as related to conceptions of aura. But if we want to find something resembling aura that is talked about in the terms of authenticity or creativity or what have you, and if we pay attention to where the fans and musicians are, it is possible to view this set of practices from another perspective. If one has one's ear to the ground, that is, if one cultivates an ethnographic perspective, there are meanings being made all over the place. The point I would like to emphasize here, though, is that not only are fans making meanings, but there is also another way of looking at this kind of cultural production. Sampling and music technology are being put to a variety of different ends, as I have already discussed with regard to New Age music and hip hop. More generally, many who write about the rise of new technologies speak of the so-called democratization of musicking—electronics makes musicking easier than ever—though this point is curiously rarely elaborated by anyone; aura usually receives the first, and usually, only, consideration in the Benjamin-inspired considerations of popular music and technology.[58]

For example, Simon Frith writes, "Technology, the shifting possibility of mechanical reproduction, has certainly been the necessary condition for the rise of the multinational entertainment business, for ever more sophisticated techniques of ideological manipulation, but technology has also made possible new forms of cultural democracy and new opportunities of individual and collective expression."[59] And this is the extent of his treatment of this issue of "cultural democracy."

But what does this "cultural democracy" mean? Alan Durant outlines three different ways the term *democracy* is used without really taking a position on any of them. One meaning, he writes, refers to democracy as "something which results from cheapness of the equipment"; the second refers to a democracy "as something which results from an input into definition of the technology"—that is, everyone can have a say in the development of music technology; and third, democracy refers to "something which results from a low or easily attainable skills-threshold for using the technology."[60]

I would like to try to move this discussion away from its emphasis on the "objectal form" of the technology-involved work—with its qualities of pastiche, bricolage, depthlessness, and more—and toward Durant's first meaning of the term *democracy*. Benjamin wrote about this, too, though this part of his essay has not been nearly so influential in considerations of popular music and technology. Rather than fetishizing or reifying "aura," I would rather draw attention to the possibility for authorship, as does Benjamin: "[T]oday there is hardly a gainfully employed European who could not, in principle, find an opportunity to publish somewhere or other comments on his work, grievances, documentary reports, or that sort of thing. Thus, the distinction between author and public is about to lose its basic character. The difference becomes merely functional; it may vary from case to case. At any moment the reader is ready to turn into a writer. As expert, which he had to become willy-nilly in an extremely specialized work process, even if only in some minor respect, the reader gains access to authorship."[61] But as that Packard Bell ad showed, the "basic character" of the distinction between the author and her public is not only blurred; at the same time, the public in the era of digital reproduction is decreasingly a realm in which there is significant discourse or interchange.

While I would be the first to decry the decline of the public, this phenomenon might at least be mitigated if one result is that more people make music for themselves. In *Noise*, Jacques Attali posits a fourth stage of musicking that he calls "composition," in which people make their own music for their own reasons and pleasure. While this argument is often cited in discussions of music and technology, it has not received the attention it has deserved because most scholars are too focused on the resulting musical object rather than the practices that produced it; or there are claims about the "democratization" that technology will bring about, claims that are infrequently investigated.

Attali writes, "We are all condemned to silence—unless we create our own relation with the world and try to tie other people into the meaning we thus create. That is what composing is. Doing solely for the sake of doing, without trying artificially to recreate the old codes in order to reinsert communication into them."[62] And later, "Composition thus leads to a staggering conception of history, a history that is open, unstable, in which labor no longer advances accumulation. . . . Time no longer flows in a linear fashion; sometimes it crystallizes in stable codes in which everyone's composition is compatible, sometimes in a multifaceted time in which rhythms, styles, and codes diverge, interdependencies become more burdensome, and rules dissolve."[63] This excerpt describes reasonably well the kinds of music I have been discussing.

It is no accident that fans of Muslimgauze, Banco de Gaia, and ambient, techno, and industrial music in general tend to speak more in technical terms than affective ones, since many of them are involved in making this music. In order for everyday people to make this music, however—in order to be "democratic"—the technology involved has to be affordable and/or available. By and large, it isn't, but these fringe dance/electronica musicians have cultivated a do-it-yourself (DIY) ethic that advocates using cheap and old equipment—that is, deliberately avoiding the newer-is-better, faster-is-better assumptions of most technophiles. More recently, software applications such as Rebirth and Acid are making the production of dance music even simpler and cheaper—all one needs now is a computer, no other hardware.

Some musicians/fans argue that the use of cheap equipment is the reason the music came into existence in the first place, as does one Australian musician who explains that

> the reason [techno] came about was because the kids who invented the form, were locked into it by economics. There was a time in the late 80s when no-one wanted those old analogue synths. They wanted the new gleaming digital stuff. It was a time when TB-303s [Roland analogue bassline synthesizers] were given away. Sold at garage sales . . . for a fiver. A time when, if a pot [volume control knob] became scratchy or broke all together on a synth, you'd probably throw it away rather than replace it. Or at most sell it for 50 bucks to someone who you considered a fool for buying it at any price. Whatever happened, it meant that people didn't place much value in these 'old buckets.'
>
> The kids were no fools. Unlike vintage synth collectors . . . the kids needed to get into it at what ever level they could. They'd most likely look at the gleaming digitals and aspire to own them but they could afford bucket loads of cheap, hand-me-down analogues. Then they discovered, more as novelties, the weird and wonderful sounds they could make. I remember them well and I remember my attitude. "Oh that's cute but we _real_ musicians have progressed somewhat." Man was I wrong. This stuff became 'Thee Shit.'[64]

By insisting on using relatively inexpensive, easy-to-find equipment, electronica musicians are ensuring that anyone who wants to make their music can. This is not just an aesthetic, or a fetishization of the cheap; according to German musician Pete Namlook (whose real name is Peter Kuhlmann; "Namlook" is "Kuhlmann" backwards, spelled phonetically; "Namlook" backwards is "koolman"), "the aim is for everyone to make a living, to bring music forward, to make innovation in music. Not to stand still. To achieve this what has happened is a social revolution where musicians are now helping each other to release music."[65]

"Forget about talent," says "How to Become a Techno God," a guide to making your own techno music; "talent just gets in the way."[66]

The efforts of the music industry early in 1997 to try to mainstream some electronica musics succeeded to some degree. At the same time, the musicians' DIY ethic, their refusal to be co-opted into the industry (which means that they make and sell their own recordings, or in the case of Banco de Gaia and Muslimgauze and other bands who don't usually appear live, make small numbers of compact discs for small, independent labels), the dissemination of information about these bands through word of mouth, zines, and the Internet rather than the mainstream press, the continued espousal of affordable equipment— all of these factors indicate that Attali's moment of composition is here, at least, on the fringes. Perhaps the day will come when our shiny new Packard Bell personal computer will be seen not just as a fancy type-writer or Internet connection, but as a machine that allows people to make their own music instead of buying it.

TURN ON,

TUNE IN,

TRANCE OUT

Of all the popular electronic dance musics today,
Goa/psychedelic trance may well be the most hidden "little culture" in
the United States, while at the same time it may well be the most
active.[1] As I write, however, its music is quickly moving into the mainstream, becoming, as Simon Reynolds has said, the "Esperanto of electronic dance music."[2] In the fall of 1999, a message circulated on the
Goa trance Internet mailing list wondering if trance music was the new
pop; it garnered many replies, for and against. Even before this moment
of incipient popularity in 1999, however—which proved to be short-
lived—there was a vast and largely connected network of Goa/psyche-
delic fans around the world, so that the Goa trance mailing list generates around a hundred messages daily; there are hundreds of websites
devoted to Goa trance musics; and there are frequent Goa parties on
every continent.

This final substantive chapter teases out several of the themes that
have appeared in various guises in earlier chapters, beginning with
the issues of anxiety and ambivalence about technology. While there
is still reason to be anxious about technology, the participants in the
Goa/psychedelic trance little culture are not anxious about it at all.
Goa trance fans don't worry about losing ground to technology; in
fact, the main goal of participation in the little culture is to lose one-
self in the collective through the use of technology. There is also the
interest in an "elsewhere"—in this case, India. This chapter also critiques theories of youths and subcultures in favor of older theories of

religion and ritual, which may be out of fashion but turn out to be far more useful in understanding the Goa trance little culture, at least as it manifested itself in New York City at the time of my fieldwork (1999).

The Gao/Psy Trance Little Culture

Goa trance is a music that has roots, like all contemporary electronic dance musics, in techno and house musics from Detroit and Chicago.[3] But Goa—now known more commonly as psychedelic trance, or psy trance for short—has a somewhat different subcultural history than these other musics. It was first called "Goa trance" because the music was associated with the leftover hippie population in Goa, a state on the west coast of India that was a Portuguese colony until 1961. American and European hippies flocked there in the 1960s looking for a paradisical beach life and cheap hashish. With the advent of digital technology, the travelers' subculture (of British New Age nomads) brought this music to those in Goa. Here, the travelers' subculture and music were, in the words of the Goa trance e-mail list FAQ, "even MORE tempered by Indian metaphors, and the music changed over time to reflect these various feelings, belief systems, etc."[4] This marked the beginning of Goa trance.[5] Goa trance music relied heavily on both U.S. techno and house music, which had become popular in Europe; in particular, the Roland TB-303 bassline, an analog piece of music technology first associated with acid house music, became a defining sound. Musicians in Goa also sampled local sounds and musics, as well as snippets of dialogue or music from old films and television programs.

By the mid-1990s, the Goa trance sound had traveled around the world, especially to the United States, Europe, and Israel. (The first major party in New York City was in September 1996 and is still talked about as legendary.) Record labels specializing in the music sprang up, as well as DJs, and some organizations dedicated to promoting Goa trance parties. The music has become so popular that there is a vast amount of information on it available on the Internet, including an extremely active mailing list devoted to Goa trance, as well as other more general trance lists.

Westernized versions of Hinduism and Buddhism became increasingly associated with this music, mainly in album and artwork hung at parties, and in a few keywords that aficionados use; e-conversations frequently concluded with "Bom!" or "Boom," short for "Bom Shankar," which is explained at one Goa trance mailing list FAQ as a phrase that is reported to be said by followers of Shiva (also known as Shankar) as they light the chillum.[6] Also, recipes for chai (a milky, spiced tea popular in South Asia) periodically surface in the Goa trance e-mail list; people occasionally greet each other with "Namaste!" the traditional greeting word used in South Asia.

Along with a somewhat different sound than electronic dance musics, Goa/psy trance is inflected both by psychedelic drug images and subculture, as well as Hinduism and Buddhism. Album and flier iconography frequently depict familiar Buddhist or Hindu imagery (occasionally with icons of spirituality from other "native" spiritual traditions) mixed with a strong psychedelic background (see figs. 8.1 and 8.2). Decorations at clubs make use of ultraviolet lights, and some clubbers dress to look their best under these lights, as well as bringing fluorescent toys such as glow sticks with them.

FIGURE 8.1.
Synthetic Sādhus Flier, January 29, 2000, New York City.

FIGURE 8.2. [LEFT]
Synthetic Sādhus Flier, March 24, 2000, New York City.
FIGURE 8.3. [RIGHT]
Tsunami name and logo.

One of the most ubiquitous symbols on album covers and fliers is the Sanskrit spelling of "Om"; the biweekly parties called "Tsunami" by their promoter in New York City use a slightly modified version of this symbol to form the letter "S" of its name, which appears on their fliers and on a banner that is displayed at their parties (see fig. 8.3). Other albums and poster art emphasize the more psychedelic aspects of the scene (see figs. 8.4 and 8.5). But even this second image has Hindu/Buddhist overtones in its round shapes and colors; it could almost be a picture of Ganesh, the Hindu elephant deity (a popular one among the more Goa-oriented fans of this music), modified by computer. Tsunami's motto is "Celestial trance for sublime people."

Participants in the little culture in New York City are almost all white, middle class, ranging in age from mid- to late teens through mid-twenties. There are a few younger and older folks, and a few people of color, but it's mainly young and white. The biggest group of nonwhites is Asian Americans, whose numbers dropped noticeably during the summer of 1999. (I assume that's because the many people who attend college in New York City left for the summer.) The psychedelic aspects of the scene are essentially holdovers from the hippie era, though most of the people involved today are too young to have been hippies. But an occasional countercultural type does make an appear-

FIGURE 8.4.
Tsunami flier (front), July 30, 1999.

FIGURE 8.5.
Tsunami flier (front), July 16, 1999.

ance; a Welshman in his late fifties, who goes by the name of Brahma, provided the artwork at one party I attended.

What mainly connects this psychedelic little culture with its progen- itor is drug use; one person told me "pot is a fact of life for me." When I was first getting involved with the New York City little culture, one of the people I knew, a bright and personable young nineteen-year-old man, asked me rather shyly, "Do you do hallucinogenics?" indicating the importance of these drugs to the scene but also the somewhat proselytizing mission of its most devout adherents. Many people also take LSD or psilocybin mushrooms before showing up at parties. They probably take these and other drugs at parties, as well, though I never witnessed this myself.

There is no single way to dress in this little culture. The men I was closest to in my study wore baggy pants and T-shirts, and occasionally they wore deliberately cheesy or outdated clothes. They also all had very short hair. The only woman I knew in the small subgroup of peo- ple I knew best always wore mismatched patterns. But other people in the scene whom I knew—partiers more than organizers—dressed as most teenagers or young adults do; only a few people dressed in the way that one occasionally reads about in the trance scene, with colors that would show up under ultraviolet lights.

Even though the little culture in New York City was fairly robust at the time of my research, Goa trance, like most contemporary electronic dance music little cultures, was slow to come to the United States in its transmogrified form of Detroit techno and Chicago house. The first major event was in September of 1996 and was organized in part by John-Emanuel Gartmann, a Swiss promoter who had worked in Europe, but who wanted to start something in New York City. He told me more than once that he thought this was the best music around and he wanted to do what he could to foster it in New York. He certainly seems committed to the city; the flipside of his business card has a pic- ture of a massive wave (tsunami) about to engulf the Statue of Liberty. Promoting Tsunami trance parties in New York has been touch and go, he said, perhaps making money on only six shows out of thirty-seven. But he's committed to it for the long haul because of his belief that this is the best music around. Part of the reason his shows are so expensive to put on is that he frequently flies in several DJs from Europe; and he flies in a person to do the decor. It's worth it, he said, because he thinks people know that they're getting a quality show. He looks down his nose at the other shows that the club Vinyl hosts in New York City, saying that "they pay no attention to decor."[7]

Gartmann has an almost Wagnerian vision. His company was called Massive Productions before he changed it to Tsunami, and his parties are more lavish than any others I have seen. It's not cheap, and it takes a lot of work. There are many headaches in putting on such a complex show. Gartmann prepares forty to forty-five press kits every other week (Tsunami parties are biweekly), he makes all the travel arrangements for the DJs and artists himself, and he coordinates everyone on the night of the show. One of the biggest problems, he said, is trying to find out a DJ's real name, which he needs to know since he is making airline reservations for them. If they're coming from abroad, their name on the ticket must match their name on their passport. (These musicians frequently hide behind their DJ names and protect their "real" identities.) Gartmann said there are as many as twenty-five people working on the day of a show. Some of the staff appears to come with the club (the clean-up crew), but the "artistic" staff would seem to be all Tsunami. Gartmann also hires a sound engineer to make sure all the equipment is working properly.

Everything about a dance club is designed to alter your senses and focus them on the music and dancing. When you go in at eleven or midnight, when the doors first open, you don't think much about the dimly lit space. But I once went early to meet some people and help them set up. It was about 8 P.M. on a bright, dry summer evening (all too rare in New York City); the sun was still out. I had to buzz the doorbell a few times but finally got in. Entering the familiar club from the bright outside was a shock. Being inside the all-black room knowing it was still sunny outside brought home the fact that clubs are really a different kind of space. Inside, you have no idea what time it is, what the weather is outside, or anything else.

In other respects, also, the Goa/psychedelic trance little cultures is similar to other kinds of electronic dance music club little cultures. As Simon Reynolds, Sarah Thornton, and others have written, there is a general desire among participants in underground dance music little cultures to come together, to transcend class and other social differences, heightened in many scenes by the use of the drug Ecstasy, technically known as methylene dioxymethamphetamine or MDMA, which heightens feelings of togetherness and community.[8]

This feeling is often referred to as "PLUR," an acronym that stands for "Peace, Love, Unity, and Respect."[9] Although they do not always use the term, mainly because of its origins in the rave scene that may Goa/psy trance people prefer to view as distinct from theirs, the Goa/psy trance little culture nonetheless strongly emphasizes PLUR, and dedicated Goa/psy trance people work hard to help cultivate and sustain it. This set of positive values I am calling the "vibe." Kai Fikentscher, in his extensive study of DJs in New York City, writes of a concept called "interactive performance," which labels "the mutual dependency of two forms of musicking in UDM [Underground Dance Music]: deejaying and dancing."[10] This "loop of nonverbal interaction between DJ and dancers, this type of energy exchange, is what shapes vibe."[11] Fikentscher talks of the importance of the vibe in the underground dance music community in New York City, and the Goa/psychedelic little culture is no different. But Goa/psy trance participants facilitate and achieve the vibe in ways unique to their particular little culture, which I will describe in a moment.

First, though, it is important to address the issue of PLUR, for in the dominant theories of music and community, electronic music is not thought to be able to engender this effect. I am referring mainly here to Charles Keil's influential ideas about "participatory discrepancies" (PDs) and the "groove." "Participatory discrepancies" are those minute "errors," differences that occur when musicians play together, and the effect of these differences, in part, helps pull musicians and listeners together into a "groove."[12]

There is little that Keil has written about the groove and PDs that I would disagree with. As an active musician myself, I relish the moments when I get together with other musicians, friends, acquaintances, strangers, and it all comes together. This doesn't happen all the time—indeed, it is all too rare—but this is part of what keeps so many of us coming back time and again. As Keil writes, "the social moments where I get these 'oneness' and 'urge to merge' feelings most forcefully are when I'm dancing at polka parties or salsa parties, swept up in a black church service, or making music."[13]

But if we are discrepant, how can we be one? I agree with Keil that it is the PDs that make the music—like the lumps that make the mashed potatoes, the yeast in the bottom of the bottle that makes the beer—this is how you know it's real. But at the same time, I think, when it all comes together, when PDs seem to drop out, this is great, too. After all, one of the best things one can say about a group of musicians is that they're "tight," they're really together.[14] I think there is something of a dialectic between PDs and the longing for the moment when it all comes together and differences disappear, however fleetingly. The tension caused by this dialectic, wondering whether, when, the groove is going to kick in and the PDs disappear, is part of the experience, part of what makes it real and exciting.

I don't consider this a critique of Keil's ideas, only an addendum. But I do have a critique. Keil's ambivalence—at best—toward technology and musicking is well represented in his writings and interviews, and it is clear that he equates the groove, and thus the possibility of PDs, as being exclusively linked with live music only, as in statements such as, "I would argue that wherever that recording thing happens, perfectionist, classicizing, Apollonian dream realizations are creeping in." On the same page he says, "All I'm arguing is that we recognize what happens in recording studios as a classicizing, perfecting, dream-world thing, and that takes it away from the dancers, which takes it away from public space, the streets, clubs."[15]

Christopher Small, on whom Keil also relies in some of his publications, similarly writes of the verb "to music" in his recent book *Musicking*: "*To music is to take part, in any capacity, in a musical performance, whether by performing, by listening, by rehearsing or practicing, by providing material for performance (what is called composition), or by dancing.*" Small's verb "to music" "covers all participation in a musical performance, whether it takes place actively or passively."[16] Questions arise immediately. First, there is the problem of just what constitutes a performance; but more to the point here, Small, like Keil, privileges live musicking. Such privileging has a long history, of course, but rebuttals have been around for quite awhile as well, most notably Alfred Schutz's landmark "Making Music Together," which argues that wherever there is music, even recorded music, something social happens.[17]

My sympathy is with Schutz's less exclusive view. Having conducted fieldwork with psy trance people in clubs in New York City, it is clear to me that something like Keil's groove—a sense of community, of oneness—happens in settings where there is no live music. Dancers achieve their groove in different ways than do musicians/listeners/dancers in live settings, but it's no less meaningful to them. Still, taking a cue from Keil, it may be useful to differentiate between the groove, referring to live music, and, drawing on some people in the scene, the "vibe," in non–live music settings such as dance clubs. I am inspired to use the word *vibe* from Keil's employment of *groove*—a word with a street valence, a word that is used by insiders to the scene.

The Vibe

Let me now flesh out what the vibe might be in this little culture. It should already be clear that *vibe* is merely an extension of, or version of, Keil's *groove*. The most significant part of this, as far as I can tell, is this coming together, this "urge to merge," in Keil's memorable phrase.[18]

Insiders refer to this music as "trance" or "psy trance," so it is necessary at this point to uncover just what trance means in this context. I think people understand that it's not technically "trance" in the premodern ritual sense, where one temporarily loses contact with everyday reality and loses control over their bodies. At the same time, however, the Goa people feel some kinship with people who undergo this kind of trance, and they're interested in achieving it themselves. Even the people least involved in the spiritual and mystical aspects of Goa/psy trance music invoke premodern musical practices when discussing this music.[19] One of the DJs I interviewed told me that even though he realized it wasn't trance in the premodern sense, "The main goal is still the same—to sort of achieve like a mental state when you're listening to it and you're dancing to it. You know, trance music has been around for millennia, you know, tribal music, trance music. The goal is still the same: to sort of achieve a trancelike mental state in your head by the music around you and by dancing. The ends are the same but the means are a little bit different."[20]

Essentially, trance is the state one is in when the vibe happens, when the "urge to merge" has succeeded, when the dancer/listener has become deindividualized, united with his fellows; as one fan wrote to the Goa trance e-mail list about a party that I attended, "there was definitely no ego, just pure vibe." People talk and write about this experience in extraordinary terms: it's a life-changing experience, it's religion, it's finding God. And the experiences that Goa/psy trance fans do have are profoundly meaningful to them. In e-mail message after e-mail message, webpage after webpage, Goa/psy trance listeners discuss how this music and scene has changed their lives for the better in the most emotional and confessional terms. It would be impossible to convey the sheer volume of such correspondences, the range of metaphors and expressions, for there are literally thousands. People use rhetorical styles ranging from the biblical to fables to parables to psychology to fairy tales to poetry, New Age, and more. A few examples will have to suffice.

One person wrote to a Goa trance e-mail list to say that what mattered to him about the music and scene was many things, but, finally, "(cliches coming now), the state u get in when u realize the importance of collectiveness, that u are no longer important as urself, but its important that u are part of it." Another in this vein: "The potential of a good techno party is having the whole party caught up in the rapture of the moment—where everyone's actions are contributing to everyone else's."

Chris Decker, in his liner notes to *Return to the Source: The Chakra Journey*, writes, "We have all felt the power of the dance floor, those expanded moments when the DJ plays that certain track that raises our energy to a peaking climax . . . As we raise our arms with an ecstatic cheer we feel our connection to each other as one tribe united in spirit—the power of the collective. This euphoric dance floor release is as ancient as human existence stretching back through time to the original campfires. It was our community ritual, our rite of passage into ecstatic oneness."[21]

One user wrote in to a website featuring comments about the music, and PLUR: "it's why you party in the first place. raves aren't about drugs, but about yourself being let go, and joining everyone else in a collective dance. long live the goa trancers everywhere. . . . peace, love, unity, and respect."[22]

Occasionally people write poems, such as this one (excerpted):

Light and Sound . . .
a perfect image of a mind-made reality
carried away by synchronity
caught in the draft of time
where no signs are left of us.
We control what we can't understand,
aeons away from wisdom . . . ,
a existance to be maintained . . .
struggling for the unspeakable.
the "Future" and the "Past" . . .
revolving spheres inside of
an infinite loop the unbearable beauty of it's fractals—

gave birth in intense climaxes of chaos
to become child-friend of the dolphin.

Others, such as the following person, invoke semireligious language: "what i referred to in my mail is that at an openair party, for example, one is open to his/her own 'rituals,' there, one doesnt find a tight etiquette to abide by, and one doesnt need a manual like a bible. one can sit on a hill-side at dawn, look down upon the wavey-trancey crowd, and feel the inevitable joy of existance and taking part. at this point my personal thoughts and reactions revolve around the fact that I'm thankful to whoever's up there, for having shown me such beauty, for having brought together thousands of people in harmony." And this one, which echoes "Amazing Grace": "I was blind and I Saw; I was deaf and I Heard; I was crippled and I Danced; I was numb and I Loved. Goa is now my lifeblood. Thanx to all you wonderful people in the UK and Greece who made it all clear. Bom!"23

Some of the people in the little culture are organic cultural theorists, such as this poster to the Goa trance mailing list from May 1999: "Summing up: what first degrades the magic [of the vibe] is excess of formalistic constraints. What is needed is a social situation of enough mutual trust and respect that there is no fear of saying ANYTHING GOES (including the guy banging drums for the first time). Where the vibe, or shared intentionality, is strong, there is a self-regulating quality to the field that draws even disruptive elements gradually into a harmony. Exercising artistic/production control to make things go right may prevent some things from going wrong, but will not necessarily make things go well. What is required for that is much more like faith in each other. Which brings us back, perhahps, to P.L.U.R."

Or, from the Goa trance mailing list of July 1999, advice to a person who said they wanted to be a DJ:

PLEASE, PLEASE, remember the magic of a 'goa trance' party. The energy. That incredible, all-pervading energy.

PLEASE, PLEASE, remember that special feeling, the 'vibe' of an underground party, or a frolic in the forest, or even a 'legit' event that managed to create an 'immersive environment', that something that was so unlike a 'rave' as to occupy a wholly different section of your brain . . . the something that makes some want to scream 'I've found my religion!', others to find a family, and most to gain friends and/or memories for life ...

To me, THAT is what I want to share with the world.

Or this: "Now with this in mind, you can apply the theory to cultural phenomena as well. the rave scene, sexual behavior, pokemon, whatever. its always the same- first there is a small group of people doing it, then it grows until a certain point where it really explodes. back to the ascension part—when enough people posess a working awareness that we are all connected via energy, that nothing is truly seperate, it will be like all of us waking up and 'getting it' all at once. one of those 'aha' moments on a global scale, where everyone is aware of each other all at once. a lot of cultures have had an 'end of the world' concept—for example, the christian second coming. but the part that's interesting is that so many cultures have a variation on this common theme."

Writing to the Goa trance mailing list, this person theorizes the vibe in a way that implies some familiarity with social theories: "Music, as a cultural factor, is a means whereby the basic unity of the collective psychism of a people (particularly in primitive societies or in special groups within a more sophisticated culture) is strengthened, sustained, and periodically revitalised. In this function music is usually associated with rites and collectively performed gestures (including shouting and applause)."

No matter what rhetorical style style is used, these experiences are powerful for many people. Even for those who don't indulge in the kinds of language I have quoted, Goa/psy trance is still a central part of their lives, as it is for the people I got to know in New York City. One person I spoke to said that for him the scene was about music and parties (he said this quite vehemently and definitively), not spirituality, and told me of another Internet mailing list on trance music that had "almost no spiritual stuff" on it. At the same time, however, this DJ clearly had something of an evangelical zeal about this music and believed in the scene's standard story about the roots of trance music going back thousands of years. What he seemed to object to was not so much the "spirituality" of the scene, but the explicit focus on spirituality rather than music.

The Vibe as Religion

However it is characterized and articulated, this vibe is widespread in all kinds of contemporary dance music little cultures and has been widely discussed in the literature on raves and other kinds of contemporary electronic music dance little cultures.[24] But if it is theorized at all, it is almost always done in the context of youth subcultures, in which it is seen as a kind of resistance; or, if the framing theory is some kind of Baudrillardian postmodernism, the vibe is seen as an instance of the hyperreal (Ben Malbon, Antonio Melechi); or, for example, this argument by Hillegonda C. Rietveld: "Since this is a moment of a 'perfect' community for which there is no original and which by the same token can be reproduced, one could call this an experience of a type of 'hyperreality' which is difficult to express in words"; or variations on themes by Gilles Deleuze and Félix Guattari (as in the writings of Georgiana Gore, Drew Hemment, Tim Jordan, Maria Pini, and Simon Reynolds).[25] Another theoretical frame employed, though less frequently than these others, is the psychoanalytical: the DJ as mother rocking her children into an altered state of consciousness, the heartbeat-like mother beat matching that of the unborn infants' in the womblike dance club (also Rietveld, and Simon Reynolds).[26]

Oddly, though, while most writers, both in and out of the academy, refer to the quasi-religious aspects of many underground dance music little cultures, anthropological and sociological theories of religion have rarely been used in any thoroughgoing way to illuminate social behavior at these clubs; to my knowledge, only one writer, Gianfranco Salvatore, has taken seriously the religious aspects of the rave scene in a couple of important writings.[27] But most references to religion are usually made in passing, though Simon Reynolds notes that, in England, traditional, organized religion noticed that raves were not all that different from Christianity, and some churches attempted to "*rejuvenate* Christianity by incorporating elements of the rave experience: dancing, lights, mass fervor, demonstrative and emotional behavior." Rave-style worship has spread, Reynolds tells us, to several English cities.[28] Reynolds, however, believes raves to be more like Buddhism in their similar quests for selflessness, or the vibe.

And, indeed, it would seem that religious forms of organization don't really have much to do with what Stuart Hall, Dick Hebdige, or Sarah Thornton found.[29] In Ken Gelder and Sarah Thornton's *Subcultures Reader*, religion drops out of the articles by the mid-1950s and reappears fleetingly only once more in the remaining articles.[30] While the youth subculture literature has been useful in understanding youth groups, at the same time it must be acknowledged that many youth subcultures, at least in the postwar era, are in many ways organized like religions, a point I will flesh below with respect to the Goa/psy trance aficionados.

Early theorists of youth subcultures were clearly more interested in resistance than religion. Classic studies such as Stuart Hall and Tony Jefferson's *Resistance through Rituals*, Dick Hebdige's *Subculture: The Meaning of Style*, and Paul Willis's *Learning to Labor* bypassed religion in favor of concerns with the ways that youths are both interpellated by, and attempt to resist, consumer culture, capitalism, and other negative aspects of the dominant culture.[31] These are concerns I am sympathetic to, but the legacy of youth subculture theory, at least in the study of youths and music, has too often meant that resistance is found where it doesn't exist. For just one example, Ben Malbon, author of one of the better articles on clubbing, writes that he wants to consider the *experience* of clubbing. This quickly morphs into an analysis of space (still useful and important), but his final words are pretty much standard Birmingham School/cultural studies, despite his attempt to distance himself: resistance is all-important, but "it is the resistance found through losing your self, paradoxically to find your self."[32] However, this "resistance" isn't resistance at all, but the organizing fact of clubbing for most people, and a widespread cultural phenomenon at that—the vibe.

A final theoretical point regarding subculture theory. Grant McCracken's "little cultures," that is, cultures that are relatively whole in and of themselves with the power "to claim the individual in broad, general ways and fine, particular ones."[33] He offers this concept in order to make a distinction between little cultures and youth subcultures. His is a useful theoretical formulation because it emphasizes the multiplicity and diversity of little cultures in this era he calls the "culture of commotion," marked by "plenitude"—of everything, where as "subculture" implies that the smaller unit is somehow a part of a whole, or dependent on a whole. It may well be, however, that this whole no longer exists, or at any rate is quickly fragmenting. The idea of "little cultures" helps move beyond the deeply essentialist assumptions of youth subculture theory; "youths" are spoken of as though everyone knows what they are, and whatever they are, they come by it naturally. McCracken, however, notes that there are dozens of species of teens (or genders or elderly or what have you); "speciation" is a feature of the contemporary, not vast collections of monolithic "youths" or other groups.

While I will continue to employ the term *little culture*, it is necessary to point out that such a term, unlike *subculture*, washes out any idea of hegemony, of domination. These still exist. I will use the *little culture* term with this important inflection, but at the same time, I would like to make it clear that little cultures (or subcultures, for that matter) are not simply *products* of their hegemons (which is essentially the conclusion that Sarah Thornton arrives at in *Club Cultures*) but that little cultures are less connected to the still powerful dominant culture(s).

If youth subculture theory doesn't really help understand the Goa/psy trance little culture, neither do the various theories usually lumped under the term *postmodern*. The tendency among nonmusicians and nonmusicologists to study music as though it were only lyrics is made more difficult in the study of music with no lyrics, and so the absence of lyrics in psy trance seems to have resulted in an even greater preponderance of so-called postmodern theories.[34] The abstractness of this theory is taken to be describing something in this lyricless music, which seems to be abstract to those who have no way of talking about music as music.[35] An example is Georgiana Gore, who takes off from Deleuze and Guattari's famous conception of the "rhizomatic" nature of contemporary social/cultural formations, and adds enthusiastically: "And so with raving!"[36]

Similarly, Antonio Melechi writes that "the trance-dance moves the body beyond the spectacle of the 'pose' and the sexuality ('romance') of the look, into a 'cyberspace' of musical sound, where one attempts to implode (get into) and disappear."[37] "Implode"? "Disappear"? This seems to have been written without reference to what people are actually doing. Drew Hemment makes a similar point, arguing that the loss of self in the rave scene is the same as the loss of self off the dancefloor "amidst a generalized loss of meaning."[38]

Likewise, this argument from Michel Gaillot, who at least notes the religious overtones of this little culture and its activities: "Techno provides an opening for that expenditure [of excess] and for the sacred, one that might seem in contradiction with its lack of political or religious commitment, although here the sacred has become something purely formal and remains only a shell."[39] It is certainly not a shell to those who practice it, however—perhaps only to those who observe it at a distance.

In insisting on this religious connection and putting theories of postmodernity and, more to the point, youth subcultures and post-modernity in the background, I am not abandoning politics that have traditionally preoccupied youth subculture theorists; politics and forms of dominance and resistance are no less interesting than they ever were, as much of the rest of this book makes clear. But many commentators on this music have found resistance and oppositionality where neither exists, or if they do, they are far from the most salient aspect of the little culture in question. Using classic theories of religion and ritual sheds more light on the Goa/psy trance crowd (and other electronic dance music subcultures) than any other body of theory I have come across.

A discussion of subcultures is probably familiar enough to most readers, since studies of subcultures at least are common in much of contemporary theoretical literature. To talk about religion needs some doing, since anthropology and ethnomusicology pay little attention to religion and ritual these days. It is thus necessary to spend some time going over classic social theories of religion, which shed a good deal of light on the Goa/psy trance little culture. The first key text for my argument is Émile Durkheim's classic *The Elementary Forms of Religions Life*, first published in 1912. This is a weighty study of Australian aboriginal religions, but the theoretical insights are useful outside this immediate context, and it is clear that Durkheim meant his observations to have wider currency, as they did. Although Durkheim's general theories are quite relevant in this context, some of his descriptions could have been written about a Goa/psy trance gathering in New York City, or, I suspect, any such similar gathering.

Durkheim's main concern, unlike the other major social theorist of the time, Max Weber, was the social group more than the individual. For Durkheim there exists a dynamic between individual and group: "far from being simple, our inner life has something that is like a double center of gravity. On the one hand is our individuality—and, more particularly, our body in which it is based; on the other is everything in us that expresses something other than ourselves."[40]

But when individuals come together, something happens. According to Durkheim,

The very act of congregating is an exceptionally powerful stimulant. Once the individuals are gathered together, a sort of electricity is generated from their closeness and quickly launches them to an extraordinary height of exaltation. Every emotion expressed resonates without interference in consciousnesses that are wide open to external impressions, each one echoing the others. . . . Probably because a collective emotion cannot be expressed collectively without some order that permits harmony and unison of movement, these gestures and cries tend to fall into rhythm and regularity, and from there into songs and dances. . . . The effervescence often becomes so intense that it leads to outlandish behavior; the passions unleashed are so torrential that nothing can hold them. People are so far outside the ordinary conditions of life, and so beyond ordinary morality.[41]

This "collective effervescence" is akin to the vibe; and, indeed, Durkheim's words aren't far from how people talk and write about the experience in the Goa/psy trance scene.

Durkheim argues that this "special world" of the moment of collective effervescence becomes seen as sacred to those who experience it, and the everyday world, profane. This distinction is predicated on the group experience:

It is not difficult to imagine that a man in such a state of exaltation should no longer know himself. Feeling possessed and led on by some sort of external power that makes him think and act differently than he normally does, he naturally feels he is no longer himself. It seems to him that he has become a new being. . . . And because his companions feel transformed in the same way at the same moment, and express this feeling by their shouts, movements, and bearing, it is as if he was in reality transported into a special world entirely different from the one in which he ordinarily lives, a special world inhabited by exceptionally intense forces that invade and transform him. Especially when repeated for weeks, day after day, how would experiences like these not leave him with the conviction that two heterogenous and incommensurable worlds exist in fact? In one world he languidly carries on his daily life; the other is one that he cannot enter without abruptly entering into relations with extraordinary power that excite him to the point of frenzy. The first is the profane world and the second, the world of sacred things.

It is in these effervescent social milieux, and indeed from that very effervescence, that the religious idea seems to have been born.[42]

It is no wonder, then, that so many trance and rave lovers talk about their experiences in religious or quasi-religious terms, sometimes invoking "God" as a way of explaining their experience, as in this post to the Goa trance mailing list from early September 1999:

> The element that made this experience so "spiritual" was the fact that while it occurred I realized I wasn't looking/finding God; I was merely worshipping him in the most public, personal way I ever have before. I've been to church plenty of times and I tell you the only difference is the energy level your on. (I think no matter what your doing, If your feeling good about it and then you start thinking of your position and who God is——you feel even better. Better than if you don't …)
>
> I believe some of this music we all love may be either influenced by or inspired from God to reach those of us who are different. When I say different it's because I have always felt different from the normal crowd and been in search of something to call my own (i.e. skater/jock/preppy).

One anonymous manifesto circulates on the Goa trance e-mail list occasionally, usually when someone feels that the conversation is straying too far from what she thinks the scene is about.

THE PSYCHEDELIC EXPIRENCE

The Psy Trance Party should remain sacred. It becomes a living art form, a beautiful theatre of light and sound where the dancers and artists all play their part no matter who they came as. A chance to be someone different, to take time out from life and be part of a non-reality zone, a totally autonomous zone that is a doorway to another dimension and which exists and is completely real until it ends and remains only in the thoughts and dreams of those who took part.

A ritual that takes all those taking part back to where it all began from. Something Mystical. Back to that tribal instinct that makes us want to stomp the ground in unison while around us swirls the entire universe. The dark night sounds break down the ego and then the daybreak and the more melodic sounds show the paradise the world can be without the ego.

A glimpse in one night of something that can only be described as COSMIC. Something you can take home only in your heart. Something they do not want us to see. [43]

This missive contains language familiar from the Internet and ethnographic quotations already offered, and resonates strongly with Durkheim's discussions.

I am also struck by the use of Durkheim's adverb *languidly* in the quotation above; in the nontrance world, the individual "languidly carries on his daily life." Many of the people I interviewed had college educations, or had decided to forgo educations, making the New York City trance little culture the primary focus of their lives. This isn't that unusual, but what struck me was how menial many of the jobs people held, even those with college educations, and how little people seemed to mind. In part, this was clearly a reaction against a dominant structure that values the Protestant work ethic and tends to judge people based on their occupations. People didn't seem to count the days until the weekend, until the next party, but were content to work at the jobs until the next party came along and would regenerate them. I talked to one person about this, a DJ with an Ivy League college education, and he said that he and his friends were "opportunistic" about parties—they happen when they happen. I thought it was a telling use of language; the term "opportunistic" conveys a certain lack—or deemphasis—of a proactive kind of agency, a stance that seemed to be pervasive in this little culture. Again, however, this is a little culture in McCracken's sense in that it is relatively self-contained. The New York City Goa/psy trance scene is a little culture in which one's job has little or nothing to do with one's identity, and, as Durkheim says, is simply a way to subsist while languidly carrying on everyday life.

From Durkheim, then, there is the notion of "collective effervescence," the vibe, that state that occurs when people are all together and tuned in to one another, an experience of "depersonalization and of a transcendent sense of participation in something larger and more powerful than themselves."[44] Durkheim, when speaking of the dynamic of individual and group, asks, "How can we belong entirely to ourselves, and entirely to others at one and the same time? The ego cannot be something completely other than itself, for, if it were, it would vanish—this is what happens in ecstasy."[45] Or the vibe.

Another somewhat more recent theorist of religion helps as well. Victor Turner, well known among anthropologists for his work on ritual, offers many insights that are of use in understanding the Goa/psy trance little culture, even though his work is now over thirty years old. It is occasionally noted that youths are liminal, a concept advanced by Turner; liminals "elude or slip through the network of classifications that normally locate states and positions in cultural space." Members of this group "tend to develop an intense comradeship and egalitarianism. Secular distinctions of rank and status disappear or are homogenized."[46] Also useful here is Turner's companion concept: where there is liminality, there is what he termed *communitas*, an alternative society that is "unstructured or rudimentarily structured and relatively undifferentiated *comitatus*, community, or even communion of equal individuals."[47]

For Turner there is a dialectical process for individuals and groups that involves successive experience of high and low, communitas and structure, homogeneity and differentiation, equality and inequality.[48] Significant for my purposes here, Turner notes that there is a striking resemblance between liminality/communitas and certain religious conditions, later writing that "in complex large-scale societies, liminality itself, as a result of the advancing division of labor, has often become a religious or quasi-religious state."[49]

Further, communitas cannot exist apart from the established social structure. "Communitas emerges where social structure is not."[50] Communitas is spontaneous, immediate, and concrete, but is only evident or accessible "through its juxtaposition to . . . aspects of social structure."[51] Communitas is everywhere structure is not, where structure falters: "communitas breaks in through the interstices of structure, in liminality; at the edges of structure, in marginality; and from beneath structure, in inferiority. It is almost everywhere held to be sacred or 'holy,' possibly because it transgresses or dissolves the norms that govern structured and institutionalized relationships and is accompanied by experiences of unprecedented potency."[52]

Perhaps this would make sense if we change "social structure" to "mainstream" (in Sarah Thornton's formulation), or to "society" among my own informants. Clubbers oppose the structure, whether it is called "society" or "mainstream," a point that Thornton misses in her study of club cultures. She is hard on her informants for not being able to articulate just what they mean by "mainstream," ultimately rejecting their claims to being oppositional. But, unlike her informants, Thornton failed to grasp that the "mainstream" is a *structure* that is opposed, or maybe just eluded, escaped from. It is not a simple set of characteristics that can be delineated under the microphone of an inquiring interviewer.

I had an experience that helps clarify this idea of the mainstream as structure. One day I received an e-mail message telling of a party in a new space. It started earlier than most parties do (10 P.M.) so this was tempting to me, since I'm not a night owl. I got there pretty much on time. There was a line outside the club so I joined. It turned out that the people in the line were all from the stock brokerage firm of Merrill Lynch; they had a block of thirty or so on the guest list (which means the price of admission is lowered to $10). After determining this, I went to the security guy, a large man with a radio earphone wire coming out of his ear. I told him I was on the guest list. He said the guest list wasn't out yet and to get back in line. He was, as I said, very large, so I went back and joined the Merrill Lynch folks. While standing in line I watched more Merrill Lynch people arriving, always by limousine. Hired limos would disgorge three or four young people at a time who would then join their buddies in line; all were in their twenties or so. There were South Asians in this group, as well as East Asians, though all seemed to be Asian Americans. It looked as though they had all gone from work to restaurants for dinner in various groups before coming to the club, so all were pretty well dressed, though I think some of the women brought something skimpier to wear on top. The men mostly wore khakis; all had long-sleeved shirts. Apparently they had taken off their ties and put them away somewhere.

Given this clientele, I wasn't surprised to discover that the club was very plush: painted black floors, copper table and countertops. Everything was very nice. The bar staff seemed professional; there were several people running around and picking up bottles and glasses. Another man was sweeping cigarette butts and other trash up off the floor. Many were apparently Mexicans, at that time the workers at or near the bottom of the economic ladder in New York City.

I spotted two people I knew who are deeply involved in the scene and chatted with them for a while. The young woman, dressed in her usual mismatched retro clothes and bandana in her hair, told me she felt dirty, that it wasn't their usual crowd. She said the main reason she was into psy trance was that it allowed you to do something other than what society wanted. But here was "society," represented by the stockbrokers. She looked chagrined.

What eventually happened was that the Goa trance people were told to continue their party in the basement while the stockbrokers and other yuppies remained on the main floor. Each group was happy in its separate little culture, though it is hard to resist not interpreting the stockbroker group as dominant, as it was, physically, over the psy trance group.

There is another factor that needs to be recalled here. The psy trance group is liminal, and it deals with this liminality in one tried-and-true way: by seeking altered states. Erika Bourguignon, another anthropological theorist (not of ritual, but of altered states of consciousness), has noted that those "who suffer greatest inability to modify their own lives in a given society under existing circumstances will be most likely to make use of altered states."[53] Connecting with Turner on this point, it is easy to pose a connection between liminal states and the use of altered states, by whatever means. Earlier, in the introduction, Bourguignon discusses this at length and says that in rigid societies, possession trance may exist in order to make possible some modifications in the social situation of individuals who have no other way of achieving this, and that possession trance may be used mainly by those who have no other option—that is, those in liminal groups.[54] Goa/psy trance fans do not enter states of possession trance, but Bourguignon's observation that those in liminal states are most likely to turn to altered states of consciousness directed at an individual situation rather than a larger, social structural one makes a good deal of sense here.

Many of these disparate strands come together in the work of French sociologist Michel Maffesoli, who has been somewhat influential on discussions of these new electronic-dance-music youth subcultures. Maffesoli does not use an explicitly religious theoretical framework as I do here, yet he draws on some of the same sources, Durkheim in particular. Durkheim's concept of "collective effervescence," his ideas about ritual, and other notions all play a role in Maffesoli's work, and he uses these and other concepts to argue that modernity "is built on the principle of individuation and of separation, whereas the empathetic period is marked by the lack of differentiation, the 'loss' in a collective subject: in other words, what I shall call neo-tribalism."[55]

Maffesoli's argument is useful, for unlike youth subculture theories, it takes into account the spiritual aspects of these new tribes. And he usefully recapitulates some of the more important ideas of the earlier scholars, as in this excerpt which might as well be by Victor Turner: "*experiencing the other* is the basis of the community."[56]

The Vibe as Hippie Relic

In both media and academic reports on the electronic dance music little cultures it has often been remarked that it is rather like that of the hippies. As Gianfranco Salvatore notes, "It simply happens that different movements process the same principles in various ways."[57] Older people involved in the scene are quick to note that it is a continuation, or perhaps to paraphrase Raymond Williams, a reemergent tradition.[58] Brahma, the late middle-age Welshman who provided the artwork at one party I attended, said, "Well, it's just leftover hippie stuff, isn't it?" Goa Gil, an American DJ who has lived in Goa since the early 1970s, argues that 1960s psychedelic culture has survived: "The Psychedelic Revolution never really stopped. It just had to go half way round the world to the end of a dirt road on a deserted beach, and there it was allowed to evolve and mutate, without government or media pressures. This is what it's come to now. The equation has met there, of this kind of vibe, it evolved into that, with the absorbing of the spiritual traditions, and the international influence. It came out in that way, and a new vibe was made from what went before it in the 60's Cyber-tribal vibe, and global."[59]

Younger people in the scene, however—the vast majority—recognize the similarity to hippies and the 1960s counterculture, though many express disgust at this comparison; some accept it with a bit of resignation; others are simply ambivalent. For the most part, they arrived at their involvement in the psy trance little culture on their own; it is not hippie nostalgia, or even a hippie-influenced little culture for most of them. As we have already seen, there can be tension between those who emphasize the spiritual/PLUR side and those who emphasize that the scene is about "music and parties," as one of my informants told me. Most people reject the hippie comparison made in journalistic reports of the scene, as does this poster to the Goa trance mailing list: "what i think is really great about the trance (the muzik & the 'scene') experience is the confirmation that we are in the right place. all the nonsense about a sad 'hippie revival' bound to sink without a point, the attacks on 'drugs' and their related scenes, the idiotic remarks about our psy trance by people who cant understand this 'electronic music which shouldnt even be considered music at all' . . . they crumble in front of the immense power which is created during the doof-doof-doof and the shhtomping of our feet :)"

For some, the knowledge of their past is viewed with more ambivalence and irony, as this post demonstrates:

> yeah !!!!
> go, team hippy!
> :)
> love, happy vibes, patchouli, nag champa, white daisy flowers, smiling faces, group hugs :)
> bright colours, and doing things for people not expecting anything in return . .
> spread the good vibes
> i am not going to pretend i live and breath these ideals, but some of the best experiences of my life have contained many of these elements :)
> open energy returns open energy
> :)

But most accept that they are part of a larger little culture with a history. As one person soberly reminded the Goa trance mailing list in early August 1999:

> this is our history. . . . its good to know the players . . . . . .
> kesey and the pranksters
> leary and league od spiritual discovery
> the gratefuldead (house band at the acid tests)
> owsley (bear)—the deads 1st soundman and the FIRST MAJOR UNDERGROUND PRODUCER OF ACID
> neal cassidy - beat writer/visionary - (the dean moriarty character in ON THE ROAD by KEROAC) was the bus driver on FURTHUR - the merry pranksters famous psychedelic bus
> and along with ALAN GINSBURG the link between beat culture and hippoe/psychedelic culture
> ginsburg, an amazing beat poet, infused the psychedelic movement with much of spiritual sense and style
> as responsible as any one person for the link between psychedelic culture and india—(setting the stage for goa as a center. . . .)[60]

This is not the space in which to recapitulate the history of the American youth counterculture in the 1960s.[61] But theorists of ritual, religion, and altered states have occasionally mentioned the hippies, and their insights are useful in understanding this group in order to differentiate it from the Goa/psy trance group.

Victor Turner, for example, compares tribesmen to hippies in their communitas and writes that it is not the same thing that arises between friends or coworkers; tribesmen and hippies seek, rather, "a transformative experience that goes to the root of each person's being and finds in that root something profoundly communal and shared." Turner goes on to make a link between "existence" and "ecstasy" and theorizes what I have been calling the vibe; "ecstasy" is a way of standing outside, standing outside of all of the "structural positions one normally occupies in a social system."[62] This characterization is little different from that of Durkheim: "the ego cannot be something completely other than itself, for, if it were, it would vanish—this is what happens in ecstasy."[63] This is, again, the vibe. It is striking that the drug used in the rave scene (though less in the Goa/psy trance little culture) is called Ecstasy.

Erika Bourguignon also considers the syncretic use of symbols from many different cultures and religions, which I have already noted with respect to the Goa/psy trance little culture in New York City.[64] She notes that American youth culture in the 1960s involved no large-scale organization, but many small groups, which differed widely in their social and religious forms. Generally there was a rejection of the "establishment" way of life, a search for a new life and new consciousness. Bourguignon also observes that there was a lack of ideological sharing among the aspects of the "movement," on the one hand, and the ideological isolation from the larger society on the other: the isolation of a segment of an age group that largely represented a particular education and economic stratum of society; a search for a new way of life, not for solutions to problems of daily living in the existing society; a wish to find alternative ways of living, and thus not only to modify the society but to modify the self. Bourguignon concludes that altered states are not gradually learned and framed within a religious tradition that has long made use of them; on the contrary, altered states are induced by drugs to result in "instant mysticism" or by dramatic conversion experiences.[65]

Despite these similarities there are differences, and the main point of cleavage concerns technology. If the hippie movement was a revolt against an increasingly technocratic society, today's Goa/psy trance fans

have embraced technology—they are far from the musicians and listeners we encountered in other chapters with anxieties about technology.[66] Fans understand its centrality to the music, but don't seem to
worry about its compromised role as a product of Western rationality.
Accepting technology, the machine, also means that the Goa/psy trance
fan is not always interested in nature; there are occasionally derisive
comments about "tree huggers" on the Goa trance mailing list. Instead
of participating in "nature," Goa/psy trance people attempt to natural-
ize technology, turn it into something ancient and inevitable, not the
product of Western scientific rationality that decreases one's humanity.
This is accomplished in part through the use of a kind of fable and
vaguely religious mode of rhetoric when describing the ancient ritual
of dancing and trance such as we have already seen; Goa/psy trance's
putative relationship to ancient musics is underlain by the familiar
Western equation of the tribal or primitive with the natural. Some such
stories mention technology explicitly, such as the following liner notes
from a trance CD:

> The all-night dance ritual is a memory that runs deep within us
> all, a memory that takes us back to a time when people had
> respect for our great Mother Earth and each other. A time when
> we came together to dance as one tribe united in spirit. We under-
> stood the cycles of nature and the power of the elements. We
> danced around great fires, we chanted and we drummed, invoking
> the great spirit to empower ourselves and our community.
>
> Then one day a new force began to take control and these great
> rites of community empowerment were suppressed. Our sacred
> sites where we once danced all night into ecstatic trance had been
> taken over by a new order of worship; forcing us to sit down in
> cold silence and listen, no love. The new forces were strong. They
> released a Papal Decree (an early draft of the CJB) which forbade
> all rituals. They smashed our temples and burnt our healers. They
> put the fire goddess in chains and burnt her at the stake.
>
> They worked hard to eradicate the memory of the dance ritual
> but it remained as a seed deep within us all, to emerge one day in a
> new age, the age of Technology.[67]

Technology can be naturalized because there is no other nature that
really concerns the people in this little culture.

Victor Turner, in his brief look at hippies in *The Ritual Process*, wrote that musical expressions of communitas were often accomplished with simple instruments.[68] He reasons that this is because of their portability, but I would say that these instruments were of interest to members of the counterculture not so much because of their portability, but because of their supposed naturalness: simple wooden instruments.[69] Few of these instruments, however, are of interest to the psy trance crowd.

And this is not a group concerned with natural health, the concern of hippies and other social activists that matured at the same time. In early August 1999 one person posted a link to a site with information about genetically modified food, prefacing her message with "At the risk of sounding like a hippocrit," and elicited this response, among others: "well, for the sake of internal fucking consistency, why don't you go back to banging on wooden drums and strumming your guitar then? fuckin' hippies."

And those who emphasize the PLUR-y aspects of the scene in ways reminiscent of hippies can come in for ridicule. Several people wrote in to the Goa trance mailing list after a big outdoor party in Nevada over Labor Day weekend in 1999, decrying the hippie influence. This party featured, among others, DJ Goa Gil. One person complained that "we were walking back from the burn and i heard some fucking hippie up on stage start wailing 'can i get a collective oommm??' so i took the hint and scarpered back to my camp ASAP." Another user, writing about the same event, said that "I didn't get to enjoy much of the community dance . . . mostly becuase it was cold. Lots of people had an issue with the e x t e n d e d ritual . . . which I can sympathize with. A ritual should be a brief, bonding experience, IMHO [in my humble opinion] . . . not a 1+ hour theaterical production of tired hippie flim flam." Last, yet another complained that this party had "a bit of the usual 'goddammed hippie' lack of internal consistency (ie, the 'you are entering a non-commercial zone' sign on the way in, only to be greeted with the huge fucking coffee tent which we referred to as Starbucks for the rest of the weekend)" although s/he generally liked the event.

Trance Music

What holds this vibe together? It's not just the crowd effervescing; it's also music. Kai Fikentscher says it's rhythm. But it's not rhythm generically, it's the beat, at roughly 140 beats per minute. The beat has almost a somatic effect; no matter how late it was or how tired I felt, being in a club environment, surrounded by the music undergirded so powerfully by the beat, I could keep going. But as soon as I left, as soon as the beat was out of earshot, my fatigue would come crashing back, as though my spine had just collapsed. It's as if the beat is a prop, something to lean on. The beat is almost always present; when it's not, it comes back quickly, or else the dance disintegrates. The presence of the beat isn't unique to this particular subgenre of contemporary electronic dance music, of course.

Another feature of much of the music is a bass drone. It's not a constant tone, but a drone that goes along with the beat or in another pattern that is reasonably unobtrusive and doesn't interfere with the melody or melodies on top. Not all techno musics have this drone, and its use in this music emphasizes the trance/vibe goals of the music and little culture; in a Western musical framework, drones are often used to signify the tribal, primitive other, and in this context probably help listeners/dancers get into the vibe, as well as facilitating the comparison between this music and the ancient, "tribal" music that trance is thought to be distantly related to.

The music has other features unique to its particular subgenre, but less related to contributing to the vibe. Fans describe some of these other sounds as interesting to people having a psychotropic experience. One of these sounds is the Roland TB-303 bass, an analog instrument used in earlier forms of dance music. This was a quirky machine that sold on its introduction in 1982 for about $1,000; a used one today can go for that much or more. Its sounds can be twangy, nasal, almost comical.[70] But the sound has taken on a near-cult status among fans of the music. Most listeners recognize the sound of it; for some, it is the defining sound of this music, even though it appears in other subgenres.

Most people in the trance music little culture like this music more than other kinds of techno; they don't understand the popularity of famous bands, such as the Chemical Brothers or Aphex Twin, that are approaching or achieving mainstream recognition and fame. In a conversation with one DJ at a party, we talked about his background as an acoustic musician—"I was always a music-head," he told me—and his preference for Goa/psychedelic trance after he becoming interested in DJing. He thinks this music is more complex and interesting than other forms of techno. Another DJ told me that he finds that Goa/psy trance has more "melodic content" than techno, and that "Aphex Twin has only done a couple of songs that moved me."

Emotionality seems to be important for many listeners, a quality linked to what the music is for: not just dancing, but facilitating the vibe, connections between people. As one person wrote to the Goa trance e-mail list, "it makes my head swim with wonder that something like beats and squeaks can invoke so many emotions inside of me." To outsiders, it may seem that this music isn't emotional at all, particularly since it is electronic and not acoustic. This is perhaps the reason that analog, not digital, electronic sounds are preferred, for they impart a certain warmth to the sound that is thought to be lacking in newer all-digital instruments. Purists would also say that the software that emulates the sound of the Roland TB-303 or other analog instrument isn't close enough to the original sound.

The structure was described by a fan as: "intro, beat, beat + melody 1, break down, build, harder beat + melody 1, big break down introducing melody 2, build, build, build, hard beat maybe a breakbeat with melody 2, small break, beat with melody 1 and 2, start removing layers of the track, end of track."[71] Not all songs obey this format, criticized as formulaic, but the general trajectory is reasonably accurate. Most tracks build, melodies change, and there are always a few moments when the beat drops out (referred to by fans as a "break down"), which makes listeners/dancers feel as though they are at the edge of an abyss, only to be rescued at the last possible moment by the return of the beat.

Even though insiders frequently describe the music as melodic, it is not always melodic in the sense that acoustic music is; many of the "melodies" are less the "tunes" of most other popular music, but the sweeps and swoops made possible by the technology that the musicians use. And many of the sounds that appear to be changing, moving the music along, are changing not in terms of pitch or rhythm—the main elements of analog music; rather, pitch and rhythm might stay the same while the producer twiddles knobs to alter the quality of the sound itself. It gets more nasal, less nasal, whatever. This is a much different way of thinking in music than analog musicians possess.

The effect of twiddling these knobs that control various parameters of the sound not only choreographs the music in some sense—spatializes it—but also puts the music in your head in a certain way; it's like a thought that you are changing, or observing while it changes. It's as though the sound, as it metamorphoses, is boring itself into your head and out again, dramatizing the move from inside to outside of the self that so many people value in the scene.

Until fairly recently, most of this music required certain hardware: a computer, a sampler, a drum machine, recording equipment, a mixer, and more. But increasingly there is software available that makes it possible to produce electronic trance (or other kinds of dance music) with nothing other than a computer and some relatively inexpensive software that emulates the sounds of the Roland TB-303 and other classic analog instruments. And increasingly there are DJs who don't have vinyl discs (or CDs, for that matter) at all, but instead bring computers with hard drives full of MP3s to their gigs, though I never witnessed this. There is now MP3 playing software that allows one to cue up and mix MP3 recordings just as though they were vinyl.[72] Some of this (and other music) software is quite expensive (VisioSonic's Digital 1200SL is nearly $700, for example) but illegal free copies circulate on the Internet, allowing anyone who is interested to use them.

As might be evident from the description of the structure above, the goal of the music is to take listeners/dancers on a journey. As one DJ told me, he thinks of a DJ set as one large piece. Each song must logically follow the previous one, and if you know you want to get from point A to point B, you have to choose songs accordingly. Each song is a journey itself, so his goal is to put these little parts together into something bigger. DJs in other electronic dance musics speak this way as well, but in Goa/psychedelic trance, the journey is less metaphorical. People are hoping to dance and listen their way outside of themselves and into the collective.

Care and Feeding of the Vibe

While the vibe experience seems to be central, it isn't the only experience that draws in listeners. Some, after all, just come to dance, some to be with their friends, some for the drugs, some to get out of the house. Nonetheless, much of what transpires in the Goa/psychedelic trance little culture in New York City can be seen as geared toward the care and feeding of the vibe. I want to talk about some factors separately, but let me lay them all out now. First, this is a remarkably apolitical little culture, apolitical in terms of interpersonal politics, and more, public politics. Second, despite the early nature of Goa music sampling Indian music and clips from movies, the preferred Goa/psy trance heard in New York City almost never has any samples or recognizable words, although music with such samples continues to be made, although less frequently now. Third, unlike some dance music little cultures, there isn't really a cult of the DJ in Goa/psy trance music. People appreciate a good DJ and criticize a bad one, but what really matters is the presence and quality of the vibe, which isn't solely due to the efforts of the DJ.

Let's take these points in order, starting with the absence of politics. If someone attempts to interject a political issue into the Goa trance e-mail list, he is asking for it. In September of 1999, the following message was in response to a poster who was attempting to inform the list members of what was going on in East Timor. The response: "This has nothing to do with trance and I personally think that this tree-huggin' hippy soap-boxism belongs elsewhere." Several people told me the only political issue that people in the trance scene cared about and could agree on was the legalization of marijuana.

However, it is not just politics in this broader, public sense that are generally avoided. At the first party I went to, the notice hanging above the coat check window struck me: "Leave your issues at the door." In other words, come in to dance, and dance only. A nineteen-year-old deeply involved in the scene told me that he doesn't tolerate "politics" in any way, by which he means no egos, no personal issues, just appreciation of the music. He likes the traditional ideas behind trance music: that it is supposed to allow listeners to be transcendent, to evolve through music. He said that the current scene is full of people who present themselves as being interested in these things, but are actually "full of crap"; they don't love the music. There are very few people who are interested in the music for the sake of music, which is what the absence of politics (or "issues") means for these people. No politics, no resistance either, as far as I can tell. But if we are viewing this little culture as a religion, the absence of politics makes more sense. Politics might get in the way of the vibe.

Many of the people I got to know in the scene are DJs or promoters. Most of these people have day jobs, and they want to keep it that way. They don't want to go professional and run the risk of losing the pleasure of doing what they do; the politics, the job, the work environment, would get in the way, and they might be branded as selling out to commercial culture.

There are also no sexual politics. These parties are not places to pick up people for sex, at least so far as I could tell. Psy trance regulars, both men and women, do not dress to be provocative; they seem to be almost deliberately unsexy. Sexual motives were so absent at all the parties I attended that I never noticed. Until, that is, the night of the party attended by the stockbrokers; in my field notes from August 13, 1999, I wrote, "This was a different crowd than the usual psy trance crowd. Testosterone levels were high; the women were girls."

The second point concerning sampling is also interesting. An early list of definitions on the Internet talks about samples from old science-fiction movies, and many of early Goa/psychedelic recordings had these sounds and many others.[73] Yet, in the New York City little culture, these are not played, partly because, of course, they're too old, but also because, I think, they're too "significant," too connected to "real world," outside sounds, and thus images and meanings. This might sound a bit tenuous, but what prompted this line of thinking is the preponderance of tracks that have sounds that are *almost* language, either samples that are mixed too far down to be audible, or synthesized sounds that emulate speech but aren't actually language. Language and meaning both are being called into question with such music—called into question but not actually utilized, for the comparative directness of language might detract from the spiritual goal of the scene and compromise the vibe.

The fact that most of this music has no recognizable samples or intelligible vocals, or samples of vocals, is clearly the point for many people. In the summer of 1999, someone wrote in to the Goa trance e-mail list requesting information on vocals in Goa trance. Given the anonymity and impersonality of Internet communications compared to f2f ("face-to-face") meetings, PLUR seem to be more difficult to sustain, and this person was widely ridiculed in the many responses that her query elicited. For most people, the absence of vocals/lyrics was the point. As one fan writes, "The great thing is with no words (or at least very few) there is no side taken and no message except the world can come together to make the words for itself (i hope that fmakes sence, oh well i know what im talkin about) any way it is a wonderfull thing!!!"[74] Another person said that it's this very ambiguity that allows him/her to interpret the music. The absence of lyrics has other benefits, as discussed before; it means there's no chance that an overt political message can be enunciated. Additionally, as users are fond of pointing out, it makes it possible for this music to travel easily around the world, since it needs no translation.

Third, the DJ in the Goa/psy trance little culture in New York City is not some kind of shaman, or god substitute, as some have said about the DJ in other electronic dance music little cultures.[75] Some clubs decorate the DJ booth a bit to make it the center of the crowd's attention, but DJs themselves do not cultivate this attention. In the Goa/psy trance little culture in New York City, DJs are simply a critical constituent in a complex interplay of site, visuals, sound system, dancers, clothes, drugs, and music. DJs are kind of hyperconsumers of this music whose performances are ritualized ways of sharing their knowledge and connoisseurship with listeners; as one DJ told me, buying all the records of certain labels or artists is "a completionism that I have." People come to clubs not so much to hear the DJ, or even for a particular kind of music, but to dance. Even in terms of making the music, one person told me that what is required is a readiness to do it, not talent.

In classic social theory of religion and group behavior, Weber and Durkheim differed on the necessity of a galvanizing individual to ignite the crowd. Durkheim thought this would happen naturally and spontaneously; Weber thought that a charismatic leader was required. Charles Lindholm, who attempted to synthesize the work of Weber, Durkheim, and crowd psychologists, used this synthesis to analyze two different nontraditional religious groups in the United States, and usefully argues that, in a Durkheimian framework, "charisma exists only in the group; the charismatic leader who is Weber's hero is here a passive symbol serving as a catalyst "around whom the collective can solidify and resonate. . . . There is communication between this figure and the collective which further heightens emotion, leading to greater challenges to the ego and more potent feelings of exaltation."[76]

In the Goa/psy trance (and other electronic dance music) little cultures, this figure is the DJ. There can't be a party without a DJ, but the DJ isn't the focal point. The DJ booth at Vinyl in New York City, at least during Tsunami events, has candles around it, which gives it more of a religious flavor. Unlike some other underground dance music little cultures, New York City Goa/psy trance DJs never talk to the crowd during their sets; their sets are all about providing music for dancing, nothing more. Individual DJ sets are not demarcated, either; when one is playing his/her last record, the next DJ is cueing up their first in order to effect a seamless transition. The important thing is to keep the energy on the dance floor going; any pause or break is not simply a pause or break, but a "trainwreck" in the words of one how-to guide written by the DJ I knew best in the scene.[77] So the concern of fans is less the quality of the DJ, who is not the solitary genius as in so much of Western culture, but the quality and presence of PLUR, or vibe. One reviewer's main complaint of one party was that, even though he thought the DJs were good, "There was no PLUR" (a sentiment actually at odds with my own impression of this particular party).[78]

Dancers and DJs understand this, and talk to each other about it. One wrote to the Goa trance e-mail list in the spring of 1999 to say, "Synergy between DJ and dancers is also vital, as you can't have an ego-surpassing experience without the cooperative effect. If you let give a DJ positive reinforcement, they will be likely to have the confidence to mix well or to choose the 'right track.' Likewise, the DJ's music has to give dancers the the journey they need without ruining the flow (how do you know if no-one's dancing)." Another wrote, "The importance probably lies in the ability to nuture and give to a vibe that is there. A DJ can attempt to move the party in a particular direction but ideally that direction was inspired by the party itself. If the DJ has his (they are mostly men) own agenda outside of being aware of the subtlties of the groove than proper openings to move and shift gears will be missed or disregarded and the vibe will become disassociative or just feel shit."

Even Moby, a superstar techno DJ if there ever was one, participated in this exchange with an online interviewer:

> *What's your take on the dynamic of the Trinity: Producer/DJ/ Dancer—what makes that complete?*
> Hopefully what makes the trinity complete is when the DJ & producer & dancer are one and the same thing/person.[79]

People involved in throwing these parties are very mindful of keeping the vibe going. Whatever social aspect might be lost in the technological/computerized making of the music is compensated for in many ways in clubs. One DJ I interviewed talked about his preferences for the DJ booth. He said that it's good to have a bit of a raised stage so you can see the crowd a little; you want to be a part of the crowd still, but you want to be able to see around a little bit. He said that you have to watch the crowd to know if you're holding their attention—that's the whole point. A producer in an online interview said that he imagines his music on the dance floor while composing it: "There is some energy, you might call it 'inspiration' that a producer feels in the process of making a track, in my case I can almost visualize the place or situation a track will be played when making it and how I would want the crowd to react. . . . The DJ is in a sense a 'channeler', they take energy from themselves, the records their playing and of course their audience and use their alchemy to enhance each and return it to the dancer. It's a perfect union."

This energy, inspiration, union are, of course, all constituents of the vibe, the electronic version of groove.

At one party in New York City—the one about which the above reviewer wrote that "there was no PLUR"—the sound system conked out. Rather than being angry, people were concerned and disappointed—anger would destroy the vibe, or the possibility of the vibe. I went downstairs where people were paying admission, and while I was talking to the person at the cash register, two girls (not more than sixteen or seventeen years old) came in to say that the sound system wasn't working. They didn't complain, they didn't get angry; rather, their tone suggested that this mishap was an unfortunate thing that had happened to their community and what could be done about it? This is the kind of care and feeding of the vibe that I witnessed all the time, by party organizers and dancers in New York City.

Eschewing, for the most part, youth subculture theory allows us to understand the nonpolitical—or postpolitical—nature of this group. I am not ready to declare that today's youth are apolitical, or, as Maffesoli says, aloof from politics. Seeking the vibe, attempting to heal the world, as one person told me his efforts in the trance scene were about, may not sound very political, but it is still worthwhile.

Goa/psy trance people do not simply deemphasize the individual, as Maffesoli would have it; after all, you can't have communitas without individuals coming together, and you can't transcend the self without having a self to transcend. The individual wanes, but temporarily. After the party, psy trancers go slowly back to their profane, languid lives, which are made tolerable by their memories and anticipations of their connectedness.

ANXIETY,

CONSUMPTION,

AND AGENCY

A piano or a violin is just as inorganic as a synthesizer or a sampler.

—*Moby, "The DJ Speaks"*

The introduction of every major new technology, at least in the course of the twentieth century, has been accompanied by a complex mixture of wonderment and anxiety. Digital technology is no different. These anxieties have at bottom serious questions about humans and humanity. Two most salient of these questions are: to what extent does today's technology diminish human agency? On a larger level, to what extent does technology have the capacity to turn human history into its own history?

Those who have celebrated new technologies throughout the twentieth century have usually sought to allay the more anxiety-producing aspects of those new technologies. Commentators about radio in the 1920s and 1930s argued that democracy will be enhanced by that new technology. You have probably heard the same thing said about the Internet. Commentators about early radio also noted the rise of an information highway. You have heard that one before. Commentators about radio also believed that the borders of countries will be rendered meaningless. You have heard that one before, too.

Mention of these claims is not intended to make the point that nothing is new with today's technology. Rather, the larger argument I would like to make concerns the fundamentally social nature of digital—or any—technology. Here we are in the putative Information Age, but the claims that one hears about the technologies that are bringing us this information, as we have seen, are not new. Claims such as the ones I have just outlined are based not on the new availability of information or the historical record but instead tend to be based on people's own experiences and memories.[1]

This does not mean, however, that history does not play a role in the cultural discourses of and reactions to a major new technology. One of the perennial anxieties that a new technology contributes to concerns history, that human history might end up being a history of technology instead (a fear registered in the 1999 film *The Matrix*, in which human "reality" is nothing other than a virtual reality created for them by artificial intelligence machines, and that the "real" reality occupied by the film's heroes is about two hundred years later). This anxiety resonates in particular with the subjects of chapters 3 and 4, but particularly chapter 3, on *musique concrète*, in which postwar musicians in France and Germany attempted to come to grips with what new technologies meant for them, and how they were going to continue, or re-create, Western European art music after the horrors of World War II. Locating themselves in a prestigious history was a way for the Austrio-German composers and their aesthetic ally Pierre Boulez to claim the greatest prestige for themselves and their work following the war. Further, these composers sought make the purest forms possible, to deny all nonmusical meanings. Failure to do so ran the risk of opening the Pandora's Box of social values, history, nationalism—all the things that these early postwar composers sought to exclude from their musical concerns while they concentrated on its formal properties. In attempting to claim the highest prestige in this era, they sought to make new electronic musics whose inclusion in the great history of Western European art music could be justified, at the same time attempting to empty out any mode of signification that might have betrayed the origins of their works in their own moment in time.

Pierre Henry, on the other hand, who professed no such anxiety about the historical significance of his music, spoke of music as something that can be expressive. Some of the sounds Henry made, especially *Messe pour le temps présent*, make it easier for today's listeners to locate Henry's music in history and find meanings, which has facilitated Henry's rehabilitation by DJs and producers, as we saw, as they construct their own histories of their music.

While I have no doubt Boulez and the Austro-German composers with whom he was aesthetically allied were just as concerned about the future—posterity—other musicians we have encountered make concerns for the future more of an identifiable theme in their works. Anxiety about the future, or whether or not there would actually be a future, was paired with a buoyant optimism about those same technologies that were causing anxiety, as we saw in the chapters on space age pop music and its resurrection. The space-age pop of the 1950s and early 1960s addressed both the hyperbolic claims about technology made in that era while at the same time frequently treating them with irony and playfulness, in sound and in graphic design. Space-age pop revivalists, as collectors and musicians, display a kind of nostalgia for that earlier optimism since the technology promised in the past never arrived in their—our—own time.

For many of these fans, though, collecting these space-age pop albums provides a way of owning those earlier values, that optimism, even though these collectors know that the promise of technology in the 1950s is largely unfulfilled. These collectors point to another theoretical issue that I want to revisit here—consumption. The consumption of music has scarcely been examined in recent writings on music, but it is an important way, even the primary way, that most people in the so-called developed countries experience music as one of many kinds of commodities they consume in their lives.[2] There is currently a fashion for—even a dominance of—theories (whether by Max Horkheimer and Theodor Adorno, or Jean Baudrillard, or Friedrich Kittler, or others) that minimize the role of the consumer and maximize the role of the theorist in order to make pessimistic (or worse) claims about the contemporary moment, as if the average listener/consumer is a mindless automaton who, wittingly or not, is being sold a bill of goods. In making this critique in chapter 1 and reiterating it here I am not simply echoing the important contributions of the Birmingham School and others who emphasize that consumers make their own meanings out of what they consume. Scholars who actually talk to consumers and find out what they are thinking and doing offer more insights into consumers and consumption. Anthropologists of consumption have demonstrated, as noted in chapter 2, the ways in which consumption is simply not a mindless pleasure for people, but instead is caught up in social and kinship relations. Meanings people make might be less an example of the polysemy of popular culture than the Birmingham School might like, yet the act of consumption itself is not simply a mindless act, but one that has social meanings, and as such should neither be uncritically dismissed by those theorists who advocate a kind of "top-down" model of consumption, and, likewise, should not be uncritically celebrated by those who advocate a somewhat more "bottom-up" model.[3] In short, I have been advocating a theory of consumption that takes seriously the position of the consumer as agent, not the hapless, helpless consumer whom markets act against as is too often assumed to be the case.

Taking the consumer seriously as a subject and agent brings me to the last, and most important, theoretical issue I would like to revisit in these remaining paragraphs. Advocating a practice theory of technology in the second chapter, I argued that technology is a special kind of structure in the classic social science sense: it is a structure that both makes agents and is made by them; a structure, unlike any other, that consists of both schemas (rules) and resources, not one or the other as structures are taken to be.

Perhaps the best example of this is the subject of the previous chapter, psy trance music and musicians. These musicians employ vinyl and turntables—old technologies both, but nonetheless the preferred technologies of this group, and of dance music "little cultures" generally. The turntable (the descendent of the gramophone) is a technology that made it possible to have music anytime, and that threatened to turn producers of music into consumers of music, that threatened, in this shift from production to consumption, to remove music and musicking from their roots as social activities. And by and large it did. People who might have once made their own music learned to buy it instead. Concepts such as genius, talent, and masterpiece that inhibit many people from making music became even more instantiated in Western European cultures. The rise of the hip hop and dance music DJ, however, redefined the function of the turntable: no longer simply a reproductive device, it became a productive one as well. Human agency struck back. And psy trance and other DJs resocialized the turntable: music sounded by turntables at parties brings people together. People care about the quality of the DJ, as we saw, not as a genius creator, but as one among them whose presence is vital but not the sole reason for their gathering. Technology as a structure in the form of the gramophone/turntable might have actively changed peoples' behavior with respect to music, but people also changed the turntable and in part retrieved what had been lost.

I can also mention here the examples of Toby Marks (Banco de Gaia) and Bryn Jones (Muslimgauze). These musicians' self-representations project a kind of cloaked superagency in that they deliberately obscure who they are as individuals, but their positionality as creators is never in doubt. Marks and Jones don't evince any anxiety about technology as a structure that might threaten their agency. They are, however, embarked on a different kind of agential project than most of the other musicians in this study. Rather than being engaged in a struggle to maintain agency in the face of an encroaching technology, their struggle is to formulate a technologized musical self without a public with whom they routinely interact.

In the absence of a social situation, as when these musicians are making their music at home alone, Marks and Jones invoke a social situation through the extensive use of samples and engagement with distant political causes. It is not coincidental that the causes espoused by these musicians are concerned with identities rooted in places (Tibet and Palestine, respectively). Marks and Jones may be actors with the agency to shape digital technology as structure, but the lack of other live actors in the making of their music renders their positionality moot; unless, that is, they make self-representations, affiliate themselves with political causes, and sample musics by other musicians, all of which serve to reintegrate these detached actor/agents with at least a simulated social environment that animates their agency in the face of the potentially dehumanizing nature of digital technology even as these particular actors do not actively project anxiety about it.

As a last consideration of the question of agency, let me return to the case of Enigma versus the Kuos. If one listened to the two tracks that sample the Kuos' song, Enigma's "Return to Innocence" and the remix by Dan Lacksman, they aren't that different. Each extensively sample the original song; Michael Cretu of Enigma adds some lyrics and a female vocalist, so his version sounds more like a "song" (with a verse/chorus format), while Lacksman's is essentially a remix. But knowledge of the circumstances under which these tracks were produced changes everything. In knowingly permitting Lacksman to remix their song, the Kuos, to adapt a phrase from Marshall Berman, were in a position to become subjects in this global/informational moment, rather than objects, as they had been in Enigma's song.[4]

Earlier I addressed the ways that celebrations of technology usually overlook histories of earlier technologies. This is a familiar strategy employed by those who seek to emphasize the benefits of technology. Negative claims, not always historically informed themselves, are usually made on what the particular commentator takes to be other peoples' experiences and memories, without, however, consulting them, in the same way that the "top-down" orientation of some scholars of consumption operate. These commentators, professionally anxious about what they perceive to be the negative effects of technology, are as guilty of oversimplification as those who celebrate technology. To the technological pessimists, technology is a kind of disease for which they are the lone diagnosticians. "I am in the position of Louis Pasteur," writes Marshall McLuhan of what for him was a particularly virulent strain of technology, the television, "telling doctors that their greatest enemy was quite invisible, and quite unrecognized by them."[5]

But McLuhan, writing in 1964, was only the most recent in a long line of pessimists with respect to technology. And he overstated his case. If we view technology as fundamentally and profoundly social, if we view it as something that people do, if we define it, as does anthropologist Bryan Pfaffenberger, as "humanized nature," then it becomes clear that blows against human agency and human history were never struck.[6] Technology, however awe inspiring and anxiety producing it may seem to be upon its introduction to the realm of human social life, quickly becomes part of social life, naturalized into quotidian normality as it helps people do things they have always done: communicate, create, labor, remember, experience pleasure, and, of course, make and listen to music.

NOTES

Chapter One

1. Jacques Attali, *Noise: The Political Economy of Music*, trans. Brian Massumi; Theory and History of Literature vol. 16 (Minneapolis: University of Minnesota Press, 1985), 47.

2. Their site's URL is http://www.mh2o.com. See N'Gai Croal and Walaika Haskins, "Music Made Easy," *Newsweek*, October 25, 1999, 91–92.

3. Michael Dertouzos, *What Will Be: How the New World of Information Will Change Our Lives* (New York: HarperCollins, 1997), 113.

4. Ibid., 154–55; emphasis in the original.

5. Langdon Winner, "Technology Today: Utopia or Dystopia?" *Social Research* 64 (fall 1997), 1000–1001.

6. I am indebted to Paul Yoon for this point.

7. For an interesting discussion of older technologies as innovations, see Carolyn Marvin, *When Old Technologies Were New: Thinking about Electric Communication in the Late Nineteenth Century* (New York: Oxford University Press, 1988).

8. See Lewis Mumford, "Technics and the Nature of Man," *Technology and Culture* 7 (summer 1966): 303–17, for a critique of this point; Mumford says this belief goes back to the nineteenth century. Carroll Pursell attributes it to Benjamin Franklin (Pursell, *White Heat: People and Technology* [Berkeley and Los Angeles: University of California Press, 1994], 15).

9. Michael Adas, *Machines As the Measure of Men: Science, Technology, and Ideologies of Western Dominance*, Cornell Studies in Comparative History (Ithaca: Cornell University Press, 1989), 3. See also Bernard Stiegler, *The Fault of Epimetheus*, vol. 1 of *Technics and Time*, trans. Richard Beardsworth and George Collins; Meridian/Crossing Aesthetics (Stanford: Stanford University Press, 1998).

10. Timothy D. Taylor, *Global Pop: World Music, World Markets* (New York: Routledge, 1997).

11. Manuel Castells, *The Rise of the Network Society*, vol. 1 of *The Information Age: Economy, Society and Culture* (Cambridge, Mass.: Blackwell, 1996), 66; empahsis in the original.

12. For another discussion of the importance of the margins in understanding larger social processes and music, see Timothy D. Taylor, "Peopling the Stage: Opera, Otherness, and New Musical Representations in the Eighteenth Century," *Cultural Critique* 36 (spring 1997): 55–88. For a more general discussion of margins and centers, see Mary Douglas, *Purity and Danger: An Analysis of Concepts of Pollution and Taboo* (Harmondsworth, England: Penguin, 1970).

13. I should note, however, that the Internet does not offer a uniform sample of listening but rather tends to be a tool of the relatively affluent, educated, Western European, English-speaking male.
14. Taylor, *Global Pop*, xvii.
15. Michel Foucault, *The Archaeology of Knowledge*, trans. A. M. Sheridan Smith (New York: Pantheon, 1972), 27.
16. Terry Eagleton, *The Illusions of Postmodernism* (Cambridge, Mass.: Blackwell, 1996), 30.
17. Taylor, *Global Pop*, xvii–xviii.
18. There is one exception, which seems to have been unnoticed by most who have written about music and technology: Jon Frederickson, "Technology and Performance in the Age of Mechanical Reproduction," *International Association of the Aesthetics and Sociology of Music* 20 (December 1989): 193–220.
19. *Electronica* is an umbrella term for a fast-growing group of musics that depend to a large extent on the use of digital technology; in 1997, electronica was touted as the next big thing by the sales-depressed music industry. See Larry Flick and Doug Reece, "Electronic Music Poised for Power Surge in States," *Billboard*, February 15, 1997, 1; Karen Schoemer, "Electronic Eden," *Newsweek*, February 10, 1997, 60–62; and Neil Strauss, "The Next Big Thing or the Next Bust?" *New York Times*, January 26, 1997, sec. H, p. 36.
20. Grant McCracken, *Plenitude* (Toronto: Periph.: Fluide, 1997), 25.

Chapter Two

1. Given the speed at which MP3 and other technologies change, a lot of what you are reading here will likely be out of date or irrelevant. There is a website (of course) that keeps up with MP3 news: MP3 Newswire, at http://www.mp3newswire.net/.
2. See Paul Théberge, *Any Sound You Can Imagine: Making Music/Consuming Technology*, Music/Culture (Hanover, N.H.: University Press of New England, 1997), for an important study of the production and use of electronic instruments. For a recent consideration of the changing nature of the music industry in the face of digital technologies, see Reebee Garofalo, "From Music Publishing to MP3: Music and Industry in the Twentieth Century," *American Music* 17 (fall 1999): 318–53.
3. Raymond Williams, *The Politics of Modernism: Against the New Conformists*, ed. Tony Pinkney (London: Verso, 1989), 120; emphasis in the original.
4. Some colleges and universities are currently acceding to threats of lawsuits from the Recording Industry Association of America (RIAA) over downloading MP3s. See Lisa Guernsey, "MP3-Trading Service Can Clog Networks on College Campuses," *New York Times*, January 20, 2000, 3; David Kushner, "Napster Terrorizes Music Biz," *Rolling Stone*, April 27, 2000, 25; and Robert Menta, "Students Fight to Save Napster," MP3 Newswire, 3 March 2000, http://www.mp3newswire.net/stories/2000/studentnap. html.
5. Once MP3s are uploaded to the World Wide Web, the owners of the MP3s are sitting ducks for the copyright holders ("We will find you," said Hilary Rosen, president of the Recording Industry Association of America), so most people post only lists of their MP3s that they're willing to trade (Arik Hesseldahl, "Rosen: SDMI Is Your Friend," *Wired*, August 10, 1999, http://www.wired.com/news/culture/0,1284,21205,00.html). But there are a growing number of Usenet newsgroups devoted to specific genres and/or decades (such as alt.binaries.sounds.country.mp3 or alt.binaries.sounds.

mp3.1950s), and people post files to these and other groups all the time; users also post requests that are usually fulfilled. Most people who post music to these and other newsgroups use pseudonyms in their e-mail addresses, though they could probably be tracked down easily enough by a savvy copyright infringement hunter. The Recording Industry Association of America (RIAA), whose main concern these days seems to be piracy—that is, the practice of making and distributing illegal copies of recordings— is now saying that they are shifting most of their attention to online piracy rather than tape duplication (Recording Industry Association of America, "Piracy," http://www.riaa.com/piracy/piracy.htm).

6. M. William Krasilovsky and Sidney Shemel, *This Business of Music*, 7th ed. (New York: Billboard Books, 1995), xxxii–xxxv.

7. As I write, a lawsuit mounted by the RIAA against MP3.com was won by the RIAA. A judged ruled that MP3.com had violated copyright law. See Amy Harmon and John Sullivan, "Music Industry Wins Ruling in U.S. Court," *New York Times*, April 29, 2000, sec. C, p. 1; and Jon Pareles, "MP3.com Hopes for Deal in Copyright Suit," *New York Times*, May 1, 2000, sec. C, p. 6.

8. See Louise Knapp, "Two Pentiums and a Microphone," *Wired*, September 21, 1999, http://www.wired.com/news/news/culture/story/19415.html. Digital 1200SL retails for $499.

9. Music Point has a website at http://www.cdwcorp.com/index.htm. I would like to thank Morgan Lang for telling me about Music Point. There were precursors to this type of personalized distribution at Tower Records and other retailers, but these failed to catch on.

10. While this quotation is somewhat incendiary, I should point out that Schoenberg was more sanguine about the possibilities of the mechanical reproduction and transmission of music elsewhere in his essay. Thanks are due to Joseph Auner for reminding me of this.

11. Simon Frith, "The Industrialization of Popular Music," in *Popular Music and Communication*, ed. James Lull, 2d ed. (Newbury Park, Calif.: Sage, 1992), 69.

12. Steven Johnson also discusses eclecticism in music consumption facilitated by digital technology in *Interface Culture: How New Technology Transforms the Way We Create and Communicate* (New York: HarperEdge, 1997), esp. 204–5.

13. David Harvey, *The Condition of Postmodernity: An Enquiry into the Origins of Cultural Change* (Cambridge, Mass.: Basil Blackwell, 1989).

14. See, most importantly, Jean Baudrillard's *Selected Writings*, ed. Mark Poster (Stanford, Calif.: Stanford University Press, 1988).

15. Scott Lash and John Urry, *Economies of Signs and Space*, Theory, Culture, and Society (Newbury Park, Calif.: Sage, 1994), 61.

16. See, for just a few histories, Jules Henry, *Culture against Man* (New York: Vintage, 1963); Jackson Lears, "A Matter of Taste: Corporate Cultural Hegemony in a Mass-Consumption Society," in *Recasting America: Culture and Politics in the Age of the Cold War*, ed. Lary May (Chicago: University of Chicago Press, 1989); and George Lipsitz, *Time Passages: Collective Memory and American Popular Culture*, American Culture (Minneapolis: University of Minnesota Press, 1990). For more theoretical arguments that discuss modernity and consumerism, see Zygmunt Bauman, *Modernity and Ambivalence* (Cambridge: Polity, 1991); Anthony Giddens, *Modernity and Self-Identity: Self and Society in the Late Modern Age* (Cambridge: Polity, 1991); and Don Slater, *Consumer Culture and Modernity* (Cambridge: Polity, 1997).

At the same time, however, I am mindful of the use of material objects in marking status and rank differences, which is an ancient practice. See, for just one discussion, Colin Renfrew, "Varna and the Emergence of Wealth in Prehistoric Europe," in *The Social Life of Things: Commodities in Cultural Perspective*, ed. Arjun Appadurai (Cambridge: Cambridge University Press, 1986).

17. I am indebted to James Manheim for this observation.

18. http://www.visiosonic.com. See Christopher Jones, "Digital DJs Phatten Up," *Wired*, November 27, 1999, http://www.wired.com/news/technology/0,1282,32705,00.html.

19. http://www.carrotinnovations.com/vtt_overview.shtml.

20. http://www.mixman.com. For more on Mixman software, see "Music Made Easier; It's All in the Mix," *New York Times*, 8 October 1998, sec. G, p. 7.

21. Langdon Winner, "Technology Today: Utopia or Dystopia?" *Social Research* 64 (fall 1997): 1000–1001.

22. Virgin's music website is at http://www.v2music.com/.

23. The Frankfurt School perspective is best represented in Max Horkheimer and Theodor Adorno, *Dialectic of Enlightenment*, trans. John Cumming (New York: Continuum, 1991). For Birmingham School discussions that operate from a "bottom-up" perspective, see Stuart Hall and Tony Jefferson, eds., *Resistance through Rituals: Youth Subcultures in Post-War Britain* (1976; reprint, New York: Routledge, 1993); Dick Hebdige, *Subculture: The Meaning of Style*, New Accents (1979; reprint, New York: Routledge, 1991); and Paul E. Willis, *Learning to Labor: How Working Class Kids Get Working Class Jobs* (New York: Columbia University Press, 1981).

    The Birmingham School, despite its welcome advances over the Frankfurt School's ideas, nonetheless is frequently overly rigid and deterministic with respect to social class. I would like to thank Steven Feld for pushing me on this point.

    Adorno's position is particularly disappointing given his participation in some quasi-ethnographic studies of music while working with Paul Lazarsfeld and others in their research into radio in the U.S. in the 1940s. Martin Jay writes that the methods of Lazarsfeld and others, involving questionnaires and interviews, were inadequate in Adorno's view "because the opinions of the listeners themselves were unreliable. Not only were they incapable of overcoming the conformity of cultural norms, but even more fundamentally, their ability to hear had itself degenerated" (Jay, *The Dialectical Imagination: A History of the Frankfurt School and the Institute of Social Research, 1923-1950*, 2d ed. [Berkeley and Los Angeles: University of California Press, 1973], 190). Jay writes in a later work that Adorno's hostility toward such empirical work later lessened (Jay, *Adorno* [Cambridge, Mass.: Harvard University Press, 1984], 39).

24. See Doug Hinman and Jason Brabazon, *You Really Got Me: An Illustrated World Discography of the Kinks, 1964–1993* (Rumford, R.I.: Doug Hinman, 1994) for a brief history of 8-track tape.

25. David Morton, "A History of Endless Loop Magnetic Recording Technology in the United States," http://www.rci.rutgers.edu/~dmorton/8track.html.

26. I would be remiss not to mention two Birmingham School ethnographies: Hebdige, *Subculture*, and Willis, *Learning to Labor*.

27. James G. Carrier and Josiah McC. Heyman, "Consumption and Political Economy," *Journal of the Royal Anthropological Institute* 3 (June 1997): 368–69.

28. For more on "New Times," see Stuart Hall and Martin Jacques, eds., *New Times: The Changing Face of Politics in the 1990s* (London and New York: Verso, 1990). For a tart rejoinder, see A. Sivanandan, "All That Melts into Air Is Solid: The Hokum of New Times," *Race and Class* 31 (1989): 1–30.

29. Daniel Miller, *A Theory of Shopping* (Ithaca, N.Y.: Cornell University Press, 1998), 35. See also Miller's "Consumption as the Vanguard of History: A Polemic by Way of an Introduction," in *Acknowledging Consumption: A Review of New Studies*, ed. Daniel Miller (New York: Routledge, 1995).

30. Stuart Hall, "Notes on Deconstructing 'The Popular,'" in *People's History and Socialist Theory*, ed. Raphael Samuel (London: Routledge and Kegan Paul, 1981), 228.

31. Leo Marx, "*Technology*: The Emergence of a Hazardous Concept," *Social Research* 64 (fall 1997): esp. 981–84.

32. Statements such as this are easy to find; here's a recent one, uttered by a senior software engineer with the Internet Technology group at IBM: "[E-mail] has already changed everything we do and changed it for good" (Michael Specter, "Your Mail Has Vanished," *New Yorker*, December 6, 1999, 103).

33. Bryan Pfaffenberger, "Fetishized Objects and Humanized Nature: Towards an Anthropology of Technology," *Man* 23 (June 1988): 241–42.

34. Robert McC. Adams, *Paths of Fire: An Anthropologist's Inquiry into Western Technology* (Princeton, N.J.: Princeton University Press, 1996), 8.

35. See Renfrew, "Varna and the Emergence of Wealth."

36. Langdon Winner, *The Whale and the Reactor: A Search for Limits in an Age of High Technology* (Chicago: University of Chicago Press, 1986), esp. 5–10.

37. There are generally thought to be two varieties of technological determinism, "hard" or "strong," and "soft" or "weak." For discussions of technological determinism, see Bruce Bimber, "Karl Marx, and the Three Faces of Technological Determinism," *Social Studies of Science* 20 (May 1990): 333–51; Ruth Finnegan, *Literacy and Orality: Studies in the Technology of Communication* (Oxford: Basil Blackwell, 1988); Nathan Rosenberg, ed., *Exploring the Black Box: Technology, Economics, and History* (Cambridge: Cambridge University Press, 1994); and Merrit Roe Smith and Leo Marx, eds., *Does Technology Drive History? The Dilemma of Technological Determinism* (Cambridge: MIT Press, 1994). See also Daniel Chandler's useful discussion on the Internet at http://www.aber.ac.uk/~dgc/tecdet.html.

38. See Winner, "Technology Today," and also "Prophets of Inevitability," *Technology Review*, March/April 1998, 62.

39. Paul Levinson, *Digital McLuhan: A Guide to the Information Millennium* (New York: Routledge, 1999).

40. Marshall McLuhan, *Understanding Media: The Extensions of Man* (1964; reprint, Cambridge, Mass.: MIT Press, 1994), 9.

41. Ibid., 18.

42. In this overstatement McLuhan was not alone. It is curious that no one, to my knowledge, has noted the correspondence between McLuhan's technological determinism and other cultural theories that similarly focus on a totalized structure that any individual subject is powerless to resist (except, of course, the theorist making this claim). This tactic of positing a total system that excludes only the omniscient theorist is, however, a common maneuver in much of modern social theory; e.g., Karl Marx wrote, in a very well-known passage from the preface to *A Contribution to the Critique of Political Economy* of 1859, "It is not the consciousness of men that determines their being, but, on the contrary, their social being that determines their consciousness" (Karl Marx, preface to *A Contribution to the Critique of Political Economy*, in *Karl Marx: Selected Writings*, ed. David McLellan [Oxford: Oxford University Press, 1977], 389). Change "being/social being" to "media" and we have McLuhan. Or we could substitute Jacques Lacan's unconscious or Jean Baudrillard's codes. This is not to declare

McLuhan a Marxist, or a pre-Lacanian or Baudrillardian, but to note his tendency, like these and other thinkers, to posit a total system that seemingly they, and only they, can rise above in order to expose.

43. Friedrich A. Kittler, *Gramophone, Film, Typewriter*, trans. Geoffrey Winthrop-Young and Michael Wutz (Stanford, Calif.: Stanford University Press, 1999), 80–81.

44. Arturo Escobar, "Welcome to Cyberia: Notes on the Anthropology of Cyberculture," *Current Anthropology* 35 (June 1994): 217.

45. Erin White, " 'Chatting' a Singer Up the Pop Charts—How Music Marketers Used the Web to Generate Buzz before an Album Debuted," *Wall Street Journal*, October 5, 1999, sec. B, p. 1.

46. See Richard Siklos, "Can RCA Records Keep on Rocking?" *Business Week*, November 29, 1999, 207.

47. http://www.electricartists.com/.

48. Ibid.

49. Raymond Williams, *Television: Technology and Cultural Form* (New York: Schocken, 1974), 14.

50. Ibid.

51. Jon Frederickson, "Technology and Performance in the Age of Mechanical Reproduction," *International Association of the Aesthetics and Sociology of Music* 20 (December 1989): 193–220; Théberge, *Any Sound You Can Imagine*, 160. Théberge emphasizes the practices surrounding technology in his more recent "Technology," in *Key Terms in Popular Music and Culture*, ed. Bruce Horner and Thomas Swiss (Malden, Mass.: Blackwell, 1999).

52. Michael Menser and Stanley Aronowitz, "On Cultural Studies, Science, and Technology," in *Technoscience and Cyberculture*, ed. Stanley Aronowitz et al. (New York: Routledge, 1996), 9; emphasis in the original.

53. José Ortega y Gasset, "Man the Technician," in *Toward a Philosophy of History*, trans. Helene Weyl (New York: W. W. Norton, 1941); Lewis Mumford, *Art and Technics* (New York: Columbia University Press, 1952). For useful overviews of the philosophy of technology, see Andrew Feenberg, *Questioning Technology* (New York: Routledge, 1999); and Carl Mitcham, *Thinking through Technology: The Path between Engineering and Philosophy* (Chicago: University of Chicago Press, 1994).

54. Martin Heidegger, "The Question Concerning Technology," in *Basic Writings*, ed. David Farrell Krell (San Francisco: HarperSanFrancisco, 1977). For useful commentaries, see Leo Marx, "On Heidegger's Conception of 'Technology' and Its Historical Validity," *Massachusetts Review* 25 (winter 1984): 638–52; and Samuel Weber, "Upsetting the Set Up: Remarks on Heidegger's Questing after Technics," *MLN* 104 (December 1989): 977–92. See also R. L. Rutsky, *High Technē: Art and Technology from the Machine Aesthetic to the Posthuman* (Minneapolis: University of Minnesota Press, 1999), esp. the introduction.

55. For other introductions/summaries, see David J. Hess, *Science Studies: An Advanced Introduction* (New York: New York University Press, 1997); Sal Restivo, "The Theory Landscape in Science Studies: Sociological Traditions," in *Handbook of Science and Technology Studies*, ed. Sheila Jasanoff et al. (Thousand Oaks, Calif.: Sage, 1995); and Ron Westrum, *Technologies and Society: The Shaping of People and Things* (Belmont, Calif.: Wadsworth, 1991).

56. Donald A. MacKenzie and Judy Wajcman, *The Social Shaping of Technology: How the Refrigerator Got Its Hum*, 2d ed. (Buckingham, England: Open University Press, 1999).

57. The systems approach is most strongly identified with the work of the American historian Thomas Hughes; see esp. *Networks of Power: Electrification in Western Society, 1880–1930* (Baltimore: Johns Hopkins University Press, 1983). For key texts of the "actor-network" approach, see Michel Callon, "Some Elements of a Sociology of Translation: Domestication of the Scallops and the Fisherman of St. Brieuc Bay," in *Power, Action, and Belief: A New Sociology of Knowledge?* ed. John Law (New York: Routledge, 1986); Bruno Latour, *Science in Action: How to Follow Scientists and Engineers through Society* (Milton Keynes, England: Open University Press, 1987), and *The Pasteurization of France* (Cambridge, Mass.: Harvard University Press, 1996); and John Law, "Technology and Heterogeneous Engineering: The Case of Portuguese Expansion," in *The Social Construction of Technological Systems*, ed. Wiebe E. Bijker, Thomas Hughes, and Trevor Pinch (Cambridge, Mass.: MIT Press, 1987). There is a comprehensive bibliography maintained by John Law online at http://www.comp.lancs.ac.uk/sociology/ant-a.html. For a lone instance of this approach employed to examine music, see Antoine Hennion, "An Intermediary between Production and Consumption: The Producer of Popular Music," *Science, Technology, and Human Values* 14 (autumn 1989): 400–424. For key texts in the SCOT approach, see Bijker, Hughes, and Pinch, eds., *Social Construction of Technological Systems*.

58. Bijker and Pinch, "The Social Construction of Facts and Artifacts, Or How the Sociology of Science and the Sociology of Technology Might Benefit Each Other," in Bijker, Hughes, and Pinch, eds., *Social Construction of Technological Systems*; see also Restivo, "The Theory Landscape in Science Studies."

59. Bruno Latour, "The Trouble with Actor-Network Theory," *Philsophia* 25 (1997), http://www.ensmp.fr/~latour/popart/p67.html; emphasis in original.

60. For a useful critique of actor network theory with respect to the problem of agency, see Andrew Pickering, "The Mangle of Practice: Agency and Emergence in the Sociology of Science," *American Journal of Sociology* 99 (November 1993): 559–89.

61. See, for just two examples among many, Wanda J. Orlikowski and Daniel Robey, "Information Technology and the Structuring of Organizations," *Information Systems Research* 2 (1991): 143–99; and Geoff Walsham, "The Emergence of Interpretivism in IS Research," *Information Systems Research* 6 (1995): 376–94.

62. See also Thomas F. Gieryn, "Riding the Action/Structure Pendulum with Those Swinging Sociologists of Science," in *The Outlook for STS: Report on an STS Symposium and Workshop*, ed. Sheila Jasanoff (Ithaca, N.Y.: Cornell University Department of Science and Technology Studies, 1992).

63. Rob Hagendijk, "Structuration Theory, Constructivism, and Scientific Change," in *Theories of Science in Society*, ed. Susan E. Cozzens and Thomas F. Gieryn, Science, Technology, and Society (Bloomington and Indianapolis: Indiana University Press, 1990), 50.

64. In Bruno Latour, "Technology Is Society Made Durable," in *A Sociology of Monsters? Essays on Power, Technology and Domination*, ed. John Law, Sociological Review Monograph vol. 38 (New York: Routledge, 1991).

65. Sherry B. Ortner, *Making Gender: The Politics and Erotics of Culture* (Boston: Beacon Press, 1996), 2; emphasis in the original.

66. Ibid. Since practice theory is less a theory than a "founding argument," there are few sources that one could recommend; practice theory is more visible in practice, as it were, than in theoretical formulations. See, however, Pierre Bourdieu's *Outline of a*

Theory of Practice, trans. Richard Nice (Cambridge: Cambridge University Press, 1977), and *The Logic of Practice,* trans. Richard Nice (Cambridge: Polity, 1990); Ortner also recommends Anthony Giddens's *Central Problems in Social Theory: Action, Structure, and Contradiction in Social Analysis* (Berkeley and Los Angeles: University of California Press, 1979); and Marshall Sahlins's *Historical Metaphors and Mythical Realities: Structure in the Early History of the Sandwich Islands Kingdom,* Association for Social Anthropology in Oceania special publications vol. 1 (Ann Arbor: University of Michigan Press, 1981). See also Sherry B. Ortner, "Theory in Anthropology since the Sixties," *Comparative Studies in Society and History* 26 (January 1984): 126–66, for a discussion of anthropological theory leading up to practice theory in the 1980s.

67. Ortner, *Making Gender,* 12.
68. Ibid., 13.
69. Bryan Pfaffenberger, "Social Anthropology of Technology," *Annual Review of Anthropology* (1992): 500.
70. William H. Sewell Jr., "A Theory of Structure: Duality, Agency, and Transformation," *American Journal of Sociology* 98 (July 1992): 6.
71. Ibid., 9.
72. Ibid., 13.
73. Ibid.; emphasis in the original.
74. Pfaffenberger, "Social Anthropology of Technology," 502.
75. Sewell, "Theory of Structure," 21.
76. Pfaffenberger, "Social Anthropology of Technology," 497. Many writers include some kind of immaterial aspect in their definition of technology. Jacques Ellul, for example, writes of "technique" by saying that it does not refer to machines or technology, but rather, "In our technological society, *technique* is the *totality of methods rationally arrived at and having absolute efficiency* (for a given stage of development) in *every* field of human activity" (Jacques Ellul, *The Technological Society,* trans. John Wilkinson [New York: Alfred A. Knopf, 1964], xxv); emphasis in the original. In this sense—that technology isn't just a thing but a kind of ideology that affects everything we do and think—Neil Postman's *Technopoly* could be considered a recent American successor to Ellul's work. And Postman is generous in his mention of Ellul in *Technopoly: The Surrender of Culture to Technology* (New York: Vintage, 1993).
77. Ortner, *Making Gender,* 2.

Chapter Three

1. Eric Hobsbawm, *The Age of Extremes: A History of the World, 1914–1991* (New York: Vintage, 1996), 265, 264.
2. Ibid., 265.
3. Ibid., 267.
4. For other discussions of the role of technology in postwar Europe, particularly France (which is the main subject of this essay, because of the focus on *musique concrète*), see Gabrielle Hecht, "Peasants, Engineers, and Atomic Cathedrals: Narrating Modernization in Postwar Provincial France," *French Historical Studies* 20 (summer 1997): 381–418, "Political Designs: Nuclear Reactors and National Policy in Postwar France," *Technology and Culture* 354 (October 1994): 657–85, and *The Radiance of France: Nuclear Power and National Identity after World War II,* Inside Technology (Cambridge, Mass.: MIT Press, 1998); and Cecil O. Smith Jr., "The Longest Run: Public Engineers and Planning in France," *American Historical Review* 95 (June 1990):

657–92. For an illuminating discussion of the era preceding the war, see Marjorie A. Beale, *The Modernist Enterprise: French Elites and the Threat of Moderinty, 1900–1940* (Stanford: Stanford University Press, 1999); and Paul Rabinow, *French Modern: Norms and Forms of the Social Environment* (Chicago: University of Chicago Press, 1995).

5. In hindsight it looks as though the immediate postwar era was uniformly proscience, but there was a good deal of public debate about the atomic bomb, which was by no means seen as a wholly salutary invention, as Paul Boyer discusses in *By the Bomb's Early Light: American Thought and Culture at the Dawn of the Atomic Age* (New York: Pantheon, 1985).

6. Pierre Schaeffer, "Introduction à la musique concrète," *Polyphonie* 6 (1950): 30–52. Carlos Palombini writes that Schaeffer was using the term by April or May of 1948 in his journals; see Carlos Palombini, "Machine Songs V: Pierre Schaeffer—from Research into Noises to Experimental Music," *Computer Music Journal* 17 (fall 1993): 16.

   For discussions of music and technology in France before World War II, see Richard James, "Expansion of Sound Resources in France, 1913–1940, and Its Relationship to Electronic Music" (Ph.D. diss., University of Michigan, 1981), and "Avant-Garde Sound-on-Film Techniques and Their Relationship to Electro-Acoustic Music," *Musical Quarterly* 72 (1986): 74–89.

7. Robert Gilpin, *France in the Age of the Scientific State* (Princeton, N.J.: Princeton University Press, 1968), 151.

8. Spencer R. Weart, *Scientists in Power* (Cambridge, Mass.: Harvard University Press, 1979), 217.

9. David Pace, "Old Wine—New Bottles: Atomic Energy and the Ideology of Science in Postwar France," *French Historical Studies* 17 (spring 1991): 48.

10. Ibid., 53.

11. Ibid., 51.

12. Walter A. McDougall, "Space-Age Europe: Gaullism, Euro-Gaullism, and the American Dilemma," *Technology and Culture* 26 (April 1985): 184.

13. Georgina Born, *Rationalizing Culture: IRCAM, Boulez, and the Institutionalization of the Musical Avant-Garde* (Berkeley and Los Angeles: University of California Press, 1995), 71.

14. Hobsbawm, *The Age of Extremes*, 501.

15. Leo Marx, "The Idea of 'Technology' and Postmodern Pessimism," in *Technology, Pessimism, and Postmodernism*, ed. Yaron Ezrahi, Everett Mendelsohn, and Howard P. Segal (Amherst: University of Massachusetts Press, 1995), 20.

16. Pierre Schaeffer, interview by Tim Hodgkinson, *Recommended Records Quarterly*, 1987. I have not been able to obtain a published copy of this interview, but it is available on a number of Internet sites such as http://pages.ripco.net/~eleon/articles/pierre-schaeffer.html.

17. See Carlos Palombini, "Machine Songs V"; and "*Musique concrète* Revisited," *Electronic Musicological Review* 4 (June 1999), http://cce.ufpr.br/~rem/REMv4/vol4/arti-palombini.htm [forthcoming in *The Twentieth-Century Music Avant-Garde*, ed. Larry Sitsky (Westport, Conn.: Greenwood)]; "Pierre Schaeffer, 1953: Towards an Experimental Music," *Music and Letters*, November 1993: 542–57; "Pierre Schaeffer's Typo-Morphology of Sonic Objects" (Ph.D. diss., University of Durham, 1993), and "Technology and Pierre Schaeffer: Pierre Schaeffer's *Arts-Relais*, Walter Benjamin's *technische Reproduzierbarkeit* and Martin Heidegger's *Ge-stell*," *Organised Sound* 3

(1998): 36–43, also published online in *MikroPolyphonie* 4 (July 1997 to December 1998), http://farben.latrobe.edu.au/mikropol/volume4/palombini-c/palombini.html.

18. Schaeffer, "Introduction à la musique concrète," 50–51. All translations are my own unless otherwise noted.

19. Mark Sinker writes that the term *concrete* is also borrowed from concrete poetry, but this art form developed after Schaeffer used the term (Sinker, "Shhhhhh!" *Musical Quarterly* 81 [summer 1997]: 212).

20. *Solfège* is a mainly pedagogical method of learning music by singing syllables; "do, re, mi" are all solfège syllables. "Pierre Schaeffer, 1910–1995: The Founder of *Musique concrète*," *Computer Music Journal* 20 (summer 1996): 10. No citation information for this quotation is provided.

21. Pierre Schaeffer, *Traité des objets musicaux* (Paris: Éditions du Seuil, 1966), 23.

22. Claude Lévi-Strauss, *The Raw and the Cooked: Introduction to a Science of Mythology*, trans. John and Doreen Weightman (1969; reprint, Harmondsworth, England: Penguin, 1986), 23.

23. Pierre Schaeffer, *À la recherche d'une musique concrète* (Paris: Éditions du Seuil, 1952), 46–47, cited in John Dack, "The Relationship between Electro-Acoustic Music and Instrumental/Vocal Composition in Europe in the Period 1948–70" (Ph.D. diss., Middlesex Polytechnic, 1989), 17.

24. John Diliberto, "Pierre Schaeffer and Pierre Henry: Pioneers in Sampling," *Electronic Musician*, December 1986, 56.

25. Palombini, "Machine Songs V," 15.

26. Schaeffer, *À la recherche d'une musique concrète*, 23.

27. Nonetheless, by the mid-1960s a new term was being applied to some of Schaeffer's and other composers' music—*musique anecdotique*; see Rodolfo Caesar, "The Composition of Electroacoustic Music" (Ph.D. diss., University of East Anglia, 1992), glossary, available online at http://riojet.area-mundi.com/lamut/lamutpgs/rcpesqs/rctese/09glos.htm.

28. Palombini, "*Musique concrète* Revisited."

29. Theodor Adorno, *Philosophy of Modern Music*, trans. Anne G. Mitchell and Wesley V. Blomster (New York: Continuum, 1994).

   Other books appeared that solidified Schoenberg's position. René Leibowitz's *Schoenberg and His School: The Contemporary Stage of the Language of Music*, trans. Dika Newlin (1949; reprint, New York: Da Capo Press, 1970) was published in French in 1946; and Dika Newlin's *Bruckner, Mahler, Schoenberg* was first published in 1947, the title alone indicating the historical trajectory to which Newlin and other Schoenberg followers were adhering (Newlin, *Bruckner, Mahler, Schoenberg*, rev. ed. [New York: W. W. Norton, 1978]). Other writers offered other trajectories. *Neue Musik-Zeitschrift*, a journal begun after the war, ran an article entitled "The Heritage of New Music" and summarized the first half of the century thus: "[Feruccio] Busoni [1866–1924] is the prophet of new music, who possessed a deep knowledge of its inner cohesion and who saw its future with an at times visionary power. If Busoni is the prophet, then the martyr's crown belongs to Arnold Schoenberg" (quoted by Joanna Ching-Yun Lee, "György Ligeti's *Aventures* and *Nouvelle Aventures*: A Documentary History" [Ph.D. diss., Columbia University, 1993], 18).

30. Pierre Boulez, *Orientations: Collected Writings*, trans. Martin Cooper, ed. Jean-Jacques Nattiez (Cambridge, Mass.: Harvard University Press, 1986), 428.

31. Pierre Boulez, "Schoenberg Is Dead," in *Notes of an Apprenticeship*, comp. Paule Thévenin, trans. Herbert Weinstock (New York: Alfred A. Knopf, 1968), 271.

32. Boulez, "Trajectories: Ravel, Stravinsky, Schoenberg," in *Notes of an Apprenticeship*, 264.

33. For more perspectives on Webern's death, see Kathryn Bailey, *The Life of Webern*, Musical Lives (Cambridge: Cambridge University Press, 1998). I would like to thank Joseph Auner for this reference.

34. Oliver Neighbour, Paul Griffiths, and George Perle, *The New Grove Second Viennese School: Schoenberg, Webern, Berg*, Composer Biography series (New York: W. W. Norton, 1983). For these arguments about the representations of these three composers I am indebted to Joseph Auner, "The Second Viennese School as a Historical Concept," in *Schoenberg, Berg, and Webern: A Companion to the Second Viennese School*, ed. Bryan Simms (Westport, Conn.: Greenwood, 1999), 15. I would like to thank Walter Frisch for telling me of this article.

35. For more on the lionization of Webern, and the importance of the Second Viennese School and its influence on postwar European composition, see Boulez, *Notes of an Apprenticeship* and *Orientations*; Andrew Clements, "Western Europe, 1945–70," in *Modern Times: From World War II to the Present*, ed. Robert P. Morgan, Music and Society (Englewood Cliffs, N.J.: Prentice Hall, 1993); and Lee, "György Ligeti's *Aventures*." This discussion of postwar musical life in Germany owes much to Lee's work.

36. Boulez, "Today's Searchings," in *Notes of an Apprenticeship*, 22.

37. Boulez, "A Time for Johann Sebastian Bach," in *Notes of an Apprenticeship*, 12; emphasis in the original.

38. Wolfgang Martin Stroh, *Zur Soziologie der elektronischen Musik* (Zürich: Amadeus Verlag, 1975), 112.

39. Boulez, "Concrete (Music)," in *Notes of an Apprenticeship*, 291.

40. Schaeffer's magnum opus is *Traité des objets musicaux*. For a discussion of Boulez's role in electronic music in France, see Born, *Rationalizing Culture*.

41. Boulez, "Concrete (Music)," in *Notes of an Apprenticeship*, 289–90.

42. Ibid., 290.

43. Jean-Jacques Nattiez includes a footnote in *Music and Discourse* in which Boulez backs up his earlier judgment of *musique concrète*: "During his lecture at Metz on 28 February 1976, I asked Boulez if his position had changed since I.R.C.A.M. [Institut de Recherche et de Coordination Acoustique/Musique] opened an electronic and computer music division. Boulez: 'only imbeciles don't change their minds, and in this case, I am an imbecile' " (*Music and Discourse: Toward a Semiology of Music*, trans. Carolyn Abbate [Princeton, N.J.: Princeton University Press, 1990], 97, n. 6).

44. Boulez, "Concrete (Music)," in *Notes of an Apprenticeship*, 290, 291.

45. In Michel Chion, *La musique electroacoustique*, Que sais-je? (Paris: Presses Universitaires de France, 1982), 74, cited in Dack, "Relationship," 19.

46. Herbert Eimert, "Der Sinus-Ton, *Melos* 21 (1954): 171, cited in Dack, "Relationship," 138.

47. See Herbert Eimert, "What Is Electronic Music?" *Die Reihe* 1 (1958): 1–10.

48. André Hodeir, *Since Debussy: A View of Contemporary Music*, trans. Noel Burch (New York: Grove Press, 1961), 140–41.

49. Vladimir Ussachevsky, "Music in the Tape Medium," *Juilliard Review*, spring 1959, 19.

50. Reginald Smith Brindle, "The Lunatic Fringe: Concrete Music," *Musical Times*, May 1956, 246. He is more sanguine about this music in his later *The New Music: The Avant-Garde since 1945* (New York: Oxford University Press, 1975).

51. Terence Dwyer, *Composing with Tape Recorders: Musique Concrète for Beginners* (London and New York: Oxford University Press, 1971), 25; emphasis in the original.

52. Ibid., 26; emphasis in the original.
53. See Dack, "Relationship," for an interesting discussion of the rise to hegemony of serialism.
54. Palombini, "Machine Songs V," 19; Pierre Schaeffer, "Vers une musique expérimentale," *La Revue musicale* 236 (1957): 16, cited in Dack, "Relationship," 20.
55. Cited in Donald Mitchell, *The Language of Modern Music* (London: Faber and Faber, 1976), 170.
56. Eduard Hanslick, *On the Beautiful in Music*, trans. Gustave Cohen, ed. Morris Weitz (New York: Liberal Arts Press, 1957), 32. For an astute discussion of absolute music, see Carl Dahlhaus, *The Idea of Absolute Music*, trans. Roger Lustig (Chicago: University of Chicago Press, 1989).
57. The continuing power of absolute music was so strong that even in contemporary considerations of copyright, *elektronische Musik* came out on top. Jean Renauld writes, for example, that "it seems that the music is just the product of the machines, which produce and combine the most diverse sounds by means of manipulating them, and of course, which in turn may be due either to artibrariness or accident as to a personal choice of the artist. However, an exception must be made for those works that use the process of serial composition" (Jean Renauld, *Concrete Music, Electronic Music, and Copyright* [New York: Copyright Society of the U.S.A., 1958], 5).
58. Schaeffer, *Traité des objets musicaux*, 22–23, cited in Dack, "Relationship," 21.
59. See Marianna Torgovnick, *Gone Primitive: Savage Intellects, Modern Lives* (Chicago: University of Chicago Press, 1990); and Glenn Watkins, *Pyramids at the Louvre: Music, Culture, and Collage from Stravinsky to the Postmodernists* (Cambridge, Mass.: Harvard University Press, 1994).
60. Palombini, "Pierre Schaeffer, 1953," 542.
61. Schaeffer, "Vers une musique expérimentale," 11. Since J. S. Bach died in 1750, Schaeffer's chronology is a little off.
62. Liner notes to *Pierre Schaeffer: l'œuvre musicale*, INA TRM 292572, 1998.
63. Palombini, "Machine Songs V," 15.
64. Paul Rivet, "Organization of an Ethnological Museum," cited in James Clifford, *The Predicament of Culture: Twentieth-Century Ethnography, Literature, and Art* (Cambridge, Mass.: Harvard University Press, 1988), 139. I am indebted to Paul Rabinow for suggesting this line of inquiry.
65. Karlheinz Stockhausen, "Advice to Clever Children . . . ," interview by Dick Witts, *The Wire*, November 1995, 33–34; emphasis and ellipsis in the original.
66. Vladimir Ussachevsky, "As Europe Takes to Tape," *American Composers Alliance Bulletin*, autumn 1953, 11.
67. Schaeffer, interview by Tim Hodgkinson.
68. Ibid.
69. Claude Lévi-Strauss, *The Savage Mind*, Nature of Human Society (Chicago: University of Chicago Press, 1966), 19.
70. Ibid., 21.
71. Ibid., 22.
72. Pierre Schaeffer, *La musique concrète* (Paris: Presses Universitaires de France, 1967), 16.
73. Quoted in Antoine Bonnet, "*Écriture* and Perception: On *Messagesquisse* by Pierre Boulez," *Contemporary Music Review* 2 (1987): 207.
74. Ibid., 207–8.

75. Olivier Nuc, "Pierre Henry: La Quête du Son Philosophial," *aden* [Paris], November 25–December 1, 1998, 5.

76. Pierre Henry, interview by Ios Smolders, http://www.ddc.net/emaurer/PierreHenry/interview.htm.

77. Rhama Khazam, "Electroacoustic Alchemist," *The Wire*, June 1997, 39.

78. Henry, interview by Ios Smolders.

79. Schaeffer, *La musique concrète*, 74.

80. "Pierre Schaeffer parle de Pierre Henry avec François Bayle," *La Revue musicale* 265–66 (1969): 118. Schaeffer used much the same language to describe Henry's music in Marc Pierret's *Entretiens avec Pierre Schaeffer* (Paris: Éditions Pierre Belfond, 1969), 30.

81. Khazam, "Electroacoustic Alchemist," 38.

82. Michel Chion, *Pierre Henry* (Paris: Fayard/Fondation SACEM, 1980), 124. A "jerk" is Henry's term for an electric guitar piece.

83. "Henry, Pierre," http://www.virgin.fr/html/cyber/tnt/dico/h.html#henry.

84. Chion, *Pierre Henry*, 126.

85. Eric Dahan, "About Mass for the Present Day," liner notes to *Métamorphose: Messe pour le temps présent, d'apres la musique du ballet de Maurice Béjart*, Philips Music Group [France] 456 294-2, 1997.

86. Dominique Frétard, "Pierre Henry a-t-il été le Pygmalion de Maurice Béjart?" *Le Monde*, July 5, 1996, 23; ellipsis in the original.

87. Chion, *Pierre Henry*, 125–26; Nuc, "Pierre Henry," 5. Henry was ambivalent about the success of this album, as reported in the interview by Ios Smolders. See also François Seloron, "Pierre Henry et le Pop," *Rock and Folk* [Paris], February 1970, 38–42.

88. "Henry, Pierre," http://www.virgin.fr/html/cyber/tnt/dico/h.html#henry.

89. See Dave Marsh, *Louie Louie: The History and Mythology of the World's Most Famous Rock 'n' Roll Song* (New York: Hyperion, 1993). Marsh does not mention this "version," however.

90. http://www.xs4all.nl/~tdg/louie2.html.

91. Frétard, "Pierre Henry a-t-il été le Pygmalion," 23. The music for *The Wild Angels* was performed mainly by Davie Allan and the Arrows, with the songs written by Mike Curb, Harley Hatcher, and Davie Allan.

92. Michael Bonner, "All 'Present' and Correct," *Melody Maker*, October 18, 1997, 53.

93. These and other quotations that follow in this chapter are from the Internet or Usenet and employ the spelling and punctuation of the originals.

94. Bonner writes in *Melody Maker* that, among DJs, Henry is the most influential composer, more so than Stockhausen, Cage, La Monte Young, or Philip Glass ("All 'Present' and Correct," 53). However, Nonesuch has recently released a remix album of music by Steve Reich entitled *Reich Remixed* (Nonesuch 79552-2, 1999).

95. Jacques Lonchampt, " 'L'Apocalypse' et 'Ceremony' de Pierre Henry, à l'Olympia," *Le Monde*, February 11, 1970, 19; ellipsis in the original. See also Olivier Alain's review of the same concert, "Variétés électroniques," *Le Figaro*, February 13, 1970, 30.

96. Henry, interview by Ios Smolders.

97. Seloron, "Pierre Henry et le Pop," 40.

98. Chion, *Pierre Henry*, 145–46.

99. Henry, interview by Ios Smolders.

100. The final track on *Freak Magnet* (Beyond Records 78058, 2000) is entitled "A Story (featuring Pierre Henry)," and is mentioned in the band's label's press kit for the

album. The song is about a young couple eaten by a monster on the interstate; Henry's contribution seems to have been to add noises to the mix, and he is listed as a producer for the track.

101. http://www.vfemmes.com/fem_html/guy_int.html.

102. Raymond Williams, *Marxism and Literature*, Marxist Introductions (Oxford and New York: Oxford University Press, 1977).

103. Susana Loza, personal communication, July 6, 2000. I would also like to thank Ron Radano for pushing me on this point.

104. Marie-Aude Roux, "Un grand-père de la techno," *Le Monde*, July 24, 1998, 1, and Nuc, "Pierre Henry," 5; *Nova* [Paris], November 1998, 38. Thanks are due to David Suisman for bringing me these magazines. See also Kurt B. Reighley, "Let's Go Discotheque: A Survey of French Dance Music," *CMJ New Music Monthly*, October 1997, 20; and Richard Wolfson, "Grandpa to Pop's Whizkids," *(London) Daily Telegraph*, May 22, 1999, 8.

105. Daniel Smith, review of *Pierre Schaeffer: l'œuvre musicale*, http://newyork.sidewalk.com/link/21953. This URL is no longer active.

106. http://www.ubl.com/.

107. http://www.perso.infonie.fr/grems/gentech.htm.

108. http://web.pncl.co.uk/~rocklist/mixmag.html.

109. The liner notes to the CD that was released following the film mentions Schaeffer along with Henry, however.

110. Greg Bowes, "The A–Z of Electronica," http://www.mg.co.za/mg/art/music/column/980702-wild.html.

111. "Pierre Henry," http://www.novaplanet.com/html/actuel/html/phenry/html/phenry.html.

112. Ios Smolders, review of Alain de Filippis, *Ton Dieu ne s'appelle-t-il pas ego? Vital*, January 1, 1995, http://enigma.v2.nl/Archief/ArchieTexten/Vitals/Vital39.html.

113. "The Techno Story," http://www.devastating-rhythm.ch/news.htm. This URL is no longer active. I should note that Edgard Varèse (1885–1965) worked in France and the United States, not Italy.

114. Shane Danielsen, "Bands That Don't Play Together, Stay Together," http://entertainment.news.com/au/music/arc90303.htm. This URL is no longer active.

115. Esther Yoon, "Buffalo Daughter: Tokyo Calling," *Resonance*, http://www.resonancemag.com/issues/15/currentissue/shortwaves/buffalodaughter.html.

116. Sielwolf, interview by Sniper Wells, *IDR Zine*, http://vr.dv.net/interviews/sie19_int.html. "Pendereckie" is the Polish composer Krzysztof Penderecki (b. 1933).

117. Susana Loza, personal communication, July 6, 2000.

118. Dahan, "About Mass for the Present Day."

Chapter Four

1. See John F. Kasson, *Civilizing the Machine: Technology and Republican Values in America, 1776–1900* (New York: Penguin, 1977); Leo Marx, *The Machine in the Garden: Technology and the Pastoral Ideal in America* (1964; reprint, New York: Oxford University Press, 2000); and Howard P. Segal, *Future Imperfect: The Mixed Blessings of Technology in America* (Amherst: University of Massachusetts Press, 1994).

2. Lynn Spigel, *Make Room for TV: Television and the Family Ideal in Postwar America* (Chicago: University of Chicago Press, 1992), esp. 46–48. I would like to thank Joanne Meyerowitz for recommending this book.

3. Jules Henry, *Culture against Man* (New York: Vintage, 1963). For more general histories of the 1950s, see David Halberstam, *The Fifties* (New York: Villard, 1993); Julián Marías, *America in the Fifties and Sixties: Julián Marías on the United States*, trans. Blanche De Puy and Harold C. Raley, ed. Michael Aaron Rockland (University Park: Pennsylvania State University Press, 1972); and Robert J. Samuelson, *The Good Life and Its Discontents: The American Dream in the Age of Entitlement, 1945–1995* (New York: Times Books, 1995).

4. Paul Boyer, *By the Bomb's Early Light: American Thought and Culture at the Dawn of the Atomic Age* (New York: Pantheon, 1985).

5. Michael Smith, "Advertising the Atom," in *Government and Environmental Politics: Essays on Historical Developments since World War Two*, ed. Michael J. Lacey (Washington, D.C.: Woodrow Wilson Center Press/Baltimore: Johns Hopkins University Press, 1991), 241.

6. Smith, "Advertising the Atom," 244.

7. For a discussion of popular songs inspired by the atom, see A. Costandina Titus and Jerry L. Simich, "From 'Atomic Bomb Baby' to 'Nuclear Funeral': Atomic Music Comes of Age, 1945–1990," *Popular Music and Society* 14 (winter 1990): 11–37.

8. Smith, "Advertising the Atom," 244.

9. Harold E. Stassen, "Atoms for Peace," *Ladies' Home Journal*, August 1945, 48, cited in Stephen L. Del Sesto, "Wasn't the Future of Nuclear Energy Wonderful?" in *Imagining Tomorrow: History, Technology, and the American Future*, ed. Joseph J. Corn (Cambridge, Mass.: MIT Press, 1986), 58.

10. In 1956, Simon and Schuster published *The Walt Disney Story of Our Friend the Atom* by physicist Heinz Haber. The title alone gives a sense of one of the directions that this public relations campaign took; language such as this was directed at children, and, judging by the illustrations and vocabulary, this book was aimed at early adolescents. Haber's physics is accurate and clear, and is preceded by a foreword from Disney in which he proclaims that "The atom is our future." The atom is so important, Disney says, that his company embarked on several atomic projects, including a Hall of Science in the Tomorrowland section of Disneyland that will educate people about atomic energy, among other things. Disney concludes his foreword with a mixture of the kinds of rhetoric used by proponents—atomic power is about exploration, adventure; it has deep historical roots; science is creative; humankind came together in the production of this knowledge. "The story of the atom is a fascinating tale of human quest for knowledge, a story of scientific adventure and success. Atomic science has borne many fruits, and the harnessing of the atom's power is only the spectacular end result. It came about through the work of many inspired men whose ideas formed a kind of chain reaction of thoughts. These men came from all civilized nations, and from all centuries as far back as 400 B.C. Atomic science began as a positive, creative thought. It has created modern science with its many benefits for mankind. In this sense our book tries to make it clear to you that we can indeed look upon the atom as our friend" (Disney, foreword to Heinz Haber, *The Walt Disney Story of Our Friend the Atom* [New York: Simon and Schuster, 1956], 11).

11. Smith, "Advertising the Atom," 245.

12. Allan C. Fisher Jr., "You and the Obedient Atom," *National Geographic*, September 1958, 303, cited in Smith, "Advertising the Atom," 246.

13. Brian Horrigan, "Popular Culture and Visions of the Future in Space, 1901–2001," in *New Perspectives on Technology and American Culture*, ed. Bruce Sinclair (Philadelphia: American Philosophical Society, 1986), 59–60.

14. Ibid., 60.
15. Randy Liebermann, "The *Collier's* and Disney Series," in *Blueprint for Space: Science Fiction to Science Fact*, ed. Frederick I. Ordway III and Randy Liebermann (Washington, D.C.: Smithsonian Institution Press, 1992), 135.
16. Ibid., 144.
17. Ibid., 145.
18. U.S. Census Bureau, http://www.census.gov/population/estimates/nation/popclockest txt.
19. Liebermann, "The *Collier's* and Disney Series," 146.
20. Michael L. Smith, "Selling the Moon: The U.S. Manned Space Program and the Triumph of Commodity Scientism," in *The Culture of Consumption: Critical Essays in American History, 1880-1980*, ed. Richard Wightman Fox and T. J. Jackson Lears (New York: Pantheon, 1982), 192.
21. Ibid.
22. Ruth Schwartz Cowan, *A Social History of American Technology* (New York: Oxford University Press, 1997), 260.
23. Ibid., 262. See also Ruth Schwartz Cowan, *More Work for Mother: The Ironies of Household Technology from the Open Hearth to the Microwave* (New York: Basic Books, 1983) for a discussion of the ways that these gadgets actually increased the amount of time women spent on housework. NASA's homepage is http://nctn.hq.nasa.gov/ and has a link labeled "Spinoffs and Commercial Technology."
24. Smith, "Selling the Moon," 196. For an analysis of similar frontier discourse surrounding the construction of the first atomic bombs, see John Canaday, *The Nuclear Muse: Literature, Physics, and the First Atomic Bombs*, Science and Literature (Madison: University of Wisconsin Press, 2000).
25. "The Sixties: The Decade of Man in Space," *Newsweek*, December 14, 1959, 34, quoted in Smith, "Selling the Moon," 199.
26. Langdon Winner, *The Whale and the Reactor: A Search for Limits in an Age of High Technology* (Chicago and London: University of Chicago Press, 1986).
27. Smith, "Selling the Moon," 182.
28. Ibid., 186.
29. Thomas Hine also writes of the neologisms in this era, a trend that he paid homage to in his book's title, *Populuxe* ("a way of referring to the moment when America found a way of turning out fantasy on an assembly line" [5]). Hine writes of this 1955 Chevrolet that it signaled the arrival of the "populuxe" era: "Its tailfins were quite modest, compared with what was to come later, but they were a strong contrast with the basic transportation image of previous years. It was, as people said at the time, a baby Cadillac, powerful, exciting, available in an array of lively color schemes. It was still a Chevy, and everyone knew that, but it allowed the Chevy buyer to partake fully of a moment when the act of breaking the sound barrier had taken on truly heroic qualities and rocketing into space was just around the corner. The Chevy buyer even had an edge over those who were buying more expensive, yet clearly more old-fashioned cars, such as Oldsmobiles and Chryslers—he was buying the future" (Hine, *Populuxe* [New York: Alfred A. Knopf, 1986], 12).
30. Laura Nader, "Energy Needs for Sustainable Human Development from an Anthropological Perspective," in *Energy as an Instrument for Socio-Economic Development*, ed. José Goldemberg and Thomas B. Johansson (New York: United Nations Development Programme, 1995), 47.

31. Hine, *Populuxe*, 134.
32. Ibid., 129-30.
33. Kristina Zarlengo, "Civilian Threat, the Suburban Citadel, and Atomic Age American Women," *Signs* 24 (summer 1999): 942–43.
34. For a recent writing on the masculinization of technology, see Ruth Oldenziel, *Making Technology Masculine: Men, Women, and Modern Machines in America, 1870–1945* (Amsterdam: Amsterdam University Press, 1999).
35. Elaine Tyler May also makes this point in "Explosive Issues: Sex, Women, and the Bomb," in *Recasting America: Culture and Politics in the Age of Cold War*, ed. Lary May (Chicago: University of Chicago Press, 1989).
36. Quoted in Zarlengo, "Civilian Threat," 940.
37. Ibid.
38. Ibid., 943.
39. A comparison to the futurist composers risks being ahistorical and I should note that, as is not widely discussed, the futurists had a political agenda that included the glorification of war, an agenda that most people today would find repugnant. For more on the futurists, see Umbro Apollonio, ed. and comp., *Futurist Manifestos*, trans. Robert Brain, Documents of 20th-Century Art (New York: Viking 1973); and Douglas Kahn, *Noise Water Meat: A History of Sound in the Arts* (Cambridge, Mass.: MIT Press, 1999). For a brief history of the futurism movement that situates it in social and cultural history of the era, see Eric Hobsbawm, *The Age of Extremes: A History of the World, 1914–1991* (New York: Vintage, 1996).
40. This is included on the reissue *Space-Capades*, vol. 3 of *Ultra-Lounge*, Capital CDP 7243 8 35176 2 6, 1996.

    Some musicians, including those whom I discuss in this chapter, looked down their noses at such sound effects; the unnamed author of a profile of Les Baxter, for example, began his article by saying that "Les Baxter is one of a handful of conductor-arrangers who can turn out hit records without the benefit of name singers or resorting to hoked-up orchestral tricks that are sound effects rather than musical inventions" (" 'Don't Have to Cheapen Music to Sell It,' Asserts Les Baxter," *Down Beat*, September 7, 1955, 10).
41. Keir Keightley, " 'Turn it Down!' She Shrieked: Gender, Domestic Space, and High Fidelity, 1948–59," *Popular Music* 15 (May 1996): 149–77.
42. Barbara Ehrenreich, *The Hearts of Men: American Dreams and the Flight from Commitment* (New York: Anchor, 1984), 49–50. I would like to thank Joanne Meyerowitz for recommending this book. For an earlier history of the gramophone in the home, see Holly Kruse, "Early Audio Technology and Domestic Space," *Stanford Humanities Review* 3 (fall 1993): 1–14.
43. Ehrenreich, *Hearts of Men*, 44. See also Keightley, " 'Turn it Down!' "

    Jennifer McKnight-Trontz's *Exotiquarium: Album Art from the Space Age* (New York: St. Martin's Griffin, 1999) contains reproductions of many covers from these albums, which usually depict a happy, well-dressed young couple in various stages of courtship and foreplay and featured titles such as *After Dinner Music*, *A Tropical Affair*, *Music for Playboys to Play By* (this one pictures a woman on a sofa with a cocktail and a man dressed up as Satan hovering over her); *Businessman's Bounce*, *Mind If I Make Love to You*, and others.
44. Spigel, *Make Room for TV*.
45. Immanuel Kant, *The Critique of Judgment*, trans. Werner S. Pluhar (Indianapolis:

Hackett, 1987), 200. I would like to thank Sam Kerstein for recommending this careful translation.

46. Ibid.

47. See Keightley, " 'Turn it Down!' " 163–69.

48. Rita Reif, "The Woman's Touch: Pressure from Hi-Fi Waves Is Sending Components Back into the Woodwork," *New York Times*, November 18, 1956, 11, cited in Keightley, " 'Turn it Down!' " 168.

49. Opal Loomis, "The High Fidelity Wife, or a Fate Worse Than Deaf," *Harper's*, August 1955, 6, cited in Keightley, " 'Turn it Down!,' " 168.

50. Ibid.

51. Susan J. Douglas, "Audio Outlaws: Radio and Phonograph Enthusiasts," in *Possible Dreams: Enthusiasm for Technology in America*, ed. John L. Wright (Dearborn, Mich.: Henry Ford Museum and Greenfield Village, 1992), 46.

52. Hine, *Populuxe*, 109. See also Richard Horn, *Fifties Style* (New York: Friedman/Fairfax, 1993).

53. McKnight-Trontz, *Exotiquarium*, 23. *Exotiquarium* reproduces some of these album covers.

54. John Ball Jr., "The Witch Doctor in Your Living Room," *Hi-Fi/Stereo Review*, March 1960, 63.

55. Paul Williams, quoted in Eric Asimov, "The New Bad-Boy Sound: Space Age Pop," *New York Times*, January 7, 1996, sec. 4, p. 2.

56. Irwin Chusid, liner notes to *Mallets in Wonderland*, vol. 2 of *The RCA History of Space Age Pop*, RCA 66646, 1995. These notes are also available online at http://www.chaoskitty.com/sabpm/sapvol2.html.

57. Rebecca Leydon, "Utopias of the Tropics: The Exotic Music of Les Baxter and Yma Sumac," in *Widening the Horizon: Exoticism in Post-War Popular Music*, ed. Philip Hayward (Sydney: John Libbey, 1999), 62.

58. Ibid., 62–63.

59. For evidence of the impact of Moog synthesizers on this music, see David Schafer, "101 Moogs!" *Cool and Strange Music!* February–April 1997, 22–23, which includes a discography.

60. Liner notes from *Les Baxter: The Sounds of Adventure*, online at "The Exotic World of Les Baxter" website, http://www.tamboo.com/baxter/baxter1.html.

   The theremin has recently been revived as a part of the revival of space-age pop, which I will discuss in chapter 5. The resurgence of interest in the instrument is registered in the appearance of a number of websites devoted to it (the most comprehensive is "The Theremin Home Page" at http://www.thereminworld.com/), as well as a Usenet group called alt.music.makers.theremin. The revival of interest in the theremin is also apparent from the availability and popularity of theremin kits from Robert Moog's company (more about this online at http://metalab.unc.edu/id/theremin/); and an award-winning documentary film by Steven M. Martin, *Theremin: An Electronic Odyssey* (Orion Classics, 1994). See also Kyle Gann, "Music For Theremin: It's Not Just for Aliens Anymore," *Village Voice*, August 31, 1999, 113.

61. See Les Baxter, "The Les Baxter Interview," by James Call and Peter Huestis, http://www.tamboo.com/baxter/baxinterview/index.html. For more on Baxter, see Joseph Lanza, *Elevator Music: A Surreal History of Muzak, Easy-Listening, and Other Moodsong* (New York: St. Martin's, 1994); and David Toop, *Exotica: Fabricated Soundscapes in a Real World* (London: Serpent's Tail, 1999).

62. The soundtrack was recently rereleased as BMG/Fox 11010, 1993.

63. I should note that the rerelease of the entire album by a small independent label lists the title as "Many Moods."

   For more on the use of vocables to convey otherness in music, see Timothy D. Taylor, "World Music in Television Ads," *American Music* 18 (summer 2000): 162–92.

64. For a recent study of the electric guitar, see Steve Waksman, *Instruments of Desire: The Electric Guitar and the Shaping of Musical Experience* (Cambridge, Mass.: Harvard University Press, 2000).

65. The term *bombshell* was first used in the title of a 1933 film featuring Jean Harlow, but MGM, so as not to imply to listeners that it was a war picture, released it as *Blonde Bombshell*, directed by Victor Fleming.

66. Zarlengo, "Civilian Threat," 946–47.

67. May, "Explosive Issues," 164. See also JoAnne Brown, " 'A Is for *Atom*, B Is for *Bomb*': Civil Defense in American Public Education, 1948–1963," *Journal of American History* 75 (June 1988): 68-90.

68. Anne McClintock, *Imperial Leather: Race, Gender, and Sexuality in the Colonial Contest* (New York and London: Routledge, 1995); see also Ella Shohat, "Gender and Culture of Empire: Toward a Feminist Ethnography of Cinema," in *Visions of the East: Orientalism in Film*, ed. Matthew Bernstein and Gaylyn Studlar (New Brunswick, N.J.: Rutgers University Press, 1997); and Zarlengo, "Civilian Threat." I would like to thank Susana Loza for recommending Shohat's article.

69. Liner notes to *Music for Heavenly Bodies*, Omega OSL-4, n.d.

70. For more on Paul Tanner, see "The Paul Tanner Electro-Theremin Page" at http://www.geocities.com/Vienna/4611/PTE-TPage.html.

71. As discussed above, the "space" connection gives leave to present the recording apparatus, and occasionally, the instruments if they are electric, in technical terms, and so the liner notes to *Music for Heavenly Bodies* contain the usual kinds of information about the electro-theremin: "The audio range of the electro-theremin covers the complete sound spectrum, from 0 to over 20,000 cycles per second. Its high and lows can only be measured on an oscilloscope. Its sounds are pure sine waves without any harmonics, making it an ideal instrument with which to test your audio equipment" (liner notes to *Music for Heavenly Bodies*, Omega OSL-4, n.d.).

72. http://www.wildsscene.com/liners/spaceesc.html.

73. Much of this music was caught up in cocktail culture: drinks were to be served in a gracious suburban home or to one's date, all while listening to this futuristic music. Space does not permit a discussion of this here; see, instead, Joseph Lanza, *The Cocktail: The Influence of Spirits on the American Psyche* (New York: St. Martin's, 1995).

74. For an article that gives a sense of the tenacity of some of the space-age pop music collectors who are discussed in the second half of this chapter, see Ken Saari, ""My Space Escapade," *Cool and Strange Music!*, November 1997/February 1998, 40–41.

75. Liner notes to *Music for Heavenly Bodies*.

76. McKnight-Trontz, *Exotiquarium*, 89. A different quotation appears in V. Vale and Andrea Juno, eds., *Incredibly Strange Music*, vol. 2 (San Francisco: Re/Search, 1994), 207. Another example of this space travelogue is Walter Schumann's *Exploring the*

Unknown (1955); a quotation from the liner notes to this album appears in Vale and Juno, *Incredibly Strange Music*, vol. 2, 204.

77. I should note that it was also in the immediate postwar era that the commercial travel industry as we now know it came into being; David Halberstam has written of the rise in the 1950s of the Holiday Inn, for example (Halberstam, *The Fifties*, chap. 12). But this is a subject of tangential interest here.

78. Little is known about the Barrons, but there is an interview with Bebe Barron in Vale and Juno, eds., *Incredibly Strange Music*, vol. 2.

79. Louis and Bebe Barron, liner notes to *Forbidden Planet*, Small Planet PR-D-001, 1989. *Leitmotif* is a term associated mainly with the music of Richard Wagner, who employed recognizable themes to represent characters, objects, and characters' states of mind in his operas.

80. Jack Diamond, liner notes to *Man in Space with Sounds*, Subliminal Sounds SUBCD-4, 1998.

81. Ibid.

82. Ibid.

Chapter Five

1. See Fred Davis, *Yearning for Yesterday: A Sociology of Nostalgia* (New York: Free Press, 1979), and J. Ronald Oakley, *God's Country: America in the Fifties* (New York: Dembner, 1986), for two considerations of 1970s nostalgia for the 1950s.

2. See Mark Vail, *Vintage Synthesizers: Pioneering Designers, Groundbreaking Instruments, Collecting Tips, Mutants of Technology* (San Francisco: Miller Freeman, 2000), for an examination of some of the instruments that are becoming popular again.

3. Chris Morris, "Bachelor Pad Music from '50s, '60s Is Swingin' Again," *Billboard*, September 9, 1995, 1.

4. See also Philip Hayward, "The Cocktail Shift: Aligning Musical Exotica," in *Widening the Horizon: Exoticism in Post-War Popular Music*, ed. Philip Hayward (Sydney: John Libbey, 1999) for a discussion of the revival.

5. See Timothy D. Taylor, *Global Pop: World Music, World Markets* (New York: Routledge, 1997), for a similar discourse used by advocates of world music in the late 1980s and early 1990s.

6. Irwin Chusid, liner notes to *The Stereo Action Dimension*, vol. 3 of *The RCA History of Space Age Pop*, RCA 66647, 1995. These notes are also available online at http://www.chaoskitty.com/sabpm/sapvol3.html.

7. All quotations from Usenet groups appear with their original spelling and punctuation unless otherwise noted.

8. "The Lounge Fad," *Revolt in Style*, http://www.revoltinstyle.com/october/lounge/. This URL is no longer active.

9. David Hinckley, "Musical Longevity," *New York Daily News*, August 5, 1996, 31.

10. Irwin Chusid, liner notes to *Melodies and Mischief*, vol. 1 of *The RCA History of Space Age Pop*, RCA 66645, 1995. These notes are also available online at http://www.chaoskitty.com/sabpm/sapvol1.html.

11. Andy Seiler, " '60s Kitsch King Finds '90s Niche," *USA Today*, August 8, 1995, sec. D, p. 5.

12. Unlike most kinds of music these days, exotica is scarcely available on MP3s. The exotica Internet mailing list rarely has any information about MP3 sites or trades, as if they collect the music for its iconography, notes, and camp more than the sound.

13. Exotica mailing list FAQ version 3.2, http://www.studio-nibble.com/lists/exofaq32.html.

14. Byron Werner, "Space Age Bachelor Pad Music: A Forward," http://atomicmule.com/kulture/byron/space1.html.

15. Vale and Juno, eds., *Incredibly Strange Music*, vols. 1 and 2 (San Francisco: Re/Search, 1993); Joseph Lanza, *Elevator Music: A Surreal History of Muzak, Easy-Listening, and Other Moodsong* (New York: St. Martin's, 1994).

16. Dana Countryman, e-mail communication, January 29, 2000.

17. Jack Diamond, e-mail communication, October 18, 1999.

18. Will Straw, "Sizing up Record Collections: Gender and Connoisseurship in Rock Music Culture," in *Sexing the Groove: Popular Music and Gender*, ed. Sheila Whitely (New York: Routledge, 1997), 12.

19. Ibid., 11.

20. Ibid., 12.

21. Ibid., 12–13.

22. Werner, "Space Age Bachelor Pad Music," http://atomicmule.com/kulture/byron/space1.html.

23. Vale and Juno, introduction to Vale and Juno, eds., *Incredibly Strange Music*, vol. 1, 3; emphasis in the original.

24. Vale and Juno, introduction to Vale and Juno, eds., *Incredibly Strange Music*, vol. 2, 4.

25. See Hayward, ed., *Widening the Horizon*; and David Toop, *Exotica: Fabricated Soundscapes in a Real World* (London: Serpent's Tail, 1999).

26. There is a fairly extensive literature on collecting, some of which considers gender. See Russell W. Belk and Melanie Wallendorf, "Of Mice and Men: Gender Identity in Collecting," in *Interpreting Objects and Collections*, ed. Susan M. Pearce, Leicester Readers in Museum Studies (New York: Routledge, 1994); Helga Dittmar, "Meanings of Material Possessions As Reflections of Identity: Gender and Social-Material Position in Society," *Journal of Social Behaviour and Personality* 6 (1991): 165–86; Katharine Martinez and Kenneth L. Ames, eds., *The Material Culture of Gender, the Gender of Material Culture* (Winterthur, Del.: Henry Francis du Pont Winterthur Museum, 1997); and Susan M. Pearce, *On Collecting: An Investigation into Collecting in the European Tradition* (New York: Routledge, 1995).

27. "Why Lounge? Why Now?" http://www.fsbassociates.com/books2/loungekit.htm. The book, which does not include this passage, is Steve Knopper, ed., *MusicHound Lounge: The Essential Album Guide to Martini Music and Easy Listening* (Detroit: Visible Ink, 1998).

28. Jennifer Ditchburn, "Lounging 'Round," *Rhythm Music*, July 1997, 20. The exotica mailing list in the summer of 1997 carried many discussions about lounge/exotica fan demographics; many posters to the list felt that they were not baby boomers and didn't feel invested in the 1960s, and thus had a more 1950s retro orientation.

29. There is a substantial literature on popular musics and authenticity; see, most importantly, Simon Frith, *Sound Effects: Youth, Leisure, and the Politics of Rock 'n' Roll*, Communication and Society Series (London: Constable, 1983); and Charles Hamm, *Putting Popular Music in Its Place* (Cambridge: Cambridge University Press, 1995).

30. For more on the commodification of the 1960s, see Thomas Frank, *The Conquest of Cool: Business Culture, Counterculture, and the Rise of Hip Consumerism* (Chicago: University of Chicago Press, 1997); and Edward P. Morgan, "Democracy in Eclipse? Media Culture and the Postmodern 'Sixties,'" *New Political Science* 40 (spring 1997): 5–31.

31. More than one commentator has argued that the revival of this music is a politically conservative move; see Richard Gehr, "Exotica Neurotica," http://www.levity.com/rubric/exotica.html; and Milo Miles, "Incredibly Bad Music," *Salon*, http://www.salon1999.com/10/reviews/lounge1.html.

32. Irwin Chusid, liner notes to *Bachelor's Guide to the Galaxy*, vol. 1 of *Cocktail Mix*, Rhino R2 72237, 1995; emphasis in the original.

33. Randall Rothenberg, "The Swank Life," *Esquire*, April 1997, 73.

34. Stephanie Coontz, *The Way We Never Were: American Families and the Nostalgia Trap* (New York: Basic Books, 1992).

35. Lyn Gardner, "Radio Lava Lamp Camp," *Guardian* (Manchester, England), February 3, 1996, 26.

36. Brian Doherty, "Matt Groening: The Creator of 'The Simpsons' on His New Sci-Fi TV Show, Why It's Nice to Be Rich, and How the ACLU Infringed on His Rights," *Mother Jones*, March 1, 1999, 34.

37. Dave Walker, " 'Futurama': 'Jetsons' Meet 'The Simpsons,' " *Arizona Republic*, March 28, 1999, sec. E, p. 1. Groening appeared in a recent documentary entitled *Yesterday's Tomorrows* directed by Barry Levinson (Cinemax, 1999) that examined past views of a future that has not come to pass. *Yesterday's Tomorrows* is also the title of a useful book by Joseph J. Corn and Brian Horrigan, *Yesterday's Tomorrows: Past Visions of the American Future* (Baltimore: Johns Hopkins University Press, 1984).

38. Perrey's music is back in part because of a Fatboy Slim remix of "E.V.A.," originally from *Moog Indigo*, Vanguard 6549-2, 1970; the remix is available on Camille Yarbrough's *Yo' Praise*, Vanguard 746-2, 1999, and was used in a television commercial for MasterCard. Also, the French band Air professes to be fans of Perrey, and collaborated with him on their debut album *Moon Safari* (1998), on the track "Remember." The members of the band enthuse about Perrey on a radio program, "Morning Becomes Eclectic," available online at http://www.kcrw.org/, and on the band's website, http://www.babelweb.freeserve.co.uk/airweb/page2.html.

39. Jean-Jacques Perrey, interviewed in Vale and Juno, eds., *Incredibly Strange Music*, vol. 1, 97; emphasis in the original.

40. See Laurent Fourier, "Jean-Jacques Perrey and the Ondioline," trans. Curtis Roads, *Computer Music Journal* 18 (winter 1994): 19–25.

41. These have been collected and released on *Good Moog: Astral Animations and Komputer Kartoons*, Kosinus 55, 1998.

42. Perrey, interviewed in Vale and Juno, eds., *Incredibly Strange Music*, vol. 1, 97; emphasis and ellipsis in the original.

43. Jean-Jacques Perrey, "The Jean Jacques Perrey Interview!" interview by Dana Countryman, *Cool and Strange Music!* February–April 1997, 29; ellipsis in the original.

44. Liner notes to Perrey-Kingsley, *The In Sound from Way Out*, Vanguard 79222-2, 1966.

45. Tim Gane, interview, http://www.2launch.com/stereolab.html. This URL is no longer active.

46. Aidin Vaziri, "Mellow Gold," http://www.jetpack.com/lounge02/beats/lounge/mellowgold/index.html.

47. As part of a 4-CD set, Wendy Carlos, *Switched On Boxed Set*, East Side Digital 81422, 1999. In 1992, Carlos released *Switched On Bach 2000*, Telarc 80323.

48. Liner notes to *Transient Random-Noise Bursts with Announcements*, Elektra 9 61536-2, 1993.

49. Tim Gane, interview, http://www.2launch.com/stereolab.html. This URL is no longer active.

50. Stereolab's engagement with music from the 1950s isn't confined to space age pop. Their 1998 album *Emperor Tomato Ketchup* contains a track entitled "Les Yper-Sound," a title that refers to Pierre Henry and Michel Colombier's "band," formed to release a single from *Messe pour le temps présent.* "Les Yper-Sound" seems to be the work of the album's producer, John McEntire, who "admits to a fondness for old-school *musique concrète*" (Joel Begleiter, review of the Sea and Cake, "Two Gentlemen," *Herald*, October 17, 1997, http://www.theherald.org/herald/issues/g101797/the-sea.f.html). Stereolab's "Les Yper-Sound" employs the kinds of swoops and buzzes that one could hear in Henry's works, combined with a fairly straight-ahead melody.

51. Régis Debray, *Media Manifestos: On the Technological Transmission of Cultural Forms,* trans. Eric Rauth (New York: Verso, 1996), 17.

52. Tim Gane, "In the Studio: Stereolab's Tim Gane on Distorted Organs," interview, http://www.maths.monash.edu.au/~rjh/stereolab/interviews/rso.html. This URL is no longer active.

53. For an example of Eno's enthusiasm for technology, see Brian Eno, "The Studio as Compositional Tool, Part 1," *Down Beat,* July 1983, 56–57, and "The Studio As Compositional Tool, Part 2," *Down Beat,* August 1983, 50–53.

54. Brian Eno, "The Revenge of the Intuitive," *Wired,* January 1999, http://www.wired.com/wired/archive/7.01/eno_pr.html.

55. Ibid.

56. Robert Moog, interview by Terry Gross, *Fresh Air,* National Public Radio, February 28, 2000.

57. Eno, "Revenge of the Intuitive."

58. Ellen Ullman, "The Dumbing-Down of Programming," *Salon,* May 1998, http://www.salonmagazine.com/21st/feature/1998/05/cov_feature.html. See also Ullman's *Close to the Machine: Technophilia and Its Discontents* (San Francisco: City Lights Books, 1997).

59. Leo Marx, "The Idea of 'Technology' and Postmodern Pessimism," in *Technology, Pessimism, and Postmodernism,* ed. Yaron Ezrahi, Everett Mendelsohn, and Howard P. Segal (Amherst: University of Massachusetts Press, 1995), 12.

60. An example of a theorist whose primary interest is exchange is Arjun Appadurai, who proposes that "*the commodity situation, in the social life of any 'thing' be defined as the situation in which its exchangeability ... for some other thing is its socially relevant feature*" ("Introduction: Commodities and the Politics of Value," in *The Social Life of Things: Commodities in Cultural Perspective,* ed. Arjun Appadurai [Cambridge: Cambridge University Press, 1986], 13; emphasis in the original).

61. Grant McCracken, "The Evocative Power of Things: Consumer Goods and the Preservation of Hopes and Ideals," in *Culture and Consumption: New Approaches to the Symbolic Character of Consumer Goods and Activities* (Bloomington and Indianapolis: Indiana University Press, 1988), 106.

62. Ibid.

63. Ibid., 109–10.

64. Ibid., 110.

65. Ibid.

66. Grant McCracken, *Plenitude* (Toronto: Periph.: Fluide, 1997), 39–42.

67. Ibid., 41.

68. Rothenberg, "Swank Life," 74.

69. Vaziri, "Mellow Gold," http://www.jetpack.com/lounge02/beats/lounge/mellowgold/index.html.

Try Combustible Edison's *I, Swinger*, Sub Pop 244, 1994; *Schizophonic*, Sub Pop 313, 1996; and *The Impossible World*, Sub Pop 431, 1998. See also their official website at http://www.subpop.com/bands/combustible/comed/.

Chapter Six

1. Manuel Castells, *The Rise of Network Society*, vol. 1 of *The Information Age: Economy, Society, and Culture* (Cambridge, Mass.: Blackwell, 1996), 66.
2. Arjun Appadurai, *Modernity at Large: Cultural Dimensions of Globalization*, Public Worlds, vol. 1 (Minneapolis: University of Minnesota Press, 1996).
3. This term is derived from Paul Virilio's idea of the "infosphere," a kind of information-scape that he believes will assume biological proportions in the near future (Virilio, *Open Sky*, trans. Julie Rose [London: Verso, 1997]), 84.
4. Doug Henwood, "Post What?" *Monthly Review* 48 (September 1996): 6–7.
5. Jerry H. Bentley, *Old World Encounters: Cross-Cultural Contacts and Exchanges in Pre-Modern Times* (New York and Oxford: Oxford University Press, 1993).
6. Ibid., 5.
7. Ibid., 26–27.
8. Immanuel Wallerstein, *The Modern World-System: Capitalist Agriculture and the Origins of the European World-Economy in the Sixteenth Century*, Studies in Social Discontinuity (New York and London: Academic Press, 1974), 102.
9. For more on this point, see Timothy D. Taylor, *Global Pop: World Music, World Markets* (New York: Routledge, 1997).
10. Stuart Hall, "The Local and the Global: Globalization and Ethnicity," in *Culture, Globalization and the World-System*, ed. Anthony D. King, Current Debates in Art History, vol. 3 (Binghamton, N.Y.: Department of Art and Art History, State University of New York at Binghamton, 1991), 34.
11. Timothy Brennan, *At Home in the World: Cosmopolitanism Now*, Convergences: Inventories of the Present (Cambridge and London: Harvard University Press, 1997).
12. Immanuel Wallerstein, *Historical Capitalism* (London: Verso, 1983), 39. Some have argued that global expansion has been driven not in searching for cheap labor, but for new markets (see, most famously, V. I. Lenin, *Imperialism, the Highest Stage of Capitalism: A Popular Outline* [New York: International, 1939)].
13. See, for just two examples, Jocelyne Guilbault, "On Redefining the 'Local' through World Music," *World of Music* 32 (1993): 33–47; and Rob Wilson and Wimal Dissanyake, eds., *Global/Local: Cultural Production and the Transnational Imaginary*, Asia-Pacific: Culture, Politics, and Society (Durham, N.C.: Duke University Press, 1996).
14. Roland Robertson, "Globalisation or Glocalisation?" *Journal of International Communication* 1 (1994): 33. See also Roland Robertson, "Glocalization: Time-Space and Homogeneity-Heterogeneity," in *Global Modernities*, ed. Mike Featherstone et al., Theory, Culture and Society (Thousand Oaks, Calif.: Sage, 1995). Virilio, *Open Sky*, also uses the term. For just two examples of the term in business discourse, see Christopher Conte, "A Special News Report on People and Their Jobs in Offices, Fields and Factories," *Wall Street Journal*, May 21, 1991, sec. A, p. 1; and Martha H. Peak, "Developing an International Style of Management," *Management Review*, February 1991, 32–35. A recent scholarly article that considers the time is Marwan M. Kraidy, "The Global, the Local, and the Hybrid: A Native Ethnography of Glocalization," *Critical Studies in Mass Communication* 16 (December 1999): 456–76. For other uses of

the term, as well as alternatives, see Philip Hayward, "Cultural Tectonics," *Convergence* 6 (Spring 2000): 39–47. Last, see Timothy D. Taylor, "World Music in Television Ads," *American Music* 18 (summer 2000): 162–92, for a discussion of American and European business attitudes toward the global and the local.

15. For a discussion of the false dichotomy of "global" and "local," see Charles Piot, *Remotely Global: Village Modernity in West Africa* (Chicago: University of Chicago Press, 1999). I would like to thank Louise Meintjes for this reference.

16. "IOC President to Thank Ami Singers," *Free China Journal*, http://ww3.sinanet. com/heartbeat/fcj/0726news/16_E.html. This URL is no longer active.

17. Pierre Bois, e-mail communication, March 29, 1999. He reiterates this rather defensively in a later e-mail, April 7, 1999.

18. By "New Age" I'm referring to a middle-class rejection of mainstream religions and a turn to other forms of spirituality. See Wouter J. Hanegraaff, *New Age Religion and Western Culture: Esotericism in the Mirror of Secular Thought*, Studies in the History of Religions, vol. 72 (Leiden: Brill Academic Publishers, 1996); Paul Heelas, *The New Age Movement: The Celebration of the Self and the Sacralization of Modernity* (Cambridge, Mass.: Blackwell, 1996); and Deborah Root, "Conquest, Appropriation, and Cultural Difference," chap. 3 in *Cannibal Culture: Art, Appropriation, and the Commodification of Difference* (Boulder: Westview Press, 1996). I should note that there has been a good deal of discussion on the Enigma Internet mailing list concerning the New Age category; some liked it, but the majority didn't.

19. Enigma FAQ, http://www.spikes.com/enigma/faq/faq5.htm.

20. Enigma Live Chat Event on the Internet, December 13, 1996.

21. Renata Huang, "Golden Oldie," *Far Eastern Economic Review*, November 2, 1995, 62.

22. Ashley Esarey, "An Ami Couple Seeks Recognition for Their Music," http://www.sinica.edu/tw/tit/special/0996_Innocence.html. This URL is no longer active.

23. There is also another story that Kuo tells: "Two years ago, my granddaughter brought a tape home and played me the song on the Enigma record. That's the first time I heard that Enigma had used my voice. I was very surprised and happy. It felt good to have people using my voice, but I was also surprised because I never sang such a song with all those other sounds, I wondered how it was made" (Lifvon Guo [Kuo Ying-nan], interview by Frank Kohler, *All Things Considered*, National Public Radio, June 11, 1996).

24. "Olympic Music from Taiwan," http://ourworld.compuserve.com/homepages/smlpp/ enigma.htm. This URL is no longer active. "Return to Innocence" has appeared on many other compilations, however, including: *Dance Mix USA*, vol. 2, Quality Music 3902, n.d.; *Dance Mix USA*, vol. 3, Quality Music 6727, 1995; *First Generation: 25 Years of Virgin*, Virgin 46589, 1998; *High on Dance*, Quality Music 6741, 1995; *Loaded*, vol. 1, EMI America 32393, 1995; and *Pure Moods*, Virgin 42186, 1997.

25. "Ami Sounds Scale Olympian Heights," http://www.gio.gov.tw/info/sinorama/ 8508/508006e1.html. This URL is no longer active.

26. Ibid.

27. "From Betelnuts to Billboard Hits," http://pathfind.com/@@CkDcMAcA0VE9Uaiw/ Asiaweek/96/1122/feat5.html. This URL is no longer active. This new recording is called *Circle of Life* (Magic Stone MSD030) and was released in October of 1998.

    Lost in the shuffle in the lawsuits and new recordings are the other singers on this song, Panay, Afan, and Kacaw, according to "True Feelings from the Bosom of Nature,"

Sinorama   Magazine,   http://www.gio.gov.tw/info/sinorama/8508/5080/161e.html. This URL is no longer active.

28. "IOC President to Thank Ami Singers," *Free China Journal,* http://ww3.sinanet.com/ heartbeat/fcj/0726news/16_E.html.

29. "Ami Sounds Scale Olympian Heights," http://www.gio.gov.tw/info/sinorama/8508/ 508006e2.html. This URL is no longer active.

30. "From Betelnuts to Billboard Hits."

31. "Ami Sounds Scale Olympian Heights," http://www.gio.gov.tw/info/sinorama/8508/ 508006e2.html.

32. "Olympic Music from Taiwan," http://ourworld.compuserve.com/homepages/smlpp/ enigma.htm. This is the figure also reported on the Internet newsgroup misc.activism.progressive by someone who seems to be an activist on behalf of the Kuos.

33. "Ami Sounds Scale Olympian Heights," http://www.gio.gov.tw/info/sinorama/8508/ 508006e2.html.

34. Deborah Kuo, "Taiwan Aborigines Sue Enigma, Music Companies," Central News Agency, March 28, 1998; and "Taiwan Couple Sue Enigma Over Vocals on International Hit," Associated Press, March 27, 1998.

35. "dcd" refers to the band Dead Can Dance. All quotations from Usenet groups on the Internet appear with their original spelling and punctuation unless otherwise indicated.

36. E. Patrick Ellisen, telephone communication, February 16, 1999.

37. E. Patrick Ellisen, telephone communication, April 21, 1999.

38. Quoted in Huang, "Golden Oldie," 62.

39. Brenda Sandburg, "Music to Their Ears," *Recorder,* June 24, 1999, 1. See also Victor Wong, "Taiwan Aboriginal Singers Settle Copyright Lawsuit," *Billboard,* July 31, 1999, 14.

40. The Hakka people were a migratory group who were persecuted at various times by the native peoples in whose territories they settled.

41. From http://www.mpath.com/~piaw/bunny/shinbao.htm. This URL is no longer active.

42. It is included on the soundtrack to the film *Chinese Box,* Blue Note 93285, 1998.

43. This is a common discourse by Western musicians and fans about non-Western musics—they are simply raw material for the genius of the Western star. See, for example, Paul Simon's discussion of his work with black South African musicians on *Graceland* in the documentary *Paul Simon: Born at the Right Time* (Warner Reprise Video, 1992), in which he clearly narrates himself as an adventurer/explorer going into the heart of darkest Africa to bring back natural, unrefined materials that he transforms into something valuable and worthy. See also Timothy D. Taylor, *Global Pop,* chap. 1, for a more general discussion of this assumption.

44. Enigma FAQ, http://www.spikes.com/enigma/.

45. Quoted in Sally Price, *Primitive Art in Civilized Places* (Chicago: University of Chicago Press, 1989), 100.

46. http://www.spikes.com/enigma/Mambo1.html. This URL is no longer active.

47. Ibid. Cretu and Enigma were sued for a sample on their earlier recording. An interview with Cretu published in Norway in 1990 says that "the Gregorian church chant is recorded in Rumania, and [Cretu] answers frenetically affirmative when we wonder if the singing monks have received their share of all the D-marks he gets" (Catharina Jacobsen, "Michael's Mystical Music" *(Oslo, Norway) Verdens Gang,* December 19, 1990

[trans. Joar Grimstvedt], available at http://www.stud.his.no/~joarg/Enigma/articles/verdensGang1290.html). But it later transpired that the recording was made in the 1970s by the Munich-based choir Kapelle Antiqua, which recognized its recording of chant sampled on the Enigma album. Even though this recording is in the public domain (and it is not clear why), the group sued, claiming that Cretu had infringed on its "right of personality." The group settled out of court. *Billboard*'s report on the suit says that "it is understood that the bulk of the money paid to Kapelle Antiqua is in recognition of the infringement of its 'right of personality.' Lesser sums have been paid to the record companies Polydor and BMG/Ariola for the unauthorized use of master recordings" (Ellie Weinert, " 'Sadeness' Creator Settles Sample Suit," *Billboard*, September 14, 1991, 80).

48. Simon Frith, "Music and Morality," in *Music and Copyright*, ed. Simon Frith, Edinburgh Law and Society Series (Edinburgh: Edinburgh University Press, 1993), 8.

49. Ellie Weinert, " 'Changes' in Works for Enigma," *Billboard*, January 8, 1994, 10.

50. Dominic Pride, "Virgin Stays with Proven Marketing for Enigma," *Billboard*, November 23, 1996, 1.

51. Review of *The Cross of Changes*, by Enigma, http://www.hyperreal.com/music/epsilon/reviews/enigma.cross. This URL is no longer active.

52. "Olympic Music from Taiwan," http://ourworld.compuserve.com/homepages/smlpp/enigma.htm.

53. See Douglas Rushkoff, "Conspiracy or Crackpot? Cyberlife US," *(Manchester) Guardian*, November 14, 1996, 13.

54. Paul Fisher, "Connected: Log and Learn Encyclopedia," *(London) Daily Telegraph*, December 11, 1999, 10.

55. Here are just some of the newspaper reports on the Encarta discrepancies: Charles Arthur, "How Many People Does It Take to Invent the Lightbulb?" *(London) Independent*, June 26, 1999, 13; Kevin J. Delaney, "Microsoft's Encarta Has Different Facts for Different Folks," *Wall Street Journal*, June 25, 1999, A1; and Stephen Moss, "Your History Is Bunk, My History Is Right," *(Manchester) Guardian*, June 29, 1999, section G2, p. 4.

56. Liner notes to *Polyphonies Vocales des aboriginès de Taïwan*, Inedit, Maison Des Cultures du Monde, W 2609 011, 1989.

57. These "ethnotechno" musics generally display a different attitude toward the sampled material, however. It's usually less foregrounded in the mix, there tend to be shorter samples, and the samples are not usually put to New Age ends as in Enigma's song. See chapter 3 for a discussion of the differences between these electronic musics and their use of samples.

  For more on "ethnotechno," see Erik Goldman, "Ethnotechno: A Sample Twist of Fate," *Rhythm Music*, July 1995, 36–39; Josh Kun, "Too Pure?" *Option*, May–June 1996, 54; and Jon Pareles, "A Small World after All. But Is That Good?" *New York Times*, March 24, 1996, sec. H, p. 34.

58. Nancy Guy, e-mail communication, March 29, 1999.

59. Juping Chang, "Ami Group Sings of Bittersweet Life in the Mountains," *Free China Journal*, January 1, 1999, http://publish.gio.gov.tw/FCJ/fcj.html. This URL is no longer active.

60. Ibid.

61. I am very grateful to Dale Wilson for translating the liner notes. For sources on the concept of self-exoticization and self-Orientalism, see Shuhei Hosokawa, "Soy Sauce Music: Harumi Hosono and Japanese Self-Orientalism," in *Widening the Horizon: Exoticism in Post-War Popular Music*, ed. Philip Hayward (Sydney: John Libby, 1999);

Koichi Iwabuchi, "Complicit Exoticism: Japan and its Other," *Continuum* 8 (1994): 49–82; and Joseph Tobin, *Re-Made in Japan: Everyday Life and Consumer Taste in a Changing Society* (New Haven, Conn.: Yale University Press, 1992).

62. Liner notes to Difang, *Circle of Life*, Magic Stone Music MSD-030, 1998.

63. *Deep Forest* sampled music from all over Africa. Released in Europe in 1992, it proved to be one of the best-selling albums on college campuses in 1993–94, selling over 1.5 million copies in the United States alone.

For more on Deep Forest, see Carrie Borzillo, "Deep Forest Growing in Popularity," *Billboard*, February 19, 1994, 8, and "U.S. Ad Use Adds to Commercial Success of *Deep Forest*," *Billboard*, June 11, 1994, 44; Steven Feld, "Pygmy Pop: A Genealogy of Schizophonic Mimesis," *Yearbook for Traditional Music* 28 (1997): 1–35 and "A Sweet Lullaby for World Music," *Public Culture* 12 (winter 2000): 145–71; René T. A. Lysloff, "Mozart in Mirrorshades: Ethnomusicology, Technology, and the Politics of Representation," *Ethnomusicology* 41 (spring/summer 1997): 206–19; Andrew Ross, review of *Deep Forest*, *Artforum* 32 (December 1993): 11–13; the extensive FAQ at http://www.spikes.com/worldmix/faq.htm; and Hugo Zemp, "The/An Ethnomusicologist and the Record Business," *Yearbook for Traditional Music* 28 (1997): 36–56.

Deep Forest took Lee's advice. Wind Records was established in Taiwan to preserve traditional musics. But it was one of their collections that found its way onto *Boheme*, on which they sampled a selection from a CD entitled *The Songs of the Yami Tribe*, vol. 3 of *The Music of Aborigines on Taiwan Island*, Wind Records, TCD-1503, 1993. According to the Deep Forest FAQ, the Ami sample on *Boheme* is "A Recitative for Describing Loneliness," a title so evocative that it would seem hard to pass up (the Deep Forest FAQ is at http://www.spikes.com/worldmix/faq.htm). The Yami are a different group than the Ami; it isn't a different transliteration. The program note accompanying the original Yami recording says that "A Recitative for Describing Loneliness" employs a scale uncommon in Yami music and is borrowed from the Ami. But to Roger Lee, it seems that an aborigine is an aborigine: Can I give you Ami? No? Yami? As usual, this appropriative act by Deep Forest becomes converted into a sales tactic. Next to the entry in Wind Records' catalog for Yami recording there is a little blurb mentioning that "A Recitative for Describing Loneliness" was "excerpted" on Deep Forest's *Boheme*.

The sampled song is "Marta's Song," Marta being the well-known Hungarian singer Marta Sebestyén. "A Recitative for Describing Loneliness" flits through the background when Sebestyén isn't singing her folk song (beginning at 1:45). A Hungarian/Transylvanian reader of the Enigma mailing list informs me that this is a traditional song about a woman who is lamenting being pregnant and alone.

64. Anita Huang, "Global Music, Inc.," http://www.gio.gov.tw/info/fcr/8/p42.htm. This URL is no longer active. See also a more recent report on the growing popularity of music with an "Aboriginal flair" in Taiwan: Victor Wong's "Taiwan's Power Station Brings Aboriginal Flair to What's Music," *Billboard*, July 11, 1998, 48.

65. Steven Feld, "From Schizophonia to Schismogenesis: On the Discourses and Commodification Practices of 'World Music' and 'World Beat,'" in Charles Keil and Steven Feld, *Music Grooves: Essays and Dialogues* (Chicago: University of Chicago Press, 1994).

Chapter Seven

1. Packard Bell was proud of this spot, and on its website offered eight different still photos from it (see fig, 7.1). The first page of their website features a new logo that asks

their trademark question, "Wouldn't you rather be at home?" They also promised an eventual trio of thirty-second ads that will "expand on the commercial's main ideas." The ad itself was once available for downloading, but the URL is no longer active.

2. Jürgen Habermas, *The Structural Transformation of the Public Sphere: An Inquiry into a Category of Bourgeois Society,* trans. Thomas Burger and Frederick Lawrence (Cambridge, Mass.: MIT Press, 1991), 27.

3. Geoff Eley, "Nations, Publics, and Political Cultures: Placing Habermas in the Nineteenth Century," in *Culture/Power/History: A Reader in Contemporary Social Theory,* ed. Nicholas B. Dirks, Geoff Eley and Sherry B. Ortner, Princeton Studies in Culture/Power/History (Princeton, N.J.: Princeton University Press, 1994), 297.

4. Nancy Fraser, *Unruly Practices: Power, Discourse and Gender in Contemporary Social Theory* (Minneapolis: University of Minnesota Press, 1989). See also Eley, "Nations, Publics, and Political Cultures."

5. Arjun Appadurai and Carol Breckenridge, "Why Public Culture?" *Public Culture* 1 (fall 1988): 5.

6. Marshall Berman, *All That Is Solid Melts into Air: The Experience of Modernity* (New York: Penguin, 1988). See also Richard Sennett, *The Fall of Public Man* (1977; reprint, New York: W. W. Norton, 1992).

7. Mike Davis, *City of Quartz: Excavating the Future in Los Angeles* (New York: Vintage, 1992); Edward W. Soja, *Postmodern Geographies: The Reassertion of Space in Critical Social Theory* (London and New York: Verso, 1989).

8. See Sarah Thornton, *Club Cultures: Music, Media and Subcultural Capital,* Music/Culture (Middletown, Conn.: Wesleyan University Press, 1996), for a discussion of the dance music underground in the United Kingdom and bands' naming practices.

9. Just as the original version of this chapter was going to press I learned that Bryn Jones died of a rare fungal infection on January 14, 1999. See Neil Strauss, "Bryn Jones, 38, Musician Known As Muslimgauze," *New York Times,* January 28, 1999, sec. C, p. 23.

10. http://www.obsolete.com/banco/.

11. Toby Marks, "Banco de Gaia," interview by Nisus, http://www.hallucinet.com/asylem/asylem4/bdg.htm.

12. http://www.obsolete.com/banco/.

13. For more on Deep Forest, see Carrie Borzillo, "U.S. Ad Use Adds to Commercial Success of *Deep Forest,*" *Billboard,* June 11, 1994, 44, and "Deep Forest Growing in Popularity," *Billboard,* February 19, 1994, 8; Steven Feld, "Pygmy Pop: A Genealogy of Schizophonic Mimesis," *Yearbook for Traditional Music* 28 (1997): 1–35; Andrew Ross, review of *Deep Forest, Artforum* 32 (December 1993): 11; Al Weisel, "Deep Forest's Lush Lullaby," *Rolling Stone,* April 21, 1994, 26; and Hugo Zemp, "The/An Ethnomusicologist and the Record Business," *Yearbook for Traditional Music* 28 (1997): 36–56.

14. Susana Loza reminds me, however, that that electronic dance music little cultures vary in different parts of the world. In the United Kingdom, DJs are much more public figures—stars—than in the United States, for example (Susana Loza, e-mail communication, July 6, 2000).

15. Bryn Jones, interview, *Eskhatos* (1995), http://pretentious.net/Muslimgauze/articles/eskatos.htm.

16. Richard Gehr, "Muslimgauze: Beyond the Veil," *Village Voice,* October 28, 1994, 67.

17. Bryn Jones, interview, *Eskhatos* (1995), http://pretentious.net/Muslimgauze/articles/eskatos.htm.

18. "Muslimgauze," a media release by Extreme, http://www.xtr.com/extreme/muslimg.htm.

19. Bryn Jones, interview, *Eskhatos* (1995), http://pretentious.net/Muslimgauze/articles/eskatos.htm.

20. Ios Smolders, review of Muslimgauze, *Blue Mosque*, Vital, November 1, 1994, http://www.v2.nl/Archief/ArchiefTexten/Vitals/Vital38.html.

21. Bryn Jones, interview, *Eskhatos* (1995), http://pretentious.net/Muslimgauze/articles/eskatos.htm.

22. Toby Marks, "Banco de Gaia—Recording and Playing Live," interview, http://www.demon.co.uk/london-calling/mbanco1.html. This URL is no longer active.

23. Ibid.

24. Ibid.

25. Marks expressed reservations in another interview, however, where he questioned this process: "But to me that always seems a bit like saying well here's the proper one and this remix album is stuff we played around with and some of it's alright and some of [it] isn't. I really want to do it that way" (Toby Marks, "Banco de Gaia," interview, http://www.chaoscontrol.com/archive2/banco/bancoten.html). Clearly there is some tension between dance-related electronica, such as that which Marks and Jones produce, and dance music for clubs, but that is the subject for another study.

26. Toby Marks, interview, http://www.demon.co.uk/london-calling/mbancocov.html.

27. Toby Marks, "From London to Lhasa," interview by Mike Kenney, http://www.outer-bass.com/resonance/banco/indexF.html. This URL is no longer active.

28. Toby Marks, "Banco de Gaia—Tibet and Last Train to Lhasa," interview, http://www.demon.co.uk/london-calling/mbanco3.html. This URL is no longer active.

29. The Banco de Gaia website is http://www.obsolete.com/banco/.

30. When I was seeking permission to reprint this cover, the person in charge of licensing at Higher Octave music asked what my writing was about. I told her it was about some electronic musicians and their political interests. I could almost hear her bristling over the phone: Eskinasi's music is *not* political, but spiritual, she told me. If I wrote about it as political, Higher Octave would deny me permission to reprint.

31. Toby Marks, "From London to Lhasa," interview by Mike Kenney, http://www.outer-bass.com/resonance/banco/indexF.html. This URL is no longer active.

32. For writings on these composers and their uses of other musics, see Lawrence Morton, "Footnotes to Stravinsky Studies: *Le Sacre du Printemps*," *Tempo* 78 (March 1979): 9–16; Richard Taruskin, "Russian Folk Melodies in *The Rite of Spring*," *Journal of the American Musicological Society* 33 (fall 1980): 501–43; Benjamin Suchoff, "Ethnomusicological Roots of Béla Bartók's Musical Language," *World of Music* 29 (1987): 43–65; and J. Peter Burkholder, *All Made of Tunes: Charles Ives and the Uses of Musical Borrowing* (New Haven, Conn.: Yale University Press, 1995).

33. Olivier Messiaen, *The Technique of My Musical Language*, trans. John Satterfield (Paris: A. Leduc, 1956).

34. Karl H. Wörner, *Stockhausen: Life and Work*, trans. and ed. Bill Hopkins (Berkeley and Los Angeles: University of California Press, 1973), 58. See also Karlheinz Stockhausen, "World Music," trans. Bernard Radloff, *Dalhousie Review* 69 (fall 1989): 318-26; and *Towards a Cosmic Music*, selected and trans. Tim Nevill (Longmead, England: Element Books, 1989).

35. For discussions of sampling in hip hop, see Andrew Bartlett, "Airshafts, Loudspeakers, and the Hip Hop Sample: Contexts and African American Musical Aesthetics," *African*

American Review 28 (winter 1994): 639–52; and Tricia Rose, *Black Noise: Rap Music and Black Culture in Contemporary America* (Middletown, Conn.: Wesleyan University Press, 1994).

36. Prince Be, interview by Terry Gross, *Fresh Air*, National Public Radio, November 29, 1995.

37. Mark Dery, "Tommy Boy X 3: Digital Underground, Coldcut, and De La Soul Jam the Beat with Audio Junkyard Collisions," *Keyboard*, March 1991, 70.

38. Mark Dery, "Public Enemy: Confrontation," *Keyboard*, September 1990, 93.

39. In the influential opening essay in Fredric Jameson, *Postmodernism, or, the Cultural Logic of Late Capitalism* (Durham, N.C.: Duke University Press, 1991).

40. Dominic Pride, "U.K.'s Nation of 'Ethno-Techno,'" *Billboard*, October 28, 1995, 52.

41. See, among others, Feld, "Pygmy Pop"; Deborah Root, *Cannibal Culture: Art, Appropriation, and the Commodification of Difference* (Boulder: Westview Press, 1996); Timothy D. Taylor, *Global Pop: World Music, World Markets* (New York: Routledge, 1997); and Marianna Torgovnick, *Gone Primitive: Savage Intellects, Modern Lives* (Chicago: University of Chicago Press, 1990).

42. Toby Marks, "Banco de Gaia," interview, http://www.chaoscontrol.com/archive2/banco/bancosamples.html.

43. Toby Marks, "From London to Lhasa," interview by Mike Kenney, http://www.outerbass.com/resonance/banco/indexF.html. This URL is no longer active.

44. Feld, "Pygmy Pop," 26.

45. Raymond Barglow, *The Crisis of the Self in the Age of Information: Computers, Dolphins, and Dreams*, Critical Psychology (New York: Routledge, 1994), 53.

46. Manuel Castells, *The Rise of the Network Society*, vol. 1 of *The Information Age: Economy, Society and Culture* (Cambridge, Mass.: Blackwell, 1996), 3.

47. Paul Virilio, *The Art of the Motor*, trans. Julie Rose (Minneapolis: University of Minnesota Press, 1995), 125, 138; emphasis in the original.

48. Thornton, *Club Cultures*, 71.

49. Andrew Goodwin, "Sample and Hold: Pop Music in the Digital Age of Reproduction," in *On Record: Rock, Pop, and the Written Word*, ed. Simon Frith and Andrew Goodwin (New York: Pantheon, 1990).

50. Jameson, *Postmodernism*.

51. All quotations from Usenet groups retain the original spelling unless otherwise indicated.

52. On this point, see, most importantly, Jean Baudrillard's *In the Shadow of Silent Majorities* (New York: Semiotext(e), 1983), and *Selected Writings*, ed. Mark Poster (Stanford, Calif.: Stanford University Press, 1988); and Jameson, *Postmodernism*.

53. Collected in Walter Benjamin, *Illuminations*, trans. Harry Zohn, ed. Hannah Arendt (New York: Schocken Books, 1969).

54. See John Mowitt, "The Sound of Music in the Era of Its Electronic Reproducibility," in *Music and Society: The Politics of Composition, Performance and Reception*, ed. Richard Leppert and Susan McClary (Cambridge: Cambridge University Press, 1987); Thomas G. Schumacher, "'This Is a Sampling Sport': Digital Sampling, Rap Music and the Law in Cultural Production," *Media, Culture and Society* 17 (April 1995): 253–73; Paul Théberge, "Random Access: Music, Technology, Postmodernism," in *The Last Post: Music after Modernism*, ed. Simon Miller, (Manchester: Manchester University Press, 1993); and many others.

55. Goodwin, "Sample and Hold," 259.

56. Andreas Huyssen, *After the Great Divide: Modernism, Mass Culture, Postmodernism, Theories of Representation and Difference* (Bloomington and Indianapolis: University of Indiana Press, 1986).

57. Pierre Bourdieu, *Distinction: A Social Critique of the Judgement of Taste*, trans. Richard Nice (Cambridge: Harvard University Press, 1984). See also Andrew Goodwin's "Popular Music and Postmodern Theory," *Cultural Studies* 5 (May 1991): 174–90 for a useful critique of the idea of the breakdown of distinctions between high and low.

58. See Alan Durant, "A New Day for Music? Digital Technologies in Contemporary Music-Making," in *Culture, Technology and Creativity*, ed. Philip Hayward (London: John Libbey, [1990]), esp. 193–95.

59. Simon Frith, "Art versus Technology: The Strange Case of Popular Music," *Media, Culture and Society* 8 (July 1986): 278.

60. Durant, "A New Day for Music?" 193.

61. Benjamin, "The Work of Art in the Age of Mechanical Reproduction," 232.

62. Jacques Attali, *Noise: The Political Economy of Music*, trans. Brian Massumi; Theory and History of Literature, vol. 16 (Minneapolis: University of Minnesota Press, 1985), 134.

63. Ibid., 147.

64. http://www2.gist.net.au/~aek/batz/paradigm.txt. This URL is no longer active. Thanks are due to Susana Loza, who gave me this URL. See also David Toop, *Ocean of Sound: Aether Talk, Ambient Sound and Imaginary Worlds* (London and New York: Serpent's Tail, 1995), 212–14 for a discussion of the importance of cheap equipment.

    As the end of this quotation indicates, the sounds of these instruments quickly became aestheticized and fetishized, sending the costs of favored used instruments through the roof.

65. Mark Prendergast, "The Chilling Fields," *New Statesman and Society*, January 13, 1995, 32.

66. From a posting to the Usenet group alt.rave on the Internet.

Chapter Eight

1. The notion of the "little culture" was forwarded by Grant McCracken, *Plenitude* (Toronto: Periph.: Fluide, 1997), 25. While probably nobody in the Goa/psy trance little culture would agree on a "must have" list of albums, here are a few favorites for those who might want to hear more: Astral Projection: *Dancing Galaxy*, Trust in Trance PHLCD2089-2, 1997; Hallucinogen: *The Lone Deranger*, Twisted Records TWSCD1, 1997, and *Twisted*, EFA 0995, 1999; Juno Reactor, *Beyond the Infinite*, Cleopatra 9739, 1996, and *Transmissions*, NovaMute 3016, 1993; Space Cat: *Beam Me Up*, Yoyo Records 34-2, 1999.

2. Simon Reynolds, "A New Invader on the Dance Floor," *New York Times*, November 29, 1998, 35. See also Simon Reynolds, "Trance International," *Spin*, June 2000, 106–112.

3. For histories of these musics and their offshoots, see Kai Fikentscher, *"You Better Work!" Underground Dance Music in New York City*, Music/Culture (Middletown, Conn.: Wesleyan University Press, 2000); Susana Loza, "Global Rhetoric, Transnational Markets: The (Post)Modern Trajectories of Electronic Dance Musics" (Ph.D. diss., University of California, Berkeley, in preparation); Ulf Poschardt, *DJ Culture*, trans. Shaun Whiteside (London: Quartet, 1998); Simon Reynolds, *Generation Ecstasy: Into the World of Techno and Rave Culture* (Boston: Little, Brown, 1998); Hillegonda C. Rietveld, *This Is Our House: House Music, Cultural Spaces and Technologies*, Popular Cultural Studies, vol. 13 (Aldershot, England: Arena, 1998); Greg Rule, *Electro Shock!*

Groundbreakers of Synth Music (San Francisco: Miller Freeman, 1999); and Dan Sicko, *Techno Rebels: The Renegades of Electronic Funk* (New York: Billboard Books, 1999).

4. All quotations from the World Wide Web, Usenet, and Internet mailing lists appear as originally spelled and punctuated unless otherwise noted. For more on the travelers, see Richard Lowe and William Shaw, *Travellers: Voices of the New Age Nomads* (London: Fourth Estate, 1993).

5. See the Goa trance mailing list FAQ at http://www.party.net/. To my knowledge, there has been no scholarly study of this little culture in Goa, though there is a good published article and a longer web version: Erik Davis, "Sampling Paradise: The Technofreak Legacy of Golden Goa," *Option*, March–April 1995, 74; the web version is at http://www.levity.com/figment/paradise.html.

6. See the 604 list FAQ at http://www.party.net/.

7. John-Emanuel Gartmann, interviews by author, New York, N.Y., June 4 and August 20, 1999.

8. For more on this, see Reynolds, *Generation Ecstasy*, and Sarah Thornton, *Club Cultures: Music, Media and Subcultural Capital*, Music/Culture (Middletown, Conn.: Wesleyan University Press, 1996). For more on dance and ecstasy, see Wayne Anthony, *Class of 88: The True Acid House Experience* (London: Virgin, 1998); Matthew Collin, *Altered State: The Story of Ecstasy Culture and Acid House* (New York: Serpent's Tail, 1997); Nicholas Saunders and Rick Doblin, *Ecstasy: Dance Trance and Transformation* (Oakland, Calif.: Quick American Archives, 1996); and Mary Anna Wright, "The Great British Ecstasy Revolution," in *DiY Culture*, ed. George McKay (London and New York: Verso, 1998).

9. The PLUR motto began in the rave scene and is still most closely bound to that particular subculture. Laura La Gassa has written a PLUR treatise, "PLUR: P(eace), L(ove), U(nity), R(espect)," online at http://www.hyperreal.org/raves/spirit/plur/PLUR.html.

10. Fikentscher, *"You Better Work!,"* 79.

11. Ibid., 81.

12. Most of Keil's writings on participatory discrepancies and the groove are collected in Charles Keil and Steven Feld, *Music Grooves: Essays and Dialogues* (Chicago: University of Chicago Press, 1994).

13. Keil and Feld, "Participatory Discrepancies and the Power of Music," in Keil and Feld, *Music Grooves*, 98.

14. See also Hans Weisethaunet, "PD-Theory: On Being 'Discrepant' or 'Playing It Right,'" in preparation, for a similar point.

15. Keil and Feld, "Dialogue 2: Grooving on Participation," in Keil and Feld, *Music Grooves*, 158.

16. Christopher Small, *Musicking: The Meanings of Performing and Listening*, Music/Culture (Hanover, N.H.: University Press of New England, 1999), 9; emphasis in the original.

17. Alfred Schutz, "Making Music Together: A Study in Social Relationships," *Social Research* 18 (1951): 76–97.

18. Keil, "Participatory Discrepancies," 98.

19. For a discussion of the admixture of technology and spiritualism, see Erik Davis, *Techgnosis: Myth, Magic and Mysticism in the Age of Information* (New York: Harmony, 1998).

20. When I first sent out a query to the Goa trance mailing list seeking input, one person wrote back and said, "Oh, you're an ethnomusicologist? Do you know Gilbert Rouget's

Music and Trance?" The trance that people talk about, though, isn't really comparable to Rouget's. Early in his book he makes a distinction between *trance* and *ecstasy*, about which he says there is some slippage in the literature. Rouget elects to use *ecstasy* "solely to describe one particular type of state—altered states, let us say, attained in silence, immobility, and solitude," and restricts *trance* to refer "solely to those [states] that are obtained by means of noise" (Rouget, *Music and Trance: A Theory of the Relations between Music and Possession*, trans. Brunhilde Biebuyck [Chicago: University of Chicago Press, 1985], 7.) The experiences described by Goa/psy trance devotees are neither, and aren't really covered in Rouget's book. But this doesn't mean that trance fans don't pursue interests in these forms of altered consciousness, or that they don't attempt to forge discursive and iconographic links with those premodern cultures that still do.

21. Chris Decker, liner notes to *Return to the Source: The Chakra Journey*, RTTS CD2, n.d., 4; ellipsis in the original.
22. http://www.third-eye.org.uk/trip/what.html.
23. Ibid.
24. See, for just a few examples, Fikentscher, *"You Better Work!"*; Ben Malbon, "Clubbing: Consumption, Identity and the Spatial Practices of Every-Night Life," in *Cool Places: Geographies of Youth Cultures*, ed. Tracey Skelton and Gill Valentine (London and New York: Routledge, 1998); Antonio Melechi, "The Ecstasy of Disappearance," in *Rave Off: Politics and Deviance in Contemporary Youth Culture*, ed. Steve Redhead, Popular Cultural Studies, vol. 1 (Aldershot, England: Avebury, 1993); Reynolds, *Generation Ecstasy*; and Rietveld, *This Is Our House*.
25. Malbon, "Clubbing"; Melechi, "Ecstasy of Disappearance." Rietveld, *This Is Our House*, 192. See Jeremy Gilbert and Ewan Pearson, *Discographies: Dance Music, Culture and the Politics of Sound* (New York: Routledge, 1999), for another recent work on contemporary electronic musics skeptical of the use of youth subcultural theory. Georgiana Gore, "The Beat Goes On: Trance, Dance and Tribalism in Rave Culture," in *Dance in the City*, ed. Helen Thomas (New York: St. Martin's Press, 1997); Drew Hemment, "e Is for *Ekstasis*," *New Formations* 31 (summer 1997): 23–38; Tim Jordan, "Collective Bodies: Raving and the Politics of Gilles Deleuze and Felix Guattari," *Body and Society* 1 (March 1995): 125–44; Maria Pini, "Women and the Early British Rave Scene," in *Back to Reality: Social Experience and Cultural Studies*, ed. Angela McRobbie (Manchester: Manchester University Press, 1997); and Reynolds, *Generation Ecstasy*.
26. Simon Reynolds, "Return to Eden," in *Psychedelia Britannica: Hallucinogenic Drugs in Britain*, ed. Antonio Melechi (London: Turnaround, 1997). I am indebted to Susana Loza for this reference.
27. Gianfranco Salvatore, "*Dea ex Machina*: La Trance, i Rave e il 'Bisogno di Trascendenza,'" and "Introduzione," both in *Techno-Trance: Una Rivoluzione Musicale di Fine Millennio*, ed. Gianfranco Salvatore (Rome: Castelvecchi, 1998). I would like to thank Gianfranco Salvatore for making English translations of these chapters available to me.

Other, tangential, exceptions include Tim Becker and Raphael Woebs, " 'Back to the Future': Hearing, Rituality and Techno," trans. Linda Fujie, *World of Music* 41 (1999): 59-71; Fikentscher, *"You Better Work!"*; and Barbara O'Connor, "Safe Sets: Women, Dance and 'Communitas,' " in *Dance in the City*, ed. Helen Thomas (New York: St. Martin's, 1997), though Victor Turner's communitas doesn't play much of a role in either Fikentscher's or O'Connor's analyses.

28. Reynolds, *Generation Ecstasy*, 242; emphasis in the original.
29. Stuart Hall and Tony Jefferson, eds., *Resistance through Rituals: Youth Subcultures in*

Post-War Britain (1976; reprint, New York: Routledge, 1993); Dick Hebdige, *Subculture: The Meaning of Style*, New Accents (1979; reprint, New York: Routledge, 1991); and Thornton, *Club Cultures*.

30. Ken Gelder and Sarah Thornton, eds., *The Subcultures Reader* (London and New York: Routledge, 1997).

31. Stuart Hall and Tony Jefferson, eds., *Resistance through Rituals*; Dick Hebdige, *Subculture*; and Paul E. Willis, *Learning to Labor: How Working Class Kids Get Working Class Jobs* (New York: Columbia University Press, 1981).

    For similar points with respect to the dominance of resistance studies, see Richard Jenkins, *Lads, Citizens, and Ordinary Kids: Working-Class Youth Life-Styles in Belfast* (London: Routledge and Kegan Paul, 1983); and Helena Wulff, "Introduction: Introducing Youth Culture in Its Own Right: The State of the Art and New Possibilities," in *Youth Cultures: A Cross-Cultural Perspective* (New York: Routledge, 1995).

32. Malbon, "Clubbing," 281.

33. McCracken, *Plenitude*, 38.

34. See Timothy D. Taylor, *Global Pop: World Music, World Markets* (New York: Routledge, 1997), xvii–xviii.

35. For a similar critique, see David Hesmondhalgh, "The Cultural Politics of Dance Music," *Soundings* [London] 5 (spring 1997): 167–78.

36. Gore, "The Beat Goes On," 57.

37. Melechi, "The Ecstasy of Disappearance," 33.

38. Hemment, "e Is for *Ekstasis*," 26.

39. Michel Gaillot, *Multiple Meaning: Techno, An Artistic and Political Laboratory of the Present*, trans. Warren Niesluchowski (Paris: Éditions Dis Voir [1998]), 23.

40. Émile Durkheim, "The Dualism of Human Nature," in *Émile Durkheim on Morality and Society*, ed. Robert Bellah (Chicago: University of Chicago Press, 1973), 152.

41. Émile Durkheim, *The Elementary Forms of Religious Life*, trans. Karen E. Fields (New York and London: Free Press, 1995), 217-18.

42. Ibid., 220.

43. With the phrase "totally autonomous zone," the writer is probably referring to Hakim Bey's idea of the "Temporary Autonomous Zone" or TAZ, the notion of a temporary space that is separate from the dominant culture. See Hakim Bey, *T.A.Z.: The Temporary Autonomous Zone, Ontological Anarchy, Poetic Terrorism*, New Autonomy series (Brooklyn, N.Y.: Autonomedia, 1991).

44. Charles Lindholm, "Charisma, Crowd Psychology and Altered States of Consciousness," *Culture, Medicine and Psychiatry* 16 (September 1992): 293.

45. Durkheim, "Dualism of Human Nature," 153.

46. Victor Turner, *The Ritual Process: Structure and Anti-Structure* (Chicago: Aldine, 1969), 95.

47. Ibid., 96.

48. Ibid., 97.

49. Ibid., 167.

50. Ibid., 126.

51. Ibid., 127.

52. Ibid., 128.

53. Erika Bourguignon, "Epilogue: Some Notes on Contemporary Americans and the Irrational," in *Religion, Altered States of Consciousness, and Social Change*, ed. Erika Bourguignon (Columbus: Ohio State University Press, 1973), 350.

54. Bourguignon, "Introduction: A Framework for the Comparative Study of Altered

States of Consciousness," in Bourguignon, ed., *Religion, Altered States of Consciousness, and Social Change*, 31.

55. Michel Maffesoli, *The Time of the Tribes: The Decline of Individualism in Mass Society*, trans. Don Smith (Thousand Oaks, Calif.: Sage, 1995), 11. For a discussion of Maffesoli's ideas with respect to music, see Andy Bennett, "Subcultures or Neo-Tribes? Rethinking the Relationship between Youth, Style and Musical Taste," *Sociology* 33 (August 1999): 599–617.

56. Maffesoli, *The Time of Tribes*, 11. Also, Maffesoli's concept of "tribes" has been fairly influential among some theorists of electronic dance music (such as Georgiana Gore and Ben Malbon), but in calling this new social formation a "tribe," we are in the same problematic territory as Sarah Thornton ("subculture") or Will Straw ("scene"; Straw, "Systems of Articulation, Logics of Change: Communities and Scenes in Popular Music," *Cultural Studies* 5 [October 1991]: 368–88). Labeling a social group implies a certain level of homogeneity, even when the theorist makes a caveat against that perception. Others theorists, such as Gore, emphasize the extreme, even rhizomatic heterogeneity.

The problem is less the label than the fact that such arguments infrequently incorporate an ethnographic perspective. One of the most interesting things to me about New York City's Goa/psy trance little culture is the fact that there are those in it who are attempting to make it a community in Will Straw's sense of the term (referring to a reasonably cohesive group), while at the same time there were those who were less interested. New York City's little culture is heterogeneous and fluid—a "scene" in Straw's usage—but its scenes have knots of greater homogeneity, of, community, even, as in the group of organizers I knew best.

57. Salvatore, "Introduzione."

58. Raymond Williams, *Marxism and Literature*, Marxist Introductions (New York: Oxford University Press, 1977); see esp. chap. 8, "Dominant, Residual, and Emergent."

59. Goa Gil, interview by Michael Gosney, *Beam*, 1999, http://www.radiov.com/production/beam/innerviews/goagil/.

60. To which list Erika Bourguignon would add Aldous Huxley and Henri Michaux. Generally, she says, there were several streams of influence on the American hippies: European literary/artistic tradition of experimentation with drugs, represented most prominently by Huxley and Michaux, and the influence of Hinduism (Bourguignon, "Epilogue," 347).

61. See instead David Farber, *The Age of Great Dreams: America in the 1960s*, American Century (New York: Hill and Wang, 1994); and Todd Gitlin, *The Sixties: Years of Hope, Days of Rage*, rev. ed. (New York: Bantam, 1993).

62. Turner, *Ritual Process*, 138–39; emphasis in the original.

63. Durkheim, "Dualism of Human Nature," 153.

64. Bourguignon, "Epilogue," 349.

65. Ibid., 352–53.

66. For a discussion of the reactions against technocratic culture, see Andrew Feenberg, "Technocracy and Rebellion: The May Events of 1968," chap 2 of *Questioning Technology* (New York: Routledge, 1999); Leo Marx, "*Technology*: The Emergence of a Hazardous Concept," *Social Research* 64 (fall 1997): 965–88; and Theodore Roszak, *The Making of a Counter Culture: Reflections on the Technocratic Society and Its Youthful Opposition* (New York: Anchor, 1969).

67. Liner notes to *Return to the Source: Deep Trance and Ritual Beats*, RTTS CD1, n.d., 2-3.

The CJB (now CJA) refers to the Criminal Justice and Public Order Act in the United Kingdom, passed in November of 1994, which attempted to ban raves.

68. Turner, *Ritual Process*, 165.
69. There is an interesting literature on the use of acoustic instruments and folk musicians; see Simon Frith, *Sound Effects: Youth, Leisure, and the Politics of Rock 'n' Roll* (New York: Pantheon Books, 1981), and "Art versus Technology: The Strange Case of Popular Music," *Media, Culture and Society* 8 (July 1986): 263–79.
70. A good Roland TB-303 page on the Internet with sound samples is at http://www.teknet.ch/tb-303/. There is also a newsgroup devoted to this instrument, alt.music.synth.roland.tb303.
71. This writer seems to be referring to a break in the beat, a usage I heard others employ. In African-American musics, however, a "breakbeat" refers to the sampled drum passages from classic recordings. The writer is probably referring to a moment in the tune when the beat drops out momentarily called a breakdown. I would like to thank Luther Elliott for clarifying this point.
72. See Louise Knapp, "Two Pentiums and a Microphone," http://www.wire.com/news/culture/story/19415.html.
73. http://www.reactor.vip.lv/readme/books/dancemus.htm. This URL is no longer active.
74. http://www.third-eye.org.uk/trip/why.html.
75. See Moby in "The Cult of the DJ," *Social Text* 43 (fall 1995), 72; and Gore, "The Beat Goes On."
76. Lindholm, "Charisma," 294.
77. http://www.sonicbarrier.org.
78. http://www.geocities.com/SouthBeach/Keys/6004/speed.htm.
79. Moby, "The DJ Speaks," *Beam*, 1999, http://www.radiov.com/production/beam/features/djspeaks/.

Chapter Nine

1. See Peter L. Berger and Thomas Luckmann, *The Social Construction of Reality: A Treatise in the Sociology of Knowledge* (1966; reprint, New York: Irvington, 1980) for an important and instructive discussion of the ways in which everyday reality presents itself as the way things have always been and thus, by extension, anything new seems to be entirely new.
2. While it doesn't consider consumption as a theoretical issue, I would be remiss not to mention Susan D. Crafts, Daniel Cavicchi, and Charles Keil, *My Music*, Music/Culture (Middletown, Conn.: Wesleyan University Press, 1993), which interviews a variety of listeners about their musical tastes.
3. Much of my recent thinking on the consumption of popular culture has been influenced by Purnima Mankekar, *Screening Culture, Viewing Politics: An Ethnography of Television, Womanhood, and Nation in Postcolonial India* (Durham, N.C.: Duke University Press, 1999).
4. Marshall Berman, *All That Is Solid Melts into Air: The Experience of Modernity* (New York: Penguin, 1988), 5.
5. Marshall McLuhan, *Understanding Media: The Extensions of Man* (1964; reprint, Cambridge, Mass.: MIT Press, 1994), 18.
6. Bryan Pfaffenberger, "Fetishized Objects and Humanized Nature: Towards an Anthropology of Technology," *Man* 23 (June 1988), 249.

REFERENCES

Music Scores
Stockhausen, Karlheinz. *Telemusik*. Vienna: Universal Edition, 1969.

Discography
101 Strings. *Astro Sounds from Beyond the Year 2000*. Scamp SCP 9717-2, 1996.
Air. *Moon Safari*. Caroline 6644, 1998.
Bachelor's Guide to the Galaxy. Vol. 1 of *Cocktail Mix*. Rhino R2 72237, 1995.
Banco de Gaia. *Last Train to Lhasa*. Mammoth/Planet Dog MR0115-2, 1995.
Carlos, Wendy. *Switched On Bach 2000*. Telarc 80323, 1992.
———. *Switched On Boxed Set*. East Side Digital 81422, 1999.
Chinese Box. Blue Note 93285, 1998.
Combustible Edison. *I, Swinger*. Sub Pop 244, 1994.
———. *The Impossible World*. Sub Pop 431, 1998.
———. *Schizophonic*. Sub Pop 313, 1996.
Dance Mix USA, vol. 2. Quality Music 3902, n.d.
Dance Mix USA, vol. 3. Quality Music 6727, 1995.
The Day the Earth Stood Still. BMG/Fox 11010, 1993.
Deep Forest. 550 Music/Epic BK-57840, 1992.
Deep Forest. *Boheme*. 550 Music/Epic BK 67115, 1995.
Difang. *Circle of Life*. Magic Stone Music MSD030, 1998.
Enigma. *MCMXC A.D.* Capitol 86224, 1991.
Enigma 2. *The Cross of Changes*. Charisma/Virgin 7243 8 39236 2 5, 1993.
Eskinasi, Alain. *Many Worlds, One Tribe*. Higher Octave Music HOMCD 7089, 1996.
Fatboy Slim. Remix of Jean Jacques Perrey's "E.V.A." On Camille Yarbrough's *Yo' Praise*. Vanguard 746-2, 1999.
First Generation: 25 Years of Virgin. Virgin 46589, 1998.
Forbidden Planet. Small Planet PR-D-001, 1989.
Hallucinogen: *The Lone Deranger*. Twisted TWSCD1, 2000.
———. *Twisted*. EFA 0995, 1999.
Henry, Pierre. *Intérieur/Extérieur*. Philips 462 132-2, 1998.
———. *Messe pour le temps présent*. Philips 456 293-2, 1997.
High on Dance. Quality Music 6741, 1995.
Juno Reactor. *Beyond the Infinite*. Cleopatra 9739, 1996.
———. *Transmissions*. NovaMute 3016, 1993.
Lacksman, Dan. *Pangea*. Eastwest World 61947-2, 1996.
Loaded, vol. 1. EMI America 32393, 1995.

Mallets in Wonderland. Vol. 2 of *The RCA History of Space Age Pop.* RCA 66646, 1995.

Melodies and Mischief. Vol. 1 of *The RCA History of Space Age Pop.* RCA 66645, 1995.

Métamorphose: Messe pour le temps présent, d'apres la Musique du Ballet de Maurice Béjart. Philips Music Group (France) 456 294-2, 1997.

Mineo, Attilio. *Man in Space with Sounds.* Subliminal Sounds SUBCD-4, 1998

Music for Heavenly Bodies. Omega OSL-4, n.d.

Muslimgauze. *Hamas Arc.* Staalplaat ST CD 051, 1993.

New Formosa Band. *Best Live and New Remix.* RD-1345, 1996.

Perrey, Jean-Jacques. *Good Moog: Astral Animations and Komputer Kartoons.* Kosinus 55, 1998.

————. *Moog Indigo.* Vanguard 6549-2, 1970.

————. *The Amazing New Electronic Sound of Jean Jacques Perrey.* Vanguard 79286-2, 1968.

Perrey/Kingsley. *The In Sound from Way Out!* Vanguard 79222-2, 1966.

Polyphonies vocales des aborigènes de Taïwan. Inedit, Maison des Cultures du Monde, W 2609 011, [1989].

Pure Moods. Virgin 42186, 1997.

Reich Remixed. Nonesuch 79552-2, 1999.

Return to the Source: Deep Trance and Ritual Beats. RTTS CD1, n.d.

Return to the Source: The Chakra Journey. RTTS CD2, n.d.

Revel, Harry. *Music Out of the Moon.* Request Records RR 231-2, 1995.

Schaeffer, Pierre. *Pierre Schaeffer: l'œuvre musicale.* INA TRM 292572, 1998.

The Songs of the Yami Tribe. Vol. 3 of *The Music of Aborigines on Taiwan Island.* Wind Records: TCD-1503, 1993.

Space-Capades. Vol. 3 of *Ultra-Lounge.* Capital CDP 7243 8 35176 2 6, 1996.

Space Cat. *Beam Me Up.* Yoyo Records 34-2, 1999.

Spooky Tooth. *Ceremony.* Edsel 565, 1998.

The Stereo Action Dimension. Vol. 3 of *The RCA History of Space Age Pop.* RCA 66647, 1995.

Stereolab. *Emperor Tomato Ketchup.* Elektra 61840, 1996.

————. *The Groop Played "Space Age Batchelor Pad Music."* Too Pure 80019, 1998.

————. *Transient Random-Noise Bursts with Announcements.* Elektra 9 61536-2, 1993.

Stockhausen, Karlheinz. *Telemusik.* Stockhausen Complete Works, 9, 1995.

Tobias. *Rainforest Rhapsody in the Key of Bali.* Malibu Records MR -09920-DA, n.d.

Violent Femmes. *Freak Magnet.* Beyond Records 78058, 2000.

Filmography

Austin Powers: International Man of Mystery. Directed by Jay Roach. New Line Studios, 1997.

Austin Powers: The Spy Who Shagged Me. Directed by Jay Roach. Warner Home Video, 1999.

Blonde Bombshell. Directed by Victor Fleming. MGM, 1933.

The Matrix. Directed by Andy Wachowski and Larry Wachowski. Grouch II Film Partnership/Silver Pictures/Village Roadshow Pictures, 1999.

Modulations. Directed by Lara Lee. Caipirinha, 1998.

Paul Simon: Born at the Right Time, Warner Reprise Video, 1992.

Pleasantville. Directed by Gary Ross. New Line Studios, 1998.

Theremin: An Electronic Odyssey. Directed by Steven M. Martin. Orion Classics, 1994.

Yesterday's Tomorrows. Directed by Barry Levinson. Cinemax, 1999.

Webography

Note: All URLs were active at the time of publication unless otherwise noted. A reasonably up-to-date list of URLs can be found at the website for this book: http://www.columbia.edu/tt327/Strange_Sounds/Strange_Sounds.htm.

http://atomicmule.com/kulture/byron/space1.html
    Vinyl Anthropology/Space Age Bachelor Pad pages.
http://difang.magicstone.com.tw/
    Difang's website at Magic Stone Music in Taiwan.
http://nctn.hq.nasa.gov/
    NASA home page.
http://perso.infonie.fr/grems/gentech.htm
    French website on the history of techno music.
http://web.pncl.co.uk/~rocklist/mixmag.html
    Mixmag's 50 tunes of 1997.
http://www.aber.ac.uk/~dgc/tecdet.html
    Daniel Chandler's useful pages on technological determinism.
http://www.alienz.com/music/alien.htm
    Information on ambient, house, trance, hip-hop, jungle, dub, and retro/disco music.
http://www.babelweb.freeserve.co.uk/airweb/page2.html
    Air's website.
http://www.carrotinnovations.com/vtt_overview.shtml
    Virtual Turntables software website.
http://www.chaoskitty.com/sabpm/sapvol1.html
http://www.chaoskitty.com/sabpm/sapvol2.html
http://www.chaoskitty.com/sabpm/sapvol3.html
    Websites with liner notes to the *RCA History of Space Age Pop.*
http://www.cdwcorp.com/index.htm
    Music Point's website.
http://www.census.gov/population/estimates/nation/popclockest.txt
    United States Census information.
http://www.comp.lancs.ac.uk/sociology/ant-a.html
    Website devoted to actor-network theory.
http://www.electricartists.com/
    Homepage of Electric Artists, an Internet marketing company.
http://www.enigma3.com
    Official Enigma website.
http://www.france.diplomatie.fr/culture/france/musique/composit/henry.html
    French Pierre Henry page.
http://www.geocities.com/SouthBeach/Keys/6004/speed.htm
    Psy trance party review site.
http://www.geocities.com/Vienna/4611/PTE-TPage.html
    The Paul Tanner Electro-Theremin Page.
www.gnutella.wego.com
    Gnutella website.
http://www.kcrw.org
    Radio station KCRW with archived interviews with members of the band Air.

http://metalab.unc.edu/id/theremin/
Robert Moog's theremin company pages.
http://www.mh2o.com
Music Hall 2000.
http://www.mixman.com
Mixman's website.
http://www.mp3newswire.net/
Website devoted to news about MP3s.
http://www.mpath.com/~piaw/bunny/shinbao.htm
Taiwanese website. This URL is no longer active.
http://www.obsolete.com/banco/
Banco de Gaia home page.
http://www.packardbell.com/ads96/television.asp
Packard Bell's television ad site. This URL is no longer active.
http://www.pretentious.net/Muslimgauze/
Muslimgauze page.
http://www.reactor.vip.lv/readme/books/dancemus.htm
Definitions of Goa trance music. This URL is no longer active.
http://www.riaa.com/
Recording Industry Association of America homepage.
http://www.sonicbarrier.org
Online Psy trance DJ guide.
http://www.spikes.com/enigma/Mambo1.html
Enigma website. This URL is no longer active.
http://www.stereolab.co.uk/
Official Stereolab site.
http://www.subpop.com/bands/combustible/comed/
Combustible Edison page at Sub Pop.
http://www.tamboo.com/baxter/baxter1.html
The Exotic World of Les Baxter.
http://www.teknet.ch/tb-303/
Roland TB-303 page.
http://www.thereminworld.com/
"The Theremin Home Page."
http://www.third-eye.org.uk/trip/how.html.
British psy trance page.
http://www.third-eye.org.uk/trip/what.html
British psy trance page.
http://www.third-eye.org.uk/trip/why.html
British psy trance page.
http://www.tsunami-trance.com
Tsunami website.
http://www.ubl.com/
Ultimate band list.
http://www.tqmcomms.co.uk/uk-dance/
UK-Dance page.
http://www.v2music.com/
Virgin's V2 Music website.

h p://www.vfemmes.com/fem_html/guy_int.html
   Violent Femmes website.
h p://www.visiosonic.com
   Software company website with MP3 playing and mixing software.
ht p://www.xs4all.nl/~tdg/louie2.html
   The complete(?) Louie Louie list.

I ernet Newsgroups

a inaries.remixes.mp3
a inaries.sounds.mp3.dance
a ulture.us.asian-indian
a music.makers.dj
a music.makers.electronic
a .music.makers.theremin
al .music.synth.roland.tb303
alt.music.tape-culture
al .music.techno
a rave
al rave.safe
j an.music.techno
r .music.ambient
r .music.industrial
    music.makers.dj
ι music.synth
r music.techno
ι music.makers.dj
ι music.rave

npublished Materials

is, Pierre. E-mail communication. March 26, 1999.
———. E-mail communication. April 7, 1999.
sar, Rodolfo. "The Composition of Electroacoustic Music." Ph.D. diss., University
   of East Anglia, 1992. http://riojet.area-mundi.com/lamut/lamutpgs/rcpesqs/rctese/
   09glos.htm.
untryman, Dana. E-mail communication, January 29, 2000.
ck, John. "The Relationship between Electro-Acoustic Music and Instrumental/Vocal
   Composition in Europe in the Period 1948–70." Ph.D. diss., Middlesex Polytechnic, 1989.
mond, Jack. E-mail communication. October 18, 1999.
sen, E. Patrick. Telephone communication. April 21, 1999.
———. Telephone communication. February 16, 1999.
irtmann, John-Emanuel. Interview by author. New York, N. Y., June 4, 1999.
———. Interview by author. New York, N.Y., August 20, 1999.
iy, Nancy. E-mail communication. March 29, 1999.
———. "Techno Hunters and Gatherers: Taiwan's Ami tribe, Enigma's 'Return to Innocence' and the Legalities of Cultural Ownership." Paper presented at the Society for Ethnomusicology, Bloomington, Indiana, October 22, 1998.
nes, Richard. "Expansion of Sound Resources in France, 1913–1940, and Its Relationship
   to Electronic Music." Ph.D. diss., the University of Michigan, 1981.

Lee, Joanna Ching-Yun. "György Ligeti's *Aventures* and *Nouvelle Aventures*: A Documentary History." Ph.D. diss., Columbia University, 1993.

Lifvon Guo. Interview by Frank Kohler. National Public Radio, *All Things Considered*. 11 June 1996.

Loza, Susana. E-mail communication. 6 July 2000.

———. "Global Rhetoric, Transnational Markets: The (Post)Modern Trajectories of Electronic Dance Musics." Ph.D. diss., University of California, Berkeley, in preparation.

Moog, Robert. Interview by Terry Gross. National Public Radio, *Fresh Air*. 28 February 2000.

Palombini, Carlos. "Pierre Schaeffer's Typo-Morphology of Sonic Objects." Ph.D. diss., University of Durham, 1993.

Prince Be. Interview by Terry Gross. *Fresh Air*. 29 November 1995.

Weisethaunet, Hans. "PD-Theory: On Being 'Discrepant' or 'Playing It Right.'" Photocopy.

Books and Articles

Adams, Robert McC. *Paths of Fire: An Anthropologist's Inquiry into Western Technology*. Princeton, N.J.: Princeton University Press, 1996.

Adas, Michael. *Machines As the Measure of Men: Science, Technology, and Ideologies of Western Dominance*. Cornell Studies in Comparative History. Ithaca: Cornell University Press, 1989.

Adorno, Theodor. *Philosophy of Modern Music*. Translated by Anne G. Mitchell and Wesley V. Blomster. New York: Continuum, 1994.

Alain, Olivier. "Variétés électroniques." *Le Figaro*, February 13, 1970, 30.

"Ami Sounds Scale Olympian Heights." [Part 1] http://www.gio.gov.tw/info/sinorama/8508/508006e1.html. [This URL is no longer active.]

"Ami Sounds Scale Olympian Heights." [Part 2] http://www.gio.gov.tw./info/sinorama/8508/508006e2.html. [This URL is no longer active.]

Anthony, Wayne. *Class of 88: The True Acid House Experience*. London: Virgin, 1998.

Appadurai, Arjun. "Introduction: Commodities and the Politics of Value." In *The Social Life of Things: Commodities in Cultural Perspective*. Edited by Arjun Appadurai. Cambridge: Cambridge University Press, 1986.

———. *Modernity at Large: Cultural Dimensions of Globalization*. Public Worlds, vol. 1. Minneapolis: University of Minnesota Press, 1996.

Appadurai, Arjun, and Carol Breckenridge. "Why Public Culture?" *Public Culture* 1 (fall 1988): 5-9.

Apollonio, Umbro, ed. and comp. *Futurist Manifestos*. Translated by Robert Brain. Documents of Twentieth-Century Art. New York: Viking 1973.

Arthur, Charles. "How Many People Does It Take to Invent the Lightbulb?" *(London) Independent*, June 26, 1999, 13.

Asimov, Eric. "The New Bad-Boy Sound: Space Age Pop." *New York Times*, January 7, 1996, section 4, p. 2.

Attali, Jacques. *Noise: The Political Economy of Music*. Translated by Brian Massumi. Theory and History of Literature, vol. 16. Minneapolis: University of Minnesota Press, 1985.

Auner, Joseph. "The Second Viennese School as a Historical Concept." In *Schoenberg, Berg, and Webern: A Companion to the Second Viennese School*. Edited by Bryan Simms. Westport, Conn.: Greenwood, 1999.

Australian DJ pages. http://www2.gist.net.au/~aek/batz/paradigm.txt. [This URL is no longer active.]

Bailey, Kathryn. *The Life of Webern*. Musical Lives. Cambridge: Cambridge University Press, 1998.

Ball, John, Jr. "The Witch Doctor in Your Living Room." *Hi-Fi/Stereo Review*, March 1960, 62–65.

Barglow, Raymond. *The Crisis of the Self in the Age of Information: Computers, Dolphins, and Dreams*. Critical Psychology. New York: Routledge, 1994.

Barron, Louis and Bebe. Liner notes to *Forbidden Planet*. Small Planet PR-D-001,1989.

Bartlett, Andrew. "Airshafts, Loudspeakers, and the Hip Hop Sample: Contexts and African American Musical Aesthetics." *African American Review* 28 (winter 1994): 639–52.

Baudrillard, Jean. *In the Shadow of Silent Majorities*. New York: Semiotext(e), 1983.

———. *Selected Writings*. Edited by Mark Poster. Stanford, Calif.: Stanford University Press, 1988.

Bauman, Zygmunt. *Modernity and Ambivalence*. Cambridge: Polity, 1991.

Baxter, Les. "The Les Baxter Interview." By James Call and Peter Huestis. http://www.tamboo.com/baxter/baxinterview/index.html.

Beale, Marjorie A. *The Modernist Enterprise: French Elites and the Threat of Moderinty, 1900–1940*. Stanford, Calif.: Stanford University Press, 1999.

Becker, Tim, and Raphael Woebs. " 'Back to the Future': Hearing, Rituality and Techno." Translated by Linda Fujie. *World of Music* 41 (1999): 59–71.

Begleiter, Joel. Review of the Sea and Cake, "Two Gentlemen." *Herald*, October 17, 1997, http://www.theherald.org/herald/issues/g101797/thesea.f.html.

Belk, Russell W., and Melanie Wallendorf. "Of Mice and Men: Gender Identity in Collecting." In *Interpreting Objects and Collections*. Edited by Susan M. Pearce. Leicester Readers in Museum Studies. New York: Routledge, 1994.

Benjamin, Walter. "The Work of Art in the Age of Mechanical Reproduction." In *Illuminations*. Translated by Harry Zohn. Edited by Hannah Arendt. New York: Schocken Books, 1969.

Bennett, Andy. "Subcultures or Neo-Tribes? Rethinking the Relationship between Youth, Style and Musical Taste." *Sociology* 33 (August 1999): 599–617.

Bentley, Jerry H. *Old World Encounters: Cross-Cultural Contacts and Exchanges in Pre-Modern Times*. New York: Oxford University Press, 1993.

Berger, Peter L., and Thomas Luckmann. *The Social Construction of Reality: A Treatise in the Sociology of Knowledge*. 1966; reprint, New York: Irvington, 1980.

Berman, Marshall. *All That Is Solid Melts into Air: The Experience of Modernity*. New York: Penguin, 1988.

Bey, Hakim. *T.A.Z.: The Temporary Autonomous Zone, Ontological Anarchy, Poetic Terrorism*. New Autonomy series. Brooklyn, N.Y.: Autonomedia, 1991.

Bijker, Wiebe E., Thomas P. Hughes, and Trevor J. Pinch, eds. *The Social Construction of Technological Systems: New Directions in the Sociology and History of Technology*. Cambridge, Mass.: MIT Press, 1987.

Bimber, Bruce. "Karl Marx, and the Three Faces of Technological Determinism." *Social Studies of Science* 20 (May 1990): 333–51.

Bonner, Michael. "All 'Present' and Correct." *Melody Maker*, October 18, 1997, 53.

Bonnet, Antoine. "*Écriture* and Perception: on *Messagesquisse* by Pierre Boulez." *Contemporary Music Review* 2 (1987): 173–209.

Born, Georgina. *Rationalizing Culture: IRCAM, Boulez, and the Institutionalization of the Musical Avant-Garde*. Berkeley and Los Angeles: University of California Press, 1995.

Borzillo, Carrie. "Deep Forest Growing in Popularity." *Billboard*, February 19, 1994, 8.

————. "U.S. Ad Use Adds to Commercial Success of *Deep Forest*." *Billboard*, June 11, 1994, 44.

Boulez, Pierre. *Notes of an Apprenticeship*. Compiled by Paule Thévenin. Translated by Herbert Weinstock. New York: Alfred A. Knopf, 1968.

————. *Orientations: Collected Writings*. Edited by Jean-Jacques Nattiez. Translated by Martin Cooper. Cambridge, Mass.: Harvard University Press, 1986.

Bourdieu, Pierre. *Distinction: A Social Critique of the Judgement of Taste*. Translated by Richard Nice. Cambridge, Mass.: Harvard University Press, 1984.

————. *The Logic of Practice*. Translated by Richard Nice. Cambridge: Polity, 1990.

————. *Outline of a Theory of Practice*. Translated by Richard Nice. Cambridge: Cambridge University Press, 1977.

Bourguignon, Erika, ed. *Religion, Altered States of Consciousness, and Social Change*. Columbus: Ohio State University Press, 1973.

Bowes, Greg. "The A–Z of Electronica." http://www.mg.co.za/mg/art/music/column/980702-wild.html.

Boyer, Paul. *By the Bomb's Early Light: American Thought and Culture at the Dawn of the Atomic Age*. New York: Pantheon, 1985.

Brennan, Timothy. *At Home in the World: Cosmopolitanism Now*. Convergences: Inventories of the Present. Cambridge, Mass.: Harvard University Press, 1997.

Brown, JoAnne. " 'A Is for *Atom*, B Is for *Bomb*': Civil Defense in American Public Education, 1948–1963." *Journal of American History* 75 (June 1988): 68–90.

Burkholder, J. Peter. *All Made of Tunes: Charles Ives and the Uses of Musical Borrowing*. New Haven, Conn.: Yale University Press, 1995.

Callon, Michel. "Some Elements of a Sociology of Translation: Domestication of the Scallops and the Fisherman of St. Brieuc Bay." In *Power, Action, Belief: A New Sociology of Knowledge?* Edited by John Law. New York: Routledge, 1986.

Canaday, John. *The Nuclear Muse: Literature, Physics, and the First Atomic Bombs*. Science and Literature. Madison and London: University of Wisconsin Press, 2000.

Carrier, James G., and Josiah McC. Heyman. "Consumption and Political Economy." *Journal of the Royal Anthropological Institute* 3 (June 1997): 355–73.

Castells, Manuel. *The Rise of the Network Society*. Vol. 1 of *The Information Age: Economy, Society and Culture*. Cambridge, Mass.: Blackwell, 1996.

Chang, Juping. "Ami Group Sings of Bittersweet Life in the Mountains." *Free China Journal*, 1 January 1999. http://publish.gio.gov.tw/FCJ/fcj.html. [This URL is no longer active.]

Chion, Michel. *La Musique electroacoustique, Que sais-je?* Paris: Presses Universitaires de France, 1982.

————. *Pierre Henry*. Paris: Fayard/Fondation SACEM, 1980.

Chusid, Irwin. Liner notes to *Bachelor's Guide to the Galaxy*. Vol. 1 of *Cocktail Mix*. Rhino R2 72237, 1995.

————. Liner notes to *Mallets in Wonderland*. Vol. 2 of *The RCA History of Space Age Pop*. RCA 66646, 1995.

————. Liner notes to *Melodies and Mischief*. Vol. 1 of *The RCA History of Space Age Pop*. RCA 66645, 1995.

————. Liner notes to *The Stereo Action Dimension*. Vol. 3 of *The RCA History of Space Age Pop*. RCA 66647, 1995.

Clements, Andrew. "Western Europe, 1945–70." In *Modern Times: From World War II to the Present*. Edited by Robert P. Morgan. Music and Society. Englewood Cliffs, N.J.: Prentice Hall, 1993.

Clifford, James. *The Predicament of Culture: Twentieth-Century Ethnography, Literature, and Art*. Cambridge, Mass.: Harvard University Press, 1988.

Collin, Matthew. *Altered State: The Story of Ecstasy Culture and Acid House.* New York: Serpent's Tail, 1997.

Conte, Christopher. "A Special News Report on People and Their Jobs in Offices, Fields and Factories." *Wall Street Journal,* May 21, 1991, sec. A, p. 1.

Coontz, Stephanie. *The Way We Never Were: American Families and the Nostalgia Trap.* New York: Basic Books, 1992.

Corn, Joseph J., and Brian Horrigan. *Yesterday's Tomorrows: Past Visions of the American Future.* Baltimore: Johns Hopkins University Press, 1984.

Cowan, Ruth Schwartz. *More Work for Mother: The Ironies of Household Technology from the Open Hearth to the Microwave.* New York: Basic Books, 1983.

———. *A Social History of American Technology.* New York: Oxford University Press, 1997.

Crafts, Susan D., Daniel Cavicchi, and Charles Keil. *My Music.* Music/Culture. Middletown, Conn.: Wesleyan University Press, 1993.

Cram, Julian. "Sample It, Loop It, Fuck It and Eat It! Or, Is Techno Postmodern?" http://www.geocities.com/Area51/Vault/3615/sample1.html. [This URL is no longer active.]

Croal, N'Gai, and Walaika Haskins. "Music Made Easy." *Newsweek,* October 25, 1999, 91–92.

"The Cult of the DJ." *Social Text* 43 (fall 1995): 67–88.

Dahan, Eric. "About Mass for the Present Day." Liner notes to *Métamorphose: Messe pour le temps présent, d'apres la musique du ballet de Maurice Béjart.* Philips Music Group (France) 456 294-2, 1997.

Dahlhaus, Carl. *The Idea of Absolute Music.* Translated by Roger Lustig. Chicago: University of Chicago Press, 1989.

Danielsen, Shane. "Bands that Don't Play Together, Stay Together." http://entertainment. news.com/ au/music/arc90303.htm. [This URL is no longer active.]

Davis, Erik. "Sampling Paradise: The Technofreak Legacy of Golden Goa." *Option,* March–April 1995, 74.

———. "Sampling Paradise: The Technofreak Legacy of Golden Goa." http://www.levity.com/figment/paradise.html.

———. *Techgnosis: Myth, Magic and Mysticism in the Age of Information.* New York: Harmony, 1998.

Davis, Fred. *Yearning for Yesterday: A Sociology of Nostalgia.* New York: Free Press, 1979.

Davis, Mike. *City of Quartz: Excavating the Future in Los Angeles.* New York: Vintage, 1992.

Debray, Régis. *Media Manifestos: On the Technological Transmission of Cultural Forms.* Translated by Eric Rauth. London: Verso, 1996.

Decker, Chris. Liner notes to *Return to the Source: The Chakra Journey.* RTTS CD2, n.d.

Deep Forest FAQ. http://www.spikes.com/worldmix/faq.htm.

Delaney, Kevin J. "Microsoft's Encarta Has Different Facts for Different Folks." *Wall Street Journal,* June 25, 1999, A1.

Del Sesto, Stephen L. "Wasn't the Future of Nuclear Energy Wonderful?" In *Imagining Tomorrow: History, Technology, and the American Future.* Edited by Joseph J. Corn. Cambridge , Mass.: MIT Press, 1986.

Dertouzos, Michael. *What Will Be: How the New World of Information Will Change Our Lives.* New York: HarperCollins, 1997.

Dery, Mark. "Public Enemy: Confrontation." *Keyboard,* September 1990, 81–96.

———. "Tommy Boy X 3: Digital Underground, Coldcut, and De La Soul Jam the Beat with Audio Junkyard Collisions." *Keyboard,* March 1991, 64–78.

Diamond, Jack. Liner notes to *Man in Space with Sounds.* Subliminal Sounds SUBCD-4, 1998.

Diliberto, John. "Pierre Schaeffer and Pierre Henry: Pioneers in Sampling." *Electronic Musician*, December 1986, 54.

Ditchburn, Jennifer. "Lounging 'Round." *Rhythm Music*, July 1997, 20.

Dittmar, Helga. "Meanings of Material Possessions As Reflections of Identity: Gender and Social-Material Position in Society." *Journal of Social Behaviour and Personality* 6 (1991): 165–86.

Doherty, Brian. "Matt Groening: The Creator of 'The Simpsons' on His New Sci-Fi TV Show, Why It's Nice to Be Rich, and How the ACLU Infringed on His Rights." *Mother Jones*, March 1, 1999, 34-37.

" 'Don't Have to Cheapen Music to Sell It,' Asserts Les Baxter." *Down Beat*, September 7, 1955, 10.

Douglas, Mary. *Purity and Danger: An Analysis of Concepts of Pollution and Taboo.* Harmondsworth, England: Penguin, 1970.

Douglas, Susan J. "Audio Outlaws: Radio and Phonograph Enthusiasts." In *Possible Dreams: Enthusiasm for Technology in America.* Edited by John L. Wright. Dearborn, Mich.: Henry Ford Museum and Greenfield Village, 1992.

Durkheim, Émile. "The Dualism of Human Nature." In *Émile Durkheim on Morality and Society.* Edited by Robert Bellah. Chicago: University of Chicago Press, 1973.

———. *The Elementary Forms of Religious Life.* Translated by Karen E. Fields. New York: Free Press, 1995.

Durant, Alan. "A New Day for Music? Digital Technologies in Contemporary Music-Making." In *Culture, Technology and Creativity.* Edited by Philip Hayward. London: John Libbey, 1990.

Dwyer, Terence. *Composing with Tape Recorders: Musique Concrète for Beginners.* London: Oxford University Press, 1971.

Eagleton, Terry. *The Illusions of Postmodernism.* Cambridge, Mass.: Blackwell, 1996.

Ehrenreich, Barbara. *The Hearts of Men: American Dreams and the Flight from Commitment.* New York: Anchor, 1984.

Eimert, Herbert. "What Is Electronic Music?" *Die Reihe* 1 (1958): 1–10.

Eley, Geoff. "Nations, Publics, and Political Cultures: Placing Habermas in the Nineteenth Century." In *Culture/Power/History: A Reader in Contemporary Social Theory.* Edited by Nicholas B. Dirks, Geoff Eley and Sherry B. Ortner. Princeton Studies in Culture/Power/History. Princeton, N.J.: Princeton University Press, 1994.

Ellul, Jacques. *The Technological Society.* Translated by John Wilkinson. New York: Alfred A. Knopf, 1964.

Enigma FAQ. http://www.spikes.com/enigma/faq/faq.htm.

Enigma Live Chat Event on the Internet, 13 December 1996.

Eno, Brian. "The Revenge of the Intuitive." *Wired*, January 1999. http://www.wired.com/wired/archive/7.01/eno_pr.html.

———. "The Studio As Compositional Tool, Part 1." *Down Beat*, July 1983, 56–57.

———. "The Studio As Compositional Tool, Part 2." *Down Beat*, August 1983, 50–53.

Exotica mailing list FAQ version 3.2. http://www.studio-nibble.com/lists/exofaq32.html.

Esarey, Ashley. "An Ami Couple Seeks Recognition for their Music." http://www.sinica.edu/tw/tit/special/0996_Innocence.html. [This URL is no longer active.]

Farber, David. *The Age of Great Dreams: America in the 1960s.* American Century. New York: Hill and Wang, 1994.

Feenberg, Andrew. *Questioning Technology.* New York: Routledge, 1999.

Feld, Steven. "From Schizophonia to Schismogenesis: On the Discourses and Commodification Practices of 'World Music' and 'World Beat.' " In Charles Keil and Steven Feld, *Music*

Grooves: Essays and Dialogues. Chicago and London: University of Chicago Press, 1994.

———. "Pygmy Pop: A Genealogy of Schizophonic Mimesis." *Yearbook for Traditional Music* 28 (1997): 1–35.

———. "A Sweet Lullaby for World Music." *Public Culture* 12 (winter 2000): 145–71.

Fikentscher, Kai. *"You Better Work!" Underground Dance Music in New York City.* Music/Culture. Middletown, Conn.: Wesleyan University Press, 2000.

Finnegan, Ruth. *Literacy and Orality: Studies in the Technology of Communication.* Oxford: Basil Blackwell, 1988.

Fisher, Paul. "Connected: Log and Learn Encyclopedia." *(London) Daily Telegraph,* December 11, 1999, 10.

Flick, Larry and Doug Reece. "Electronic Music Poised for Power Surge in States." *Billboard,* February 15, 1997, 1.

Foucault, Michel. *The Archaeology of Knowledge.* Translated by A. M. Sheridan Smith. New York: Pantheon, 1972.

Fourier, Laurent. "Jean-Jacques Perrey and the Ondioline." Translated by Curtis Roads. *Computer Music Journal* 18 (winter 1994): 19–25.

Frank, Thomas. *The Conquest of Cool: Business Culture, Counterculture, and the Rise of Hip Consumerism.* Chicago: University of Chicago Press, 1997.

Fraser, Nancy. *Unruly Practices: Power, Discourse and Gender in Contemporary Social Theory.* Minneapolis: University of Minnesota Press, 1989.

Frederickson, Jon. "Technology and Performance in the Age of Mechanical Reproduction." *International Association of the Aesthetics and Sociology of Music* 20 (December 1989): 193–220.

Frétard, Dominique. "Pierre Henry a-t-il été le Pygmalion de Maurice Béjart?" *Le Monde,* 5 July 1996, 23.

Frith, Simon. "Art versus Technology: The Strange Case of Popular Music." *Media, Culture and Society* 8 (July 1986): 263–79.

———. "The Industrialization of Popular Music." In *Popular Music and Communication.* Edited by James Lull. 2d ed. Sage Focus Editions. Newbury Park, Calif.: Sage, 1992.

———. "Music and Morality." In *Music and Copyright.* Edited by Simon Frith. Edinburgh Law and Society Series. Edinburgh: Edinburgh University Press, 1993.

Frith, Simon. *Sound Effects: Youth, Leisure, and the Politics of Rock 'n' Roll.* New York: Pantheon Books, 1981.

"From Betelnuts to Billboard Hits." http://pathfind.com/@@CkDcMAcA0VE9Uaiw/Asiaweek/96/1122/feat5.html. [This URL is no longer active.]

Gaillot, Michel. *Multiple Meaning: Techno, An Artistic and Political Laboratory of the Present.* Translated by Warren Niesluchowski. Paris: Éditions Dis Voir [1998].

Gane, Tim. Interview. http://www.2launch.com/stereolab.html

———. "In the Studio: Stereolab's Tim Gane on Distorted Organs." Interview. http://www.maths.monash.edu.au/~rjh/stereolab/interviews/rso.html. [This URL is no longer active.]

Gann, Kyle. "Music For Theremin: It's Not Just for Aliens Anymore." *Village Voice,* August 31, 1999, 113.

———. "Sampling: Plundering for Art." *Village Voice,* May 1, 1990, 102.

Gardner, Lyn. "Radio: Lava Lamp Camp." *(Manchester) Guardian,* February 3, 1996, 26.

Garofalo, Reebee. "From Music Publishing to MP3: Music and Industry in the Twentieth Century." *American Music* 17 (fall 1999): 318-53.

Gehr, Richard. "Exotica Neurotica." http://www.levity.com/rubric/exotica.html.

———. "Muslimgauze: Beyond the Veil." *Village Voice,* October 28, 1994, 67.

Gelder, Ken, and Sarah Thornton, eds. *The Subcultures Reader.* New York: Routledge, 1997.

Giddens, Anthony. *Central Problems in Social Theory: Action, Structure, and Contradiction in Social Analysis.* Berkeley and Los Angeles: University of California Press, 1979.

————. *Modernity and Self-Identity: Self and Society in the Late Modern Age.* Cambridge: Polity, 1991.

Gieryn, Thomas F. "Riding the Action/Structure Pendulum with Those Swinging Sociologists of Science." In *The Outlook for STS: Report on an STS Symposium and Workshop.* Edited by Sheila Jasanoff. Ithaca, N.Y.: Cornell University Department of Science and Technology Studies, 1992.

Gilbert, Jeremy, and Ewan Pearson. *Discographies: Dance Music, Culture and the Politics of Sound.* New York: Routledge, 1999.

Gilpin, Robert. *France in the Age of the Scientific State.* Princeton, N.J.: Princeton University Press, 1968.

Gitlin, Todd. *The Sixties: Years of Hope, Days of Rage.* Rev. ed. New York: Bantam, 1993.

Goa/604 mailing list FAQ. http://www.party.net/.

Goa Gil. Interview by Michael Gosney. *Beam,* 1999, http://www.radiov.com/production/beam/innerviews/goagil/.

Goldman, Erik. "Ethnotechno: A Sample Twist of Fate." *Rhythm Music,* July 1995, 36–9.

Goodwin, Andrew. "Popular Music and Postmodern Theory." *Cultural Studies* 5 (May 1991): 174–90.

————. "Sample and Hold: Pop Music in the Digital Age of Reproduction." In *On Record: Rock, Pop, and the Written Word.* Edited by Simon Frith and Andrew Goodwin. New York: Pantheon, 1990.

Gore, Georgiana. "The Beat Goes On: Trance, Dance and Tribalism in Rave Culture." In *Dance in the City.* Edited by Helen Thomas. New York: St. Martin's, 1997.

Guernsey, Lisa. "MP3-Trading Service Can Clog Networks on College Campuses." *New York Times,* January 20, 2000, 3.

Guilbault, Jocelyne. "On Redefining the 'Local' through World Music." *World of Music* 32 (1993): 33–47.

Haber, Hans. *The Walt Disney Story of Our Friend the Atom.* New York: Simon and Schuster, 1956.

Habermas, Jürgen. *The Structural Transformation of the Public Sphere: An Inquiry into a Category of Bourgeois Society.* Translated by Thomas Burger and Frederick Lawrence. Cambridge, Mass.: MIT Press, 1991.

Hagendijk, Rob. "Structuration Theory, Constructivism, and Scientific Change." In *Theories of Science in Society.* Edited by Susan E. Cozzens and Thomas F. Gieryn. Science, Technology, and Society. Bloomington and Indianapolis: Indiana University Press, 1990.

Halberstam, David. *The Fifties.* New York: Villard, 1993.

Hall, Stuart. "The Local and the Global: Globalization and Ethnicity." In *Culture, Globalization and the World-System.* Edited by Anthony D. King. Current Debates in Art History, vol. 3. Binghamton, N.Y.: Department of Art and Art History, State University of New York at Binghamton, 1991.

————. "Notes on Deconstructing 'The Popular.' " In *People's History and Socialist Theory.* Edited by Raphael Samuel. London: Routledge and Kegan Paul, 1981.

Hall, Stuart, and Martin Jacques, eds. *New Times: The Changing Face of Politics in the 1990s.* London: Verso, 1990.

Hall, Stuart, and Tony Jefferson, eds. *Resistance through Rituals: Youth Subcultures in Postwar Britain.* 1976; reprint, New York: Routledge, 1993.

Hamm, Charles. *Putting Popular Music in Its Place*. Cambridge: Cambridge University Press, 1995.

Hanegraaff, Wouter J. *New Age Religion and Western Culture: Esotericism in the Mirror of Secular Thought*. Studies in the History of Religions, vol. 72. Leiden: Brill Academic Publishers, 1996.

Hanslick, Eduard. *On the Beautiful in Music*. Translated by Gustave Cohen. Edited by Morris Weitz. New York: Liberal Arts Press, 1957.

Harmon, Amy, and John Sullivan. "Music Industry Wins Ruling in U.S. Court." *New York Times*, April 29, 2000, sec. C, p. 1.

Harvey, David. *The Condition of Postmodernity: An Enquiry into the Origins of Cultural Change*. Cambridge, Mass.: Basil Blackwell, 1989.

Hayward, Philip. "The Cocktail Shift: Aligning Musical Exotica." In *Widening the Horizon: Exoticism in Post-War Popular Music*. Edited by Philip Hayward. Sydney: John Libbey, 1999.

———. "Cultural Tectonics." *Convergence* 6 (Spring 2000): 39–47.

Hayward, Philip, ed. *Widening the Horizon: Exoticism in Post-War Popular Music*. Sydney: John Libbey, 1999.

Hebdige, Dick. *Subculture: The Meaning of Style*. New Accents. 1979; reprint, New York: Routledge, 1991.

Hecht, Gabrielle. "Peasants, Engineers, and Atomic Cathedrals: Narrating Modernization in Postwar Provincial France." *French Historical Studies* 20 (summer 1997): 381–418.

———. "Political Designs: Nuclear Reactors and National Policy in Postwar France." *Technology and Culture* 354 (October 1994): 657–85.

———. *The Radiance of France: Nuclear Power and National Identity after World War II*. Inside Technology. Cambridge, Mass.: MIT Press, 1998.

Heidegger, Martin. *Basic Writings*. Edited by David Farrell Krell. San Francisco: HarperSanFrancisco, 1977.

Hemment, Drew. "e Is for *Ekstasis*." *New Formations* 31 (summer 1997): 23–38.

Heelas, Paul. *The New Age Movement: The Celebration of the Self and the Sacralization of Modernity*. Cambridge, Mass.: Blackwell, 1996.

Hennion, Antoine. "An Intermediary between Production and Consumption: The Producer of Popular Music." *Science, Technology, and Human Values* 14 (autumn 1989): 400–424.

Henry, Jules. *Culture against Man*. New York: Vintage, 1963.

"Henry, Pierre." http://www.virgin.fr/html/cyber/tnt/dico/h.html#henry.

Henry, Pierre. Interview by Ios Smolders. http://www.ddc.net/emaurer/PierreHenry/interview.htm.

Henwood, Doug. "Post What?" *Monthly Review* 48 (September 1996): 1–11.

Hesmondhalgh, David. "The Cultural Politics of Dance Music." *Soundings* [London] 5 (spring 1997): 167–78.

Hess, David J. *Science Studies: An Advanced Introduction*. New York: New York University Press, 1997.

Hesseldahl, Arik. "Rosen: SDMI Is Your Friend." *Wired*, August 10, 1999. http://www.wired.com/news/culture/0,1284,21205,00.html.

Hinckley, David. "Musical Longevity." *(New York) Daily News*, August 5, 1996, 31.

Hine, Thomas. *Populuxe*. New York: Alfred A. Knopf, 1986.

Hinman, Doug, and Jason Brabazon. *You Really Got Me: An Illustrated World Discography of the Kinks, 1964–1993*. Rumford, R.I.: Doug Hinman, 1994.

Hobsbawm, Eric. *The Age of Extremes: A History of the World, 1914–1991.* New York: Vintage, 1996.

Hodeir, André. *Since Debussy: A View of Contemporary Music.* Translated by Noel Burch. New York: Grove Press, 1961.

Horkheimer, Max, and Theodor Adorno. *Dialectic of Enlightenment.* Translated by John Cumming. New York: Continuum, 1991.

Horn, Richard. *Fifties Style.* New York: Friedman/Fairfax, 1993.

Horrigan, Brian. "Popular Culture and Visions of the Future in Space, 1901–2001." In *New Perspectives on Technology and American Culture.* Edited by Bruce Sinclair. Philadelphia: American Philosophical Society, 1986.

Hosokawa, Shuhei. "Soy Sauce Music: Harumi Hosono and Japanese Self-Orientalism." In *Widening the Horizon: Exoticism in Post-War Popular Music.* Edited by Philip Hayward. Sydney: John Libbey, 1999.

Huang, Anita. "Global Music, Inc." http://www.gio.gov.tw/info/fcr/8/p42.htm. [This URL is no longer active.]

Huang, Renata. "Golden Oldie." *Far Eastern Economic Review,* November 2, 1995, 62.

Hughes, Thomas P. *Networks of Power: Electrification in Western Society, 1880–1930.* Baltimore: Johns Hopkins University Press, 1983.

Huyssen, Andreas. *After the Great Divide: Modernism, Mass Culture, Postmodernism.* Theories of Representation and Difference. Bloomington and Indianapolis: University of Indiana Press, 1986.

"IOC President to Thank Ami Singers." *Free China Journal,* http://ww3.sinanet.com/heartbeat/fcj/0726news/16_E.html. [This URL is no longer active.]

Iwabuchi, Koichi. "Complicit Exoticism: Japan and its Other." *Continuum* 8 (1994): 49–82.

Jacobsen, Catharina. "Michael's Mystical Music." Translated by Joar Grimstvedt. *(Oslo, Norway) Verdens Gang,* December 19, 1990, http://www.stud.his.no/~joarg/Enigma/articles/verdensGang1290.html.

James, Richard. "Avant-Garde Sound-on-Film Techniques and Their Relationship to Electro-Acoustic Music." *Musical Quarterly* 72 (1986): 74–89.

Jameson, Fredric. *Postmodernism, or, the Cultural Logic of Late Capitalism.* Post-Contemporary Interventions. Durham, N.C.: Duke University Press, 1991.

Jay, Martin. *Adorno.* Cambridge, Mass.: Harvard University Press, 1984.

———. *The Dialectical Imagination: a History of the Frankfurt School and the Institute of Social Research, 1923–1950.* 2d. ed. Weimar and Now, vol. 10. Berkeley and Los Angeles: University of California Press, 1996.

Jenkins, Richard. *Lads, Citizens, and Ordinary Kids: Working-Class Youth Life-Styles in Belfast.* London: Routledge and Kegan Paul, 1983.

Johnson, Steven. *Interface Culture: How New Technology Transforms the Way We Create and Communicate.* [New York]: HarperEdge, 1997.

Jones, Bryn. Interview. *Eskhatos* (1995). http://pretentious.net/Muslimgauze/articles/eskatos.htm.

Jones, Christopher. "Digital DJs Phatten Up." *Wired,* November 27, 1999. http://www.wired.com/news/technology/0,1282,32705,00.html.

Jordan, Tim. "Collective Bodies: Raving and the Politics of Gilles Deleuze and Felix Guattari." *Body and Society* 1 (March 1995): 125–44.

Kahn, Douglas. *Noise Water Meat: A History of Sound in the Arts.* Cambridge, Mass.: MIT Press, 1999.

Kant, Immanuel. *Critique of Judgment.* Translated by Werner S. Pluhar. Indianapolis: Hackett, 1987.

Kasson, John F. *Civilizing the Machine: Technology and Republican Values in America, 1776–1900.* New York: Penguin, 1977.

Keil, Charles, and Steven Feld. *Music Grooves: Essays and Dialogues.* Chicago: University of Chicago Press, 1994.

Keightley, Keir. " 'Turn it Down!' She Shrieked: Gender, Domestic Space, and High Fidelity, 1948–59." *Popular* Music 15 (May 1996): 149–77.

Khazam, Rhama. "Electroacoustic Alchemist." *The Wire*, June 1997, 36–40.

Kittler, Friedrich A. *Gramophone, Film, Typewriter.* Translated by Geoffrey Winthrop-Young and Michael Wutz. Stanford, Calif.: Stanford University Press, 1999.

Knapp, Louise. "Two Pentiums and a Microphone." *Wired*, September 21, 1999, http://www.wired.com/news/news/culture/story/19415.html.

Knopper, Steve, ed. *MusicHound Lounge: The Essential Album Guide to Martini Music and Easy Listening.* Detroit: Visible Ink, 1998.

Kraidy, Marwan M. "The Global, the Local, and the Hybrid: A Native Ethnography of Glocalization." *Critical Studies in Mass Communication* 16 (December 1999): 456–76.

Krasilovsky, M. William, and Sidney Shemel. *This Business of Music.* 7th ed. New York: Billboard Books, 1995.

Kun, Josh. "Too Pure?" *Option*, May–June 1996, 54.

Kuo, Deborah. "Taiwan Aborigines Sue Enigma, Music Companies." Central News Agency, March 28, 1998.

Kruse, Holly. "Early Audio Technology and Domestic Space." *Stanford Humanities Review* 3 (fall 1993): 1–14.

Kushner, David. "Napster Terrorizes Music Biz." *Rolling Stone*, April 27, 2000, 25.

Lanza, Joseph. *The Cocktail: The Influence of Spirits on the American Psyche.* New York: St. Martin's, 1995.

Lanza, Joseph. *Elevator Music: A Surreal History of Muzak, Easy-Listening, and Other Moodsong.* New York: St. Martin's, 1994.

La Gassa, Laura. "PLUR: P(eace), L(ove), U(nity), R(espect)." http://www.hyperreal.org/raves/spirit/plur/PLUR.html.

Lash, Scott, and John Urry. *Economies of Signs and Space.* Theory, Culture, and Society. Newbury Park, Calif.: Sage, 1994.

Latour, Bruno. *Science in Action: How to Follow Scientists and Engineers through Society.* Milton Keynes, England: Open University Press, 1987.

———. *The Pasteurization of France.* Cambridge, Mass.: Harvard University Press, 1996.

———. "Technology Is Society Made Durable." In *A Sociology of Monsters? Essays on Power, Technology and Domination.* Edited by John Law. Sociological Review Monograph, vol. 38. New York: Routledge, 1991.

———. "The Trouble with Actor-Network Theory." *Philosophia* 25 (1997): 47–64. English version, http://www.ensmp.fr/~latour/popart/p67.html.

Law, John. "Technology and Heterogeneous Engineering: The Case of Portuguese Expansion." In *The Social Construction of Technological Systems*, ed. Wiebe E. Bijker and Trevor Pinch. Cambridge: MIT Press, 1987.

Lears, Jackson. "A Matter of Taste: Corporate Cultural Hegemony in a Mass-Consumption Society." In *Recasting America: Culture and Politics in the Age of the Cold War.* Edited by Lary May. Chicago: University of Chicago Press, 1989.

Leibowitz, René. *Schoenberg and His School: The Contemporary Stage of the Language of Music.* Translated by Dika Newlin. 1949; reprint, New York: Da Capo Press, 1970.

Lenin, V. I. *Imperialism, the Highest Stage of Capitalism: A Popular Outline.* New York: International, 1939.

Lévi-Strauss, Claude. *The Raw and the Cooked: Introduction to a Science of Mythology.* Translated by John and Doreen Weightman. 1964; reprint, Harmondsworth, England: Penguin, 1986.

——. *The Savage Mind.* Nature of Human Society. Chicago: University of Chicago Press, 1966.

Levinson, Paul. *Digital McLuhan: A Guide to the Information Millennium.* New York: Routledge, 1999.

Leydon, Rebecca. "Utopias of the Tropics: The Exotic Music of Les Baxter and Yma Sumac." In *Widening the Horizon: Exoticism in Post-War Popular Music.* Edited by Philip Hayward. Sydney: John Libbey, 1999.

Liebermann, Randy. "The *Collier's* and Disney Series." In *Blueprint for Space: Science Fiction to Science Fact.* Edited by Frederick I. Ordway III and Randy Liebermann. Washington and London: Smithsonian Institution Press, 1992.

Lindholm, Charles. "Charisma, Crowd Psychology and Altered States of Consciousness." *Culture, Medicine, and Psychiatry* 16 (September 1992): 287–310.

Liner notes to Difang, *Circle of Life.* Magic Stone Music MSD-030, 1998.

Liner notes to *Les Baxter: The Sounds of Adventure.* http://www.tamboo.com/baxter/baxter1.html.

Liner notes to Les Baxter, *Space Escapade.* http://www.wildsscene.com/liners/spaceesc.html.

Liner notes to *Music for Heavenly Bodies.* Omega OSL-4, n.d.

Liner notes to Perrey/Kingsely, *The In Sound from Way Out!* Vanguard 79222-2, 1966.

Liner notes to *Pierre Schaeffer: L'œuvre musicale.* INA TRM 292572, 1998.

Liner notes to *Polyphonies vocales des aborigènes de Taïwan.* Inedit, Maison Des Cultures du Monde, W 2609 011 [1989].

Liner notes to *Return to the Source: Deep Trance and Ritual Beats.* RTTS CD1, n.d.

Liner notes to Stereolab, *Transient Random-Noise Bursts with Announcements.* Elektra 9 61536-2, 1993.

Lipsitz, George. *Time Passages: Collective Memory and American Popular Culture.* American Culture. Minneapolis: University of Minnesota Press, 1990.

Lonchampt, Jacques. " 'L'Apocalypse' et 'Ceremony' de Pierre Henry, à l'Olympia." *Le Monde,* February 11, 1970, 19.

"The Lounge Fad." *Revolt in Style.* http://www.revoltinstyle.com/october/lounge/. [This URL is no longer active.]

Lowe, Richard, and William Shaw. *Travellers: Voices of the New Age Nomads.* London: Fourth Estate, 1993.

Lysloff, René T. A. "Mozart in Mirrorshades: Ethnomusicology, Technology, and the Politics of Representation." *Ethnomusicology* 41 (spring/summer 1997): 206–19

MacKenzie, Donald A., and Judy Wajcman, eds. *The Social Shaping of Technology.* 2d ed. Buckingham, England: Open University Press, 1999.

Maffesoli, Michel. *The Time of the Tribes: The Decline of Individualism in Mass Society.* Translated by Don Smith. Thousand Oaks, Calif.: Sage, 1995.

Malbon, Ben. "Clubbing: Consumption, Identity and the Spatial Practices of Every-Night Life." In *Cool Places: Geographies of Youth Cultures.* Edited by Tracey Skelton and Gill Valentine. New York: Routledge, 1998.

Mankekar, Purnima. *Screening Culture, Viewing Politics: An Ethnography of Television, Womanhood, and Nation in Postcolonial India.* Durham, N.C.: Duke University Press, 1999.

Manning, Peter. *Electronic and Computer Music.* 2d ed. Oxford: Clarendon, 1993.

Marías, Julián. *America in the Fifties and Sixties: Julián Marías on the United States.* Edited by Michael Aaron Rockland. Translated by Blanche De Puy and Harold C. Raley. University Park: Pennsylvania State University Press, 1972.

Marks, Toby. "Banco de Gaia." Interview by Nisus. http://www.hallucinet.com/asylem/asylem4/bdg.htm.

———. "Banco de Gaia—Tibet and Last Train to Lhasa." Interview. http://www.demon.co.uk/london-calling/mbanco3.html. [This URL is no longer active.]

———. "Banco de Gaia—Recording and Playing Live." Interview. http://www.demon.co.uk/london-calling/mbanco1.html. [This URL is no longer active.]

———. "From London to Lhasa." Interview by Mike Kenney. http://www.outerbass.com/resonance/banco/indexF.html. [This URL is no longer active.]

———. Interview. http://www.demon.co.uk/london-calling/mbancocov.html. [This URL is no longer active.]

———. "Banco de Gaia." http://www.chaoscontrol.com/archive2/banco/bancoten.html.

———. "Banco de Gaia." Interview. http://www.chaoscontrol.com/archive2/banco/bancosamples.html.

Marsh, Dave. *Louie Louie: The History and Mythology of the World's Most Famous Rock 'n' Roll Song.* New York: Hyperion, 1993.

Martinez, Katharine, and Kenneth L. Ames, eds. *The Material Culture of Gender, the Gender of Material Culture.* Winterthur, Del.: Henry Francis du Pont Winterthur Museum, 1997.

Marvin, Carolyn. *When Old Technologies Were New: Thinking about Electric Communication in the Late Nineteenth Century.* New York: Oxford University Press, 1988.

Marx, Karl. *Readings from Karl Marx.* Edited by Derek Sayer. Key Texts. New York: Routledge, 1989.

Marx, Leo. "The Idea of 'Technology' and Postmodern Pessimism." In *Technology, Pessimism, and Postmodernism.* Edited by Yaron Ezrahi, Everett Mendelsohn, and Howard P. Segal. Amherst: University of Massachusetts Press, 1995.

———. *The Machine in the Garden: Technology and the Pastoral Ideal in America.* 1964; reprint, New York: Oxford University Press, 2000.

———. "On Heidegger's Conception of 'Technology' and its Historical Validity." *Massachusetts Review* 25 (winter 1984): 638–52.

———. "*Technology:* The Emergence of a Hazardous Concept." *Social Research* 64 (fall 1997): 965–88.

May, Elaine Tyler. "Explosive Issues: Sex, Women, and the Bomb." In *Recasting America: Culture and Politics in the Age of Cold War.* Edited by Lary May. Chicago: University of Chicago Press, 1989.

McClintock, Anne. *Imperial Leather: Race, Gender, and Sexuality in the Colonial Contest.* New York: Routledge, 1995.

McCracken, Grant. *Culture and Consumption: New Approaches to the Symbolic Character of Consumer Goods and Activities.* Bloomington and Indianapolis: Indiana University Press, 1988.

———. *Plenitude.* Toronto: Periph.: Fluide, 1997.

McDougall, Walter A. "Space-Age Europe: Gaullism, Euro-Gaullism, and the American Dilemma." *Technology and Culture* 26 (April 1985): 179–203.

McKnight-Trontz, Jennifer. *Exotiquarium: Album Art from the Space Age.* New York: St. Martin's Griffin, 1999.

Melechi, Antonio. "The Ecstasy of Disappearance." In *Rave Off: Politics and Deviance in*

Contemporary Youth Culture. Edited by Steve Redhead. Popular Cultural Studies, vol. 1. Aldershot, England: Avebury, 1993.

Menser, Michael, and Stanley Aronowitz. "On Cultural Studies, Science, and Technology." In *Technoscience and Cyberculture.* Edited by Stanley Aronowitz, Barbara Martinsons, Michael Menser, and Jennifer Rich. New York: Routledge, 1996.

Menta, Robert. "Students Fight to Save Napster." MP3 Newswire, March 3, 2000, http://www.mp3newswire.net/stories/2000/studentnap.html.

Messiaen, Olivier. *The Technique of My Musical Language.* Translated by John Satterfield. Paris: A. Leduc, 1956.

Miles, Milo. "Incredibly Bad Music." *Salon.* http://www.salon1999.com/10/reviews/lounge1.html.

Miller, Daniel. *A Theory of Shopping.* Ithaca, N.Y.: Cornell University Press, 1998.

Miller, Daniel, ed. "Consumption as the Vanguard of History: A Polemic by Way of an Introduction." In *Acknowledging Consumption: A Review of New Studies.* Edited by Daniel Miller. Material Cultures. New York: Routledge, 1995.

Mitcham, Carl. *Thinking through Technology: The Path between Engineering and Philosophy.* Chicago: University of Chicago Press, 1994.

Mitchell, Donald. *The Language of Modern Music.* London: Faber and Faber, 1976.

Moby. "The DJ Speaks." *Beam,* 1999, http://www.radiov.com/production/beam/features/djspeaks/.

———. "Media Diet." *Utne Reader,* January–February 2000, 111–112.

Morgan, Edward P. "Democracy in Eclipse? Media Culture and the Postmodern 'Sixties.' " *New Political Science* 40 (spring 1997): 5–31.

Morris, Chris. "Bachelor Pad Music from '50s, '60s Is Swingin' Again." *Billboard,* September 9, 1995, 1.

Morton, David. "A History of Endless Loop Magnetic Recording Technology in the United States." http://www.rci.rutgers.edu/~dmorton/8track.html.

Morton, Lawrence. "Footnotes to Stravinsky Studies: *Le Sacre du Printemps.*" *Tempo* 128 (March 1979): 9–16.

Moss, Stephen. "Your History Is Bunk, My History Is Right." *(Manchester) Guardian,* 29 June 1999, section G2, p. 4.

Mowitt, John. "The Sound of Music in the Era of Its Electronic Reproducibility." In *Music and Society: The Politics of Composition, Performance and Reception.* Edited by Richard Leppert and Susan McClary. Cambridge: Cambridge University Press, 1987.

Mumford, Lewis. *Art and Technics.* New York: Columbia University Press, 1952.

———. "Technics and the Nature of Man." *Technology and Culture* 7 (summer 1966): 303–17.

"Music Made Easier; It's All in the Mix." *New York Times,* October 8, 1998, sec. G, p. 7.

"Muslimgauze" [media release by Extreme]. http://www.xtr.com/extreme/muslimg.htm.

Nader, Laura. "Energy Needs for Sustainable Human Development from an Anthropological Perspective." In *Energy as an Instrument for Socio-Economic Development.* Edited by José Goldemberg and Thomas B. Johansson. New York: United Nations Development Programme, 1995.

Nattiez, Jean-Jacques. *Music and Discourse: Toward a Semiology of Music.* Translated by Carolyn Abbate. Princeton, N.J.: Princeton University Press, 1990.

Neighbour, Oliver, Paul Griffiths, and George Perle. *The New Grove Second Viennese School: Schoenberg, Webern, Berg.* Composer Biography Series. New York: W. W. Norton, 1983.

Newlin, Dika. *Bruckner, Mahler, Schoenberg.* Rev. ed. New York: W. W. Norton, 1978.

Nuc, Olivier. "Pierre Henry: La quête du son philosophial." *aden* [Paris], November 25–December 1, 1998, 5.

Oakley, J. Ronald. *God's Country: America in the Fifties.* New York: Dembner, 1986.

O'Connor, Barbara. "Safe Sets: Women, Dance and 'Communitas.'" In *Dance in the City.* Edited by Helen Thomas. New York: St. Martin's, 1997.

Oldenziel, Ruth. *Making Technology Masculine: Men, Women, and Modern Machines in America, 1870–1945.* Amsterdam: Amsterdam University Press, 1999.

"Olympic Music from Taiwan." http://ourworld.compuserve.com/homepages/smlpp/enigma.htm. [This URL is no longer active.]

Orlikowski, Wanda J., and Daniel Robey. "Information Technology and the Structuring of Organizations." *Information Systems Research* 2 (1991): 143–99.

Ortega y Gasset, José. *Toward a Philosophy of History.* Translated by Helene Weyl. New York: W. W. Norton, 1941.

Ortner, Sherry B. *Making Gender: The Politics and Erotics of Culture.* Boston: Beacon Press, 1996.

_____. "Theory in Anthropology since the Sixties." *Comparative Studies in Society and History* 26 (January 1984): 126–66.

Pace, David. "Old Wine—New Bottles: Atomic Energy and the Ideology of Science in Postwar France." *French Historical Studies* 17 (spring 1991): 38–61.

Palombini, Carlos. "Machine Songs V: Pierre Schaeffer—from Research into Noises to Experimental Music." *Computer Music Journal* 17 (fall 1993): 14–19.

———. "Musique Concrète Revisited." *Electronic Musicological Review* 4 (June 1999), http://cce.ufpr.br/~rem/REMv4/vol4/arti-palombini.htm.

———. "Musique Concrète Revisited." *The Twentieth-Century Music Avant-Garde.* Edited by Larry Sitsky. Westport, Conn.: Greenwood, forthcoming.

———. "Pierre Schaeffer, 1953: Towards an Experimental Music." *Music and Letters* (November 1993): 542–57.

———. "Technology and Pierre Schaeffer: Pierre Schaeffer's *Arts-Relais*, Walter Benjamin's *technische Reproduzierbarkeit* and Martin Heidegger's *Ge-stell.*" *Organised Sound* 3 (1998): 36–43.

———. "Technology and Pierre Schaeffer." *MikroPolyphonie* 4 (July 1997–December 1998). http://farben.latrobe.edu.au/mikropol/volume4/palombini-c/palombini.html.

Pareles, Jon. "MP3.com Hopes for Deal in Copyright Suit." *New York Times,* May 1, 2000, sec. C, p. 6.

———. "A Small World after All. But Is That Good?" *The New York Times,* March 24, 1996, sec. H, p. 34.

Peak, Martha H. "Developing an International Style of Management." *Management Review,* February 1991, 32–35.

Pearce, Susan M. *On Collecting: An Investigation into Collecting in the European Tradition.* New York: Routledge, 1995.

Perrey, Jean-Jacques. "The Jean Jacques Perrey Interview!" By Dana Countryman. *Cool and Strange Music!* February–April 1997, 29–32.

Pfaffenberger, Bryan. "Fetishized Objects and Humanised Nature: Towards an Anthropology of Technology." *Man* 23 (June 1988): 236–52.

———. "Social Anthropology of Technology." *Annual Review of Anthropology* (1992): 491–516.

Pickering, Andrew. "The Mangle of Practice: Agency and Emergence in the Sociology of Science." *American Journal of Sociology* 99 (November 1993): 559–89.

"Pierre Henry." http://www.novaplanet.com/html/actuel/html/phenry/html/phenry.html.

"Pierre Schaeffer, 1910-1995: The Founder of *Musique Concrète*." *Computer Music Journal* 20 (summer 1996): 10–11.

"Pierre Schaeffer parle de Pierre Henry avec François Bayle." *La Revue Musicale* 265–66 (1969): 109–118.

Pierret, Marc. *Entretiens avec Pierre Schaeffer*. Paris: Éditions Pierre Belfond, 1969.

Pini, Maria. "Women and the Early British Rave Scene." In *Back to Reality: Social Experience and Cultural Studies*. Edited by Angela McRobbie. Manchester: Manchester University Press, 1997.

Piot, Charles. *Remotely Global: Village Modernity in West Africa*. Chicago: University of Chicago Press, 1999.

Poschardt, Ulf. *DJ Culture*. Translated by Shaun Whiteside. London: Quartet, 1998.

Postman, Neil. *Technopoly: The Surrender of Culture to Technology*. New York: Vintage, 1993.

Prendergast, Mark. "The Chilling Fields." *New Statesman and Society*, January 13, 1995, 32–33.

Price, Sally. *Primitive Art in Civilized Places*. Chicago: University of Chicago Press, 1989.

Pride, Dominic. "Virgin Stays with Proven Marketing for Enigma." *Billboard*, November 23, 1996, 1.

———. "U.K.'s Nation of 'Ethno-Techno.'" *Billboard*, October 28, 1995, 1.

Pursell, Carroll. *White Heat: People and Technology*. Berkeley and Los Angeles: University of California Press, 1994.

Rabinow, Paul. *French Modern: Norms and Forms of the Social Environment*. Chicago: University of Chicago Press, 1995.

Recording Industry Association of America. "Piracy." http://www.riaa.com/piracy/piracy.htm.

Reighley, Kurt B. "Let's Go Discotheque: A Survey of French Dance Music." *CMJ New Music Monthly*, October 1997, 20.

Renauld, Jean. *Concrete Music, Electronic Music, and Copyright*. New York: Copyright Society of the U.S.A., 1958.

Renfrew, Colin. "Varna and the Emergence of Wealth in Prehistoric Europe." In *The Social Life of Things: Commodities in Cultural Perspective*. Edited by Arjun Appadurai. Cambridge: Cambridge University Press, 1986.

Restivo, Sal. "The Theory Landscape in Science Studies: Sociological Traditions." In *Handbook of Science and Technology Studies*. Edited by Sheila Jasanoff, Gerald E. Markle, James C. Petersen, and Trevor Pinch. Thousand Oaks, Calif.: Sage, 1995.

Review of Enigma, *The Cross of Changes*. http://www.hyperreal.com/music/epsilon/reviews/enigma.cross. [This URL is no longer active.]

Reynolds, Simon. *Generation Ecstasy: Into the World of Techno and Rave Culture*. Boston: Little, Brown, 1998.

———. "A New Invader on the Dance Floor." *New York Times*, November 29, 1998, 35.

———. "Return to Eden." In *Psychedelia Britannica: Hallucinogenic Drugs in Britain*. Edited by Antonio Melechi. London: Turnaround, 1997.

———. "Trance International." *Spin*, June 2000, 106–12.

Rietveld, Hillegonda C. *This Is Our House: House Music, Cultural Spaces and Technologies*. Popular Cultural Studies, vol. 13. Aldershot, England: Arena, 1998.

Robertson, Roland. "Globalisation or Glocalisation?" *Journal of International Communication* 1 (1994): 33–52.

———. "Glocalization: Time-Space and Homogeneity-Heterogeneity." In *Global Moderni-*

ties. Edited by Mike Featherstone, Scott Lash, and Roland Robertson. Theory, Culture and Society. Thousand Oaks, Calif.: Sage, 1995.

Root, Deborah. *Cannibal Culture: Art, Appropriation, and the Commodification of Difference.* Boulder: Westview Press, 1996.

Rose, Tricia. *Black Noise: Rap Music and Black Culture in Contemporary America.* Music/Culture. Middletown, Conn.: Wesleyan University Press, 1994.

Rosenberg, Nathan, ed. *Exploring the Black Box: Technology, Economics, and History.* Cambridge: Cambridge University Press, 1994.

Ross, Andrew. Review of *Deep Forest. Artforum* 32 (December 1993): 11–13.

Roszak, Theodore. *The Making of a Counter Culture: Reflections on the Technocratic Society and Its Youthful Opposition.* New York: Anchor, 1969.

Rothenberg, Randall. "The Swank Life." *Esquire,* April 1997, 70–79.

Rouget, Gilbert. *Music and Trance: A Theory of the Relations between Music and Possession.* Translated by Brunhilde Biebuyck. Chicago and London: University of Chicago Press, 1985.

Roux, Marie-Aude. "Un Grand-père de la techno." *Le Monde,* July 24, 1998, 1.

Rule, Greg. *Electro Shock! Groundbreakers of Synth Music.* San Francisco: Miller Freeman, 1999.

Rushkoff, Douglas. "Conspiracy or Crackpot? Cyberlife US." *(Manchester) Guardian,* 14 November 1996, 13.

Rutsky, R. L. *High Technē: Art and Technology from the Machine Aesthetic to the Posthuman.* Electronic Mediations. Minneapolis: University of Minnesota Press, 1999.

Saari, Ken. "My Space Escapade." *Cool and Strange Music!,* November 1997–February 1998, 40 41.

Sahlins, Marshall. *Historical Metaphors and Mythical Realities: Structure in the Early History of the Sandwich Islands Kingdom.* Association for Social Anthropology in Oceania, ASAO special publications, vol. 1. Ann Arbor: University of Michigan Press, 1981.

Salvatore, Gianfranco. *"Dea ex Machina:* La Trance, i Rave e il 'Bisogno di Trascendenza.' " In *Techno-Trance: Una Rivoluzione Musicale di Fine Millennio.* Edited by Gianfranco Salvatore. Rome: Castelvecchi, 1998.

———. "Introduzione." In *Techno-Trance: Una Rivoluzione Musicale di Fine Millennio.* Edited by Gianfranco Salvatore. Roma: Castelvecchi, 1998.

Samuelson, Robert J. *The Good Life and Its Discontents: The American Dream in the Age of Entitlement, 1945–1995.* New York: Times Books, 1995.

Sandburg, Brenda. "Music to Their Ears." *Recorder,* June 24, 1999, 1.

Saunders, Nicholas, and Rick Doblin. *Ecstasy: Dance Trance and Transformation.* Oakland, Calif.: Quick American Archives, 1996.

Schaeffer, Pierre. *À la recherche d'une musique concrète.* Paris: Èditions du Seuil, 1952.

———. Interview by Tim Hodgkinson. *Recommended Records Quarterly,* 1987. http://pages.ripco.net/~eleon/articles/pierre-schaeffer.html.

———. "Introduction à la musique concrète." *Polyphonie* 6 (1950): 30–52.

———. *La musique concrète.* Paris: Presses Universitaires de France, 1967.

———. *Traité des objets musicaux.* Paris: Èditions du Seuil, 1966.

———. "Vers une musique expérimentale." *La Revue Musicale,* 236 (1957): 11–27.

Schafer, David. "101 Moogs!" *Cool and Strange Music!,* February–April 1997, 22–23.

Schoemer, Karen. "Electronic Eden." *Newsweek,* February 10, 1997, 60–62.

Schoenberg, Arnold. *Style and Idea: Selected Writings of Arnold Schoenberg.* Translated by Leo Black. Edited by Leonard Stein. New York: St. Martin's, 1975.

Schumacher, T. G. "This Is a Sampling Sport': Digital Sampling, Rap Music and the Law in Cultural Production." *Media, Culture and Society* 17 (April 1995): 253–73.

Schutz, Alfred. "Making Music Together: A Study in Social Relationships." *Social Research* 18 (1951): 76–97.

Segal, Howard P. *Future Imperfect: The Mixed Blessings of Technology in America.* Amherst: University of Massachusetts Press, 1994.

Seiler, Andy. " '60s Kitsch King Finds '90s Niche." *USA Today,* August 8, 1995, 5D.

Seloron, François. "Pierre Henry et le Pop." *Rock and Folk* [Paris], February 1970, 38–42.

Sennett, Richard. *The Fall of Public Man.* 1977; reprint, New York: W. W. Norton, 1992.

Sewell, William H., Jr. "A Theory of Structure: Duality, Agency, and Transformation." *American Journal of Sociology* 98 (July 1992): 1–29.

Shohat, Ella. "Gender and Culture of Empire: Toward a Feminist Ethnography of Cinema." In *Visions of the East: Orientalism in Film.* Edited by Matthew Bernstein and Gaylyn Studlar. New Brunswick, N.J.: Rutgers University Press, 1997.

Sicko, Dan. *Techno Rebels: The Renegades of Electronic Funk.* New York: Billboard Books, 1999.

Sielwolf. Interview by Sniper Wells. *IDR Zine,* http://vr.dv.net/interviews/sie19_int.html.

Siklos, Richard. "Can RCA Records Keep on Rocking?" *Business Week,* November 29, 1999, 207.

Sinker, Mark. "Shhhhhh!" *Musical Quarterly* 81 (summer 1997): 211–41.

Sivanandan, A. "All That Melts into Air Is Solid: The Hokum of New Times." *Race and Class* 31 (1989): 1–30.

Size, Roni. "Better Music through Technology." Interview by Benjamin Diaz. *VHF* [supplement to *Option*], July–August 1998.

Slater, Don. *Consumer Culture and Modernity.* Cambridge: Polity, 1997.

Small, Christopher. *Musicking: The Meanings of Performing and Listening.* Music/Culture. Hanover, N.H.: University Press of New England, 1999.

Smith, Cecil O., Jr. "The Longest Run: Public Engineers and Planning in France." *American Historical Review* 95 (June 1990): 657–92.

Smith, Daniel. Review of *Pierre Schaeffer: L'œuvre musicale.* http://newyork.sidewalk.com/link/21953. [This URL is no longer active.]

Smith, Merrit Roe, and Leo Marx, eds. *Does Technology Drive History? The Dilemma of Technological Determinism.* Cambridge: MIT Press, 1994.

Smith, Michael. "Advertising the Atom." In *Government and Environmental Politics: Essays on Historical Developments since World War Two.* Edited by Michael J. Lacey. Washington, D.C.: The Woodrow Wilson Center Press/Baltimore: The Johns Hopkins University Press, 1991.

Smith, Michael L. "Selling the Moon: The U.S. Manned Space Program and the Triumph of Commodity Scientism." In *The Culture of Consumption: Critical Essays in American History, 1880–1980.* Edited by Richard Wightman Fox and T. J. Jackson Lears. New York: Pantheon, 1982.

Smith Brindle, Reginald. "The Lunatic Fringe: Concrete Music." *Musical Times,* May 1956, 246.

———. *The New Music: The Avant-Garde since 1945.* New York: Oxford University Press, 1975.

Smolders, Ios. Review of Alain de Filippis, *Ton Dieu ne s'appelle-t-il pas ego? Vital,* January 1, 1995. http://enigma.v2.nl/Archief/ArchiefTexten/Vitals/Vital39.html.

———. Review of Muslimgauze, *Blue Mosque. Vital,* November 1, 1994. http://www.v2.nl/Archief/ArchiefTexten/Vitals/Vital38.html.

Soja, Edward W. *Postmodern Geographies: The Reassertion of Space in Critical Social Theory.* London and New York: Verso, 1989.

Specter, Michael. "Your Mail Has Vanished." *New Yorker,* December 6, 1999, 96–104.

Spigel, Lynn. *Make Room for TV: Television and the Family Ideal in Postwar America.* Chicago: University of Chicago Press, 1992.

Stiegler, Bernard. *The Fault of Epimetheus.* Vol. 1 of *Technics and Time.* Translated by Richard Beardsworth and George Collins. Meridian series. Stanford, Calif.: Stanford University Press, 1998.

Stockhausen, Karlheinz. "Advice to Clever Children . . ." Interview by Dick Witts. *The Wire,* November 1995, 32–35.

———. *Towards a Cosmic Music.* Selected and translated by Tim Nevill. Longmead, England: Element Books, 1989.

———. "World Music." Translated by Bernard Radloff. *Dalhousie Review* 69 (fall 1989): 318–26.

Strauss, Neil. "Bryn Jones, 38, Musician Known As Muslimgauze." *New York Times,* January 28, 1999, sec. C, p.23.

———. "The Next Big Thing or the Next Bust?" *New York Times,* January 26, 1997, sec. H, p. 36.

Straw, Will. "Sizing up Record Collections: Gender and Connoisseurship in Rock Music Culture." In *Sexing the Groove: Popular Music and Gender.* Edited by Sheila Whitely. New York: Routledge, 1997.

———. "Systems of Articulation, Logics of Change: Communities and Scenes in Popular Music." *Cultural Studies* 5 (October 1991): 368–88.

Stroh, Wolfgang Martin. *Zur Soziologie der elektronischen Musik.* Zürich: Amadeus, 1975.

Suchoff, Benjamin. "Ethnomusicological Roots of Béla Bartók's Musical Language." *World of Music* 29 (1987): 43–65.

"Taiwan Couple Sue Enigma Over Vocals on International Hit." Associated Press, March 27, 1998.

Taruskin, Richard. "Russian Folk Melodies in *The Rite of Spring.*" *Journal of the American Musicological Society* 33 (fall 1980): 501–43.

Taylor, Timothy D. *Global Pop: World Music, World Markets.* New York: Routledge, 1997.

———. "Peopling the Stage: Opera, Otherness, and New Musical Representations in the Eighteenth Century." *Cultural Critique* 36 (spring 1997): 55–88.

———. "World Music in Television Ads." *American Music* 18 (summer 2000): 162–92.

"The Techno Story." http://www.devastating-rhythm.ch/news.htm. [This URL is no longer active.]

Théberge, Paul. *Any Sound You Can Imagine: Making Music/Consuming Technology.* Music/Culture. Hanover, N.H.: University Press of New England, 1997.

———. "Random Access: Music, Technology, Postmodernism." In *The Last Post: Music after Modernism.* Edited by Simon Miller. Music and Society. Manchester: Manchester University Press, 1993.

———. "Technology." In *Key Terms in Popular Music and Culture.* Edited by Bruce Horner and Thomas Swiss. Malden, Mass.: Blackwell, 1999.

Thornton, Sarah. *Club Cultures: Music, Media and Subcultural Capital.* Music/Culture. Middletown, Conn.: Wesleyan University Press, 1996.

Titus, A. Costandina, and Jerry L. Simich. "From 'Atomic Bomb Baby' to 'Nuclear Funeral': Atomic Music Comes of Age, 1945–1990." *Popular Music and Society* 14 (winter 1990): 11–37.

Tobin, Joseph. *Re-Made in Japan: Everyday Life and Consumer Taste in a Changing Society.* New Haven, Conn.: Yale University Press, 1992.

Toop, David. *Exotica: Fabricated Soundscapes in a Real World.* London: Serpent's Tail, 1999.

———. *Ocean of Sound: Aether Talk, Ambient Sound and Imaginary Worlds.* London: Serpent's Tail, 1995.

Torgovnick, Marianna. *Gone Primitive: Savage Intellects, Modern Lives.* Chicago: University of Chicago Press, 1990.

"True Feelings from the Bosom of Nature." *Sinorama Magazine,* http://www.gio.gov.tw/info/sinorama/8508/5080/161e.html. [This URL is no longer active.]

Turner, Victor. *The Ritual Process: Structure and Anti-Structure.* Chicago: Aldine, 1969.

Ullman, Ellen. *Close to the Machine: Technophilia and Its Discontents.* San Francisco: City Lights Books, 1997.

———. "The Dumbing-Down of Programming." *Salon,* May 1998, http://www.salon-magazine.com/21st/feature/1998/05/cov_feature.html.

Ussachevsky, Vladimir. "As Europe Takes to Tape." *American Composers Alliance Bulletin* (autumn 1953): 10–11.

———. "Music in the Tape Medium." *Juilliard Review,* spring 1959, 8.

Vail, Mark. *Vintage Synthesizers: Pioneering Designers, Groundbreaking Instruments, Collecting Tips, Mutants of Technology.* San Francisco: Miller Freeman, 2000.

Vale, V., and Andrea Juno, eds. *Incredibly Strange Music.* Vol. 1. San Francisco: Re/Search, 1993.

———. *Incredibly Strange Music.* Vol. 2. San Francisco: Re/Search, 1994.

Vaziri, Aidin. "Mellow Gold." http://www.jetpack.com/lounge02/beats/lounge/mellow-gold/index.html.

Virilio, Paul. *The Art of the Motor.* Translated by Julie Rose. Minneapolis: University of Minnesota Press, 1995.

———. *Open Sky.* Translated by Julie Rose. London: Verso, 1997.

Waksman, Steve. *Instruments of Desire: The Electric Guitar and the Shaping of Musical Experience.* Cambridge, Mass.: Harvard University Press, 2000.

Walker, Dave. " 'Futurama': 'Jetsons' Meet 'The Simpsons.' " *Arizona Republic,* March 28, 1999, E1.

Wallerstein, Immanuel. *Historical Capitalism.* London: Verso, 1983.

———. *The Modern World-System: Capitalist Agriculture and the Origins of the European World-Economy in the Sixteenth Century.* Studies in Social Discontinuity. New York: Academic Press, 1974.

Walsham, Geoff. "The Emergence of Interpretivism in IS Research." *Information Systems Research* 6 (1995): 376–94.

Watkins, Glenn. *Pyramids at the Louvre: Music, Culture, and Collage from Stravinsky to the Postmodernists.* Cambridge, Mass.: Harvard University Press, 1994.

Weart, Spencer R. *Scientists in Power.* Cambridge, Mass.: Harvard University Press, 1979.

Weber, Samuel. "Upsetting the Set Up: Remarks on Heidegger's Questing after Technics." *MLN* 104 (December 1989): 977–92.

Weinert, Ellie. " 'Changes' in Works for Enigma." *Billboard,* January 8, 1994, 10.

———. " 'Sadeness' Creator Settles Sample Suit." *Billboard,* September 14, 1991, 80.

Weisel, Al. "Deep Forest's Lush Lullaby." *Rolling Stone,* April 21, 1994, 26.

Werner, Byron. "Space Age Bachelor Pad Music: A Forward." http://atomicmule.com/kulture/byron/space1.html.

Westrum, Ron. *Technologies and Society: The Shaping of People and Things.* Belmont, Calif.: Wadsworth, 1991.

White, Erin. " 'Chatting' a Singer Up the Pop Charts—How Music Marketers Used the Web to Generate Buzz before an Album Debuted." *Wall Street Journal*, October 5, 1999, sec. B, p. 1.

"Why Lounge? Why Now?" http://www.fsbassociates.com/books2/loungekit.htm.

Williams, Raymond. *Marxism and Literature*. Marxist Introductions. Oxford: Oxford University Press, 1977.

———. *The Politics of Modernism: Against the New Conformists*. Edited by Tony Pinkney. London: Verso, 1989.

———. *Television: Technology and Cultural Form*. New York: Schocken, 1974.

Willis, Paul E. *Learning to Labor: How Working Class Kids Get Working Class Jobs*. New York: Columbia University Press, 1981.

Wilson, Rob, and Wimal Dissanayake, eds. *Global/Local: Cultural Production and the Transnational Imaginary*. Asia-Pacific: Culture, Politics, and Society. Durham, N.C.: Duke University Press, 1996.

Winner, Langdon. "Prophets of Inevitability." *Technology Review*, March–April 1998, 62.

———. "Technology Today: Utopia or Dystopia?" *Social Research* 64 (fall 1997): 989-1017.

———. *The Whale and the Reactor: A Search for Limits in an Age of High Technology*. Chicago: University of Chicago Press, 1986.

Wishart, Trevor. *On Sonic Art*. Edited by Simon Emmerson. Contemporary Music Studies, vol. 12. Rev. ed. Amsterdam: Harwood Academic, 1996.

———. "Sound Symbols and Landscapes." In *The Language of Electroacoustic Music*. Edited by Simon Emmerson. London: Macmillan, 1986.

Wolfson, Richard. "Grandpa to Pop's Whizkids." *(London) Daily Telegraph*, May 22, 1999, 8.

Wong, Victor. "Taiwan Aboriginal Singers Settle Copyright Lawsuit." *Billboard*, July 31, 1999, 14.

———. "Taiwan's Power Station Brings Aboriginal Flair to What's Music." *Billboard*, July 11, 1998, 48.

Wörner, Karl. *Stockhausen: Life and Work*. Translated and edited by Bill Hopkins. Berkeley and Los Angeles: University of California Press, 1976.

Wouk, Herman. *Marjorie Morningstar*. New York: Doubleday, 1955.

Wright, Mary Anna. "The Great British Ecstasy Revolution." In *DiY Culture*. Edited by George McKay. London and New York: Verso, 1998.

Wulff, Helena. "Introduction: Introducing Youth Culture in Its Own Right: The State of the Art and New Possibilities." In *Youth Cultures: A Cross-Cultural Perspective*. London and New York: Routledge, 1995.

Yoon, Esther. "Buffalo Daughter: Tokyo Calling." *Resonance*, http://www.resonancemag.com/issues/15/currentissue/shortwaves/buffalodaughter.html.

Zarlengo, Kristina. "Civilian Threat, the Suburban Citadel, and Atomic Age American Women." *Signs* 24 (summer 1999): 925–58.

Zemp, Hugo. "The/An Ethnomusicologist and the Record Business." *Yearbook for Traditional Music* 28 (1997): 36–56.

INDEX

Lightning Source UK Ltd.
Milton Keynes UK

177065UK00007B/31/P

9 780415 936842